Notable British Trials ~~Series No.~~

TRIAL OF

RONALD LIGHT

THE GREEN BICYCLE CASE

EDITED BY

Sally Smith

MANGO BOOKS

First edition published 2019

Copyright © Sally Smith, 2019

ISBN: 978-1-911273-76-9 (hardback)
ISBN: 978-1-914277-13-9 (softcover)

Notable British Trials imprint ©William Hodge & Company (Holdings) Ltd
Used with kind permission.

General Editors:
David Green - M.W. Oldridge - Adam Wood

Published by Mango Books
www.MangoBooks.co.uk
18 Soho Square
London W1D 3QL

Notable British Trials Series No. 87

TRIAL OF

RONALD LIGHT

THE GREEN BICYCLE CASE

EDITED BY

Sally Smith

CONTENTS.

RONALD LIGHT.

INTRODUCTION.

I.

'... reflect on this poor girl taken from us ... '[1]

It was 1919. The long war was over. The horizon was bright. Bella Wright was twenty-one years old, everyone's daughter and sister and sweetheart, everyone's girl next door, everyone's hope for the future – and that is why everyone was fascinated and appalled by what happened to her on 5 July of that year.

During the preceding four years, there had been slaughter on a scale unprecedented in modern times. All over England there were grieving families, and everywhere war memorials were sprouting up on village greens with their tragic lists of the young lives lost.

And not all the killing had stopped when the war ended. Crime has always been a social barometer; witches and counterfeiters, highwaymen and poisoners all committed crimes that were the products of their times in history. Now, in the summer of 1919, there was still easy access to service revolvers that had not been surrendered to the authorities when hostilities ceased, and there were young men who had learned how to use them and who had become hardened to suffering. These men were the lucky ones who had come home, but in many cases their personal wars were not over. Violent crime and sometimes murder had increased, particularly in a domestic context: men struggled to come to terms with a return to quiet civilian life, and to wives who had found independence, and to children who scarcely knew them.

Thousands upon thousands dead. Yet somehow the murder of an apparently innocent girl in a country lane in 1919 pierced the carapace of a nation which had begun to think that it was inured to death. All those young lives had been sacrificed, but still Bella's death mattered; and there was a public outcry for her killer to be brought to justice. In the feverish desire for the perpetrator to be found and punished, the irony that the mandatory punishment would involve yet another death was completely lost.

The death penalty overshadowed murder trials in a way we can scarcely imagine. Such trials, even nowadays, seem to have a tension that is palpable, but before the abolition of the death penalty they were infused with almost

---

1   From the funeral address by the Reverend W. N. Westmore at Bella's funeral.

Light.

unbearable drama: every nuanced decision, every tiny twist of the evidence, every impression given by a witness or formed by a jury might mean the difference between the continuing life and ghastly death of the healthy, feeling, living man or woman in the dock.

For sheer theatre, what became known as the Green Bicycle Case would be hard to beat. The murder (if indeed that is what it was) of Bella Wright was a classic, defined by its conundrums of space and time, of distance and of opportunity. And the trial that followed the crime was quite something, watched by all those who could cram inside the court while hundreds more stood outside and tens of thousands all over England followed it in the newspapers.

Bella Wright was a nice-looking girl with defined features and a determined chin, wide-apart eyes and a direct gaze. The much-loved daughter of an illiterate farm labourer, she had been brought up with the rural values of her family: hard work, respect for the land, deference to her 'betters', loyalty to those she loved, devotion to her God. She was outgoing, friendly and physically strong. Having left school aged thirteen, she had entered domestic service; but perhaps a surfeit of domesticity at home (she was the eldest of seven) made her turn to factory work and, by the summer of 1919, she was employed at Bates's Rubber Works, a pneumatic tyre manufacturer in Leicester. She was still living with her parents and her younger brothers and sisters in the tied cottage in the little village of Stoughton, about five miles from town. She had always wanted to better herself, her mother said. Perhaps she also hoped that factory work would be more lucrative than domestic service – she had a future to save up for, a sweetheart whom she hoped to marry. He was a stoker in the Navy, and his name was Archibald Ward.[2] Archibald, still aboard his ship in Portsmouth, was to be demobilised, at last, in August 1919. Only a month away, now. Unsurprising, then, her mother's poignant evidence: Bella went out that day in 'high spirits'.

Ronald Light was a pleasant, ordinary-looking thirty five year old man. He came from a middle class background, with the advantages that the phrase then implied. His family were relatively prosperous: his father had been the manager of a local colliery, and his maternal grandfather a solicitor. He had been sent to public school – Oakham, in Rutland – and, in 1906, had qualified as an engineer

---

2   Ward's sister, Sarah, worked alongside Bella at the tyre factory. According to the *Leicester Mail* (8 July 1919), Sarah 'broke down when she learned her companion's fate. "She was such a bright, good girl … that I cannot believe it is true. Poor Bella! She was a good cyclist and was going to teach me to ride. Indeed, she promised to come to my home at Braunstone on Sunday to give me a lesson. But she did not come. I was not disappointed because she was one of those girls who are always willing to do more than they are really able to. I remarked to my friend, 'Bella could not pull it in'. We were like sisters. Before her parents removed from Braunstone to Stoughton we were almost always together. I did not know that she had any male friend, nor do I think she had. She was very fond of my brother, who is in the Navy, and he thought much of her. It will be an awful blow to him."'

Introduction.

at the Central Technical College in South Kensington, part of the University of London. Some of Light's contemporaries in the class of 1906 achieved significant heights later on – amongst them, F. A. Meier in education, James Edward Montgomrey in mechanical engineering, A. P. Thurston in aeronautics and aerodynamics, and Harold Saunders (later Sir Harold) in patents and philanthropy – but Light seemed not to be on quite such an illustrious path. Leaving university with a third-class degree, he went to work as a draughtsman for the Midland Railway Company, based in Derby, living in lodgings there from 1906 to 1914. In February 1915, a few months after war broke out, he enlisted with the Royal Engineers.

Unusually, after a few weeks of active service in France, he came back to England and re-enlisted, this time as a gunner in the Honourable Artillery Company. By November 1917, he had returned to fight in France; a little over nine months later, he was invalided home to England suffering from deafness and other symptoms associated with shellshock. The war ended, and Ronald, like many others, struggled to find his way back into civilian life and into employment. Living at home with mother was, for the time being, the only option.

These two people, Bella and Ronald, occupied different worlds in which there seems no room for overlap. But separated by gender and age, background, education and experience, they had in fact a common interest: bicycling.

A bicycle had provided Bella with independence, freedom, exercise and amusement. Women's lives at that time, constrained by convention, often lacked all those things. Bella was probably not consciously 'riding to suffrage on a bicycle'[3] but, nonetheless, she had found a key to a life of her own. She cycled everywhere – to and from her job at the factory, on errands for her mother, on visits to relatives, and sometimes just for the fun of a jaunt into open countryside, further and further from home. Perhaps, like factory work, cycling interrupted the routine of the cottage, the domesticity and the drudgery. Did she regard her bicycle as her escape? And, if so, did the escape also entail secrets from her family and friends?

Ronald's interest in cycling also stemmed from a practical need for transport at a time when automobiles were still playthings for the rich – but he too liked to go on rides for the sheer pleasure of easy escape into the countryside. And perhaps he was also seeking freedom from a different kind of home life: from the house in which he now lived with his devoted, widowed mother, at 54 Highfield Street, Leicester. The house was an archetype of Edwardian respectability, with

---

3   At least two women – Susan B. Anthony and Elizabeth Cady Stanton – have been credited with coining this phrase, which was printed and reprinted in newspapers at the turn of the century.

Light.

its elaborate curtains, busy wallpaper, huge aspidistras, Chinese pots, fringed lamps, and the floral plates which hung on every wall.[4] Was it a refuge or a prison to Ronald Light, fresh from the trenches, haunted by their recurring images of horror? And his mother: with the emotional demands of her love and worry and increasing dependency, was she an anchor, or a shackle?

We know enough about Ronald and Bella to ask these questions, but not enough to answer them. We only know two things for certain: we know that, at about seven o'clock on the evening of 5 July 1919, Bella and Ronald were both out on their bicycles on the country roads around Leicester. And we know where they both were three hours later, at about ten o'clock. It is the hours between those known facts, the bit in the middle, that are a mystery. Those three hours have made the Green Bicycle case one of the most famous unsolved crimes of the twentieth century.

At about ten o'clock,[5] Ronald returned home. His mother was preparing for a visit to relatives in Rhyl, and Mary Webb, his mother's faithful domestic servant, had spent two hours keeping his supper warm. Hot supper was a rare treat in July, and Mr Ronald had been specifically instructed to be home by eight o'clock. By the time he appeared, Mary was not very pleased with Mr Ronald. Where on earth had he been? she demanded, with the familiarity of years of devoted service. His bicycle had broken down, he told her, and he deposited it in the back kitchen before tucking into the waiting supper.

At the same time, about ten o'clock, Bella Wright was lying dead beside a country road, locally referred to as the Gartree Road. It was in fact the remote Via Devana, part of the old Roman road that links Leicester and Market Harborough. Her body had been found about forty minutes earlier, at 9.20 pm, by a farmer, Joseph Cowell; she was lying half into the road, still neatly attired in her coat with her purse and handkerchief in the pocket, the little brooch still intact on her blouse and her hat still on her head. Her bicycle lay askew on the road with its front wheel pointing in the direction of Leicester.

Believing her to be injured, Cowell had lifted her onto the verge, only to realise he was holding in his arms a still-warm corpse. Leaving his farmhands to guard the body, and propping the bicycle against a gate, he had gone to summon the police and a doctor. The light had just about faded by ten o'clock, the narrow, straight little road dwindling quickly into invisibility, the overgrown vegetation looming in dark bulk over it. It must have been very quiet. Had it not been for

---

4   Description of Mrs Light's room derived from a photograph in the *Daily Sketch*, 14 June 1920.

5   Although prosecuting counsel in his opening speech said 10.30 pm, Mary Webb's evidence both at the magistrates' court committal proceedings and at the trial was that Light returned at ten o'clock, and this is likely to be more accurate.

Introduction.

the blood covering the left side of her head, matting the neat hair and pooling around it, Bella might have been asleep.

It took Joseph Cowell some time to get help. No rapid communications in those days; the evocative details are set out in the police statements, building the picture of that lost past when dramas unfolded slowly, accompanied not by the sirens and the close-to-instant communications of today, but by horses and bicycles and candlelight. Cowell had to return to his farm, harness his horses and cart and drive to the nearest police station at Glen Magna. There he reported his discovery to Police Constable Alfred Hall, who asked him to go to the post office to telephone the local doctor. In the meantime, the constable went off home to fetch his own bicycle.

It was probably not until about 11.15 pm that the doctor arrived at the scene of the crime.[6] He found a body still warm and expressed the view (not wholly reliable, given subsequent views expressed by him) that she could not have been dead for more than two hours. If correct, that meant of course, that Joseph Cowell may have found her only five minutes or so after she died.

A tragic accident was the doctor's immediate assumption. There was nothing on the body to identify Bella. She could not be left all night where she was. Cowell's cart was his milk float, large enough to carry the body, and by the time the doctor arrived Bella had been lifted onto it. The doctor, Dr Edward Williams, clambered in the dark onto the float and performed a brief investigation; the girl must have collapsed with exhaustion and fallen off her bicycle, the bleeding caused by sudden haemorrhage, he said. Concerned by the cursory opinion, PC Hall asked the doctor to accompany him to somewhere more suitable for an examination. Assisted by Hall, the farmer took the float to a small brick building – a cottage last used, appropriately enough, as a chapel, now deserted. The resourceful constable obtained some candles, and the doctor again examined the body. Natural causes, all very unfortunate, he said. And there Bella's body was left for the night, as yet unidentified, unclaimed, unmourned.

It all seemed very rum to Hall. Strong, healthy, well-nourished girls did not, in his experience, just collapse off bicycles. Furthermore, he had himself not so long ago come home from the trenches; something about the neat, focussed distribution of blood on Bella's head – and the lack of it elsewhere on her body – seemed to him inconsistent with the doctor's explanation. He could not have

---

6   The timing is uncertain: at the coroner's court, Dr Williams said he arrived at 11.15 pm; in the magistrates' court, he said 11.00 pm; at trial, he said 10.45 pm, but readily accepted in cross-examination that it may have been 11.15 pm. Any suggestion that he may have arrived earlier – at 10.45 pm – is inconsistent with his estimation that Bella had by then been dead two hours, since it seems she left her uncle's at 8.30 pm at the very earliest, and more probably at 8.45 pm.

Light.

been in his bed much before midnight at the earliest, but by six o'clock the next morning he had returned to the Via Devana – now light in the dawn – and had begun to search, though he did not know what he was searching for.

All by himself on that deserted road, Hall carried out the kind of inch-by-inch examination of the ground that we see undertaken by vigilant lines of modern police officers. He found nothing, but nonetheless he went back that afternoon, and again after his day's work, and that evening his persistence (curious or impressive, depending on your point of view) was rewarded when he found, at last, two things.

Lying on the highway about six yards from where Bella's body had fallen, he found a bullet embedded in the road. It was now a little mangled by what he deduced to be a horse's hoof. In addition, he noticed a bloodstain on the top of a field gate close to the body.

Later, in an adjacent field, a dead crow was found, its feet covered with congealed blood. Could it have been shot? There was no sign of it when the body was opened, but the bird's crop was found to be full of blood, and so a macabre theory was formulated by the police that became the final, eerie, Edgar Allan Poe touch to the mystery. The crow, the police said, had alighted by Bella's body, 'gorged' itself on the pool of blood around her head, hopped onto the gate, flown into the field, and there choked on the blood. The great black bird, its bloody claws clutching the gate, the carrion predator choking to death on what it could not resist: it was all the case needed to propel it into the mythology of England's greatest murders.

The picturesque overhanging hedgerows for some miles around were cut back in an attempt to find the weapon from which the bullet had been fired, but with no success. If that bullet had been fired by Bella's attacker, it was the only clue he had left.

Contacting Dr Williams and requesting his return must have been a little embarrassing, so plain was it that the doctor's examination the previous night had been perfunctory. This time, the blood was washed from Bella's face and there, indeed, was an unmistakable bullet wound, a small puncture – about the diameter of a lead pencil, lying behind and half an inch below the level of the left eye – where the bullet had entered, and a larger exit wound high up in Bella's hair under the right parietal bone.[7] A subsequent post mortem by two doctors confirmed these injuries and, upon their dissecting the skull, it was deduced from the injury to the brain matter that the bullet had passed 'upwards,

---

7   This is the evidence in the post mortem report and at trial by the doctors; prosecuting counsel's opening statement, which refers to 'a wound of exit just above the right cheekbone' is – surprisingly for such an important issue – incorrect.

Introduction.

inwards and backwards'.

The death from natural causes had now become a suspected murder.

Bella's anxious parents had, of course, reported her missing, and once formal identification of the body had been made, the police began their investigations with the certainties: when had her family last seen her?

On Friday 4 July 1919, Bella had arrived home on her bicycle at about 11.00 pm after a late shift at the factory. She 'went to bed and stopped there, as was her usual custom' until four o'clock on Saturday afternoon,[8] and then wrote to her sweetheart Archie and cycled to the local post office to post the letter. That evening, she was to visit her uncle, who lived in a small village called Gaulby, about four miles from her home. He was a Mr George Measures, a roadman, and on the day Bella visited, by coincidence, his married daughter and her husband James Evans were also visiting. Bella arrived at Gaulby at about 7.30 pm. During the course of the visit, which lasted about an hour or a little more, George Measures noticed a stranger idling around outside the cottage. He asked Bella if she knew who it was. 'No,' she said, 'he is a perfect stranger to me. I'll sit down a little while, and he will, perhaps, be gone.'

When she rose to leave, her family accompanied her to the door. The man was still there. While she and Evans bent over the wheel of her bicycle that had been giving her trouble on her journey, the man approached. George Measures and James Evans both recalled – to within a reasonable margin of error – what the man then said: 'Bella, you were gone a long time. I thought you had gone the other way.' But Evans was a bicycling enthusiast, and it was the stranger's bicycle, not its unfamiliar owner, that interested him: a splendid bike, pea green, with a three-speed gear, and, unusually, a back-pedalling brake. They had a chat about bicycles, he and the stranger, until Bella was ready to leave – and then off she pedalled, apparently comfortable in the stranger's company. And so the two of them, Bella and the man on the green bicycle, vanished over the horizon of the road, and into the mystery, as Bella's family turned back into the cottage. It was then probably about 8.45 in the evening.[9]

The road they took led directly from Gaulby to Stoughton, where Bella lived, and on, eventually, to Leicester. It was known as the 'Upper' or 'Leicester' Road. The first village after Gaulby was King's Norton, and just after that a turning to the left led to the smaller and less-used road to Leicester, running parallel to the Upper Road: the Via Devana. It was here, in this little-used road which was not on her direct journey home, at a point just over two miles from

---

8   *Leicester Mercury*, 23 March 1920.

9   Although there are some differences in the timings given by the witnesses, they vary between 8.30 pm and 8.45 pm, the predominance of the evidence is that Bella left at 8.45 pm.

Light.

her uncle's cottage, that Bella was found dead a short time later. She had been halfway home.

From then on the green bicycle became the symbol of all the violence and mystery of Bella's death.

'Romantic' seems a curious word to apply to the first proceedings to take place after a violent death; but nonetheless the coroner's inquest that immediately followed the discovery of a body had, in those days, a mystery and history and intimacy which did indeed give it an aura of romance.

The coroner's jurisdiction is one of the oldest in England, established in the twelfth century; the inquest into the identity of the deceased and the time, place, cause and manner of their death is a very special kind of legal hearing, and, in 1919, a very limited one, concerned only with those questions, and taking place with an immediacy and solemn formality guaranteed to bring home the reality of death far more vividly than any subsequent ritualised murder trials.

At the very first possible moment after Bella's body was discovered, the local coroner swung into action. It was customary in those days to hold the first hearing in the immediate locality of the death, sometimes even in the building in which the body had been found, and the nearest suitable building was Joseph Cowell's farm, across the fields from the road in which Bella had died. So Cowell, a man who had merely stumbled on Bella's body, found himself, curiously, intimately involved in the life and death of that unknown girl, hosting in the parlour of his farmhouse in the nearby village of Little Stretton (otherwise Stretton Parva) a grim assembly. It was by then 8 July, three days after the death.

Crammed into Cowell's best room were the coroner, a man of considerable importance in the area, Bella's family, still numb with grief, and nine 'good and lawful men of Leicester', the jurors who had been sworn and had viewed her body. Bella's mother had had to see it too and now identified her daughter with a poignant brevity, a family's tragedy summarised in a few broken sentences: 'I identify the body the jury have viewed as being that of my daughter ... she was single and twenty one years of age ... she said she was going to catch the post at Evington ... I did not see her again alive.' For Mrs Wright, there was really little more to be said.

In those days, there was no legal representation at an inquest. The immediately available witnesses were called to give evidence by the coroner and the jurors could, if they so wished, ask questions. There were no rules of evidence, and the accounts of the witnesses were written down rapidly and verbatim, often by the coroner himself, his pen flying across the page, so that the lasting record reads evocatively as if in the present; careful copperplate for the formalities, speedier more personalised manuscript as the dramas unfold,

Introduction.

the inevitable blots and smears of rapidly turned pages. As for the witnesses, these were usually the most closely involved, shocked with surprise, numb with grief, who had only hours to collect their thoughts; opinions are divided as to whether their accounts are in consequence the most reliable of all those given in the proceedings following the death, or the least.

The inquest adjourned after that first day in Joseph Cowell's parlour, and reconvened in the village hall at nearby Glen Magna. There, the jury heard the detailed story of Bella's last day. Some of the timings differ significantly from those given in the police statements, and in oral evidence in the murder trial. The absence of rules of evidence resulted in accounts which contained material which would be inadmissible in a trial, most particularly the details of the conversation between Bella's relatives about the strange man who had apparently accompanied her to, and then accompanied her from, Gaulby. Inadmissible, but the reader will find them illuminating, as, no doubt, did the coroner's jury.[10]

They had little difficulty in reaching their verdict: 'That the said Annie Bella Wright had been found dead ... and that the cause of her death was a gunshot wound in the head inflicted by a man whose name is unknown ... and [that] the said unknown man ... did feloniously murder [her]'. Whose body was it, what was the manner of her death, how was it caused? All those questions had been answered. The jury had performed their solemn duty.

The villagers in the small, close-knit village of Stoughton were numb with disbelief; a murder in that friendly little community seemed unimaginable. In the days after Bella's death, instinctively drawn out of their cottages to huddle together for comfort, they had gathered at last into a crowd outside the building in which her body had lain[11] and so, ultimately, on 11 July, to the church where her funeral took place before a congregation of hundreds – the press, the prurient and the grieving crammed together into the church and spilling outside into the graveyard, where she was then buried.

And the mystery was as deep as ever.

The case touched the heart of the whole country. 'My one thought and hope of course is to elucidate the mystery of the crime,' the Chief Constable of Leicestershire wrote to the Director of Public Prosecutions, 'and I shall be most grateful for useful assistance from any and every quarter.'[12]

On the day the inquest began, a police notice had been circulated throughout

---

10   The oral evidence given at the inquest can be found in Appendix I, and the written depositions (or statements) taken when the oral evidence was given are at Appendix II.

11   *Leicester Daily Post*, 19 July 1919.

12   TNA: PRO DPP 1/61.

Light.

England, Scotland and Wales; a substantial reward was offered. Suddenly it seemed the green bicycle had become the murderer; thanks to James Evans's passion for bicycles, a careful description of the culprit could be given: 'Green enamelled frame ... upturned handlebar, three-speed gear, control lever on right of handlebar, lever front brake, back-pedalling brake worked from crank, of unusual pattern ... "Brooks" saddle.' In contrast, the description of the rider seemed shadowy, almost irrelevant. The average-height man with his greying hair, his grey suit and cap, his black boots and cycle clips, was, it seemed, almost any man on a bicycle. No one appeared to think he was very dangerous either; if you meet him, detain him and wire the Chief Constable of Leicestershire, the public were advised. Then claim your £5 reward.

The task of the police in finding the murderer was not facilitated by the widespread demobilisation of troops now taking place. In the villages surrounding Leicester, before the First World War, the village policemen had had a good knowledge of their communities; but now men were returning from the conflict seeking new opportunities, or returning to their homes after years away. The former were strangers; the latter had changed after four years in a warzone. The once-cosy familiarity between the local policeman and the community was yet to be regained. Trust had to be rebuilt; information was less readily given. It was a new world, post-war.

There had been one small breakthrough. Although the unknown man remained elusive, a bicycle repairer called Harry Cox recognised the description of the bike. He had been asked to undertake repairs on it – repairs which were completed on 5 July, the day of Bella's death. The owner had ridden away on it at about 2.00 pm, saying he was going for a spin in the country. The shop owner did not know who he was, though he answered broadly to the police description.

When the police had grown desperate for information, the reward had been increased to £20. But, even with that incentive, no one seemed able to provide the identity of the rider, or the whereabouts of the bicycle.

Eventually, the publicity did result in two young girls – aged twelve and fourteen – coming forward. On the afternoon of the day Bella died, they too had been out on their bicycles, they said, and at about 5.00 or 5.30 in the afternoon had encountered a man who had pestered them. His bicycle had been green. It was not much, but it was something.

The police searched for men with green bicycles, scoured the area fruitlessly for the gun, continued to advertise beseechingly for witnesses, called for further assistance from Scotland Yard, and, six months later, gave it up. And in the end, with Bella long buried by her grieving family, the crime receded into the mythology of the villages concerned, and the Leicestershire countryside settled

Introduction.

into the remote gold of autumn and then into bleak winter.

And then against all odds an extraordinary thing happened.

II.

'I never had a green bicycle... '[13]

On 24 February 1920, a canal man named Whitehouse was taking his barge, loaded with coal, down the river Soar; the light dim, the two horses plodding dutifully along the towpath, the barge low in the water; a quiet timeless scene, a journey Whitehouse had taken many times. Suddenly, his towrope slackened down in the water, and then it tightened, and, as it tightened, it drew up with it a part of a green bicycle frame. He glimpsed it only for a moment before it fell back into the water, but the green bicycle was famous by now, as was the reward associated with it. For a working man, the reward was worth having, and so the bargeman returned hopefully the next day to the same place and dragged the river bed until he found most of the frame and the front wheel, and these he took triumphantly to the police.

Instructed by the police to drag with the borough dredger, labourers from the Leicester Corporation found the rear wheel, and subsequently the gear wheel cranks and pedals. The green bicycle, almost in its entirety, had emerged symbolically from the dark depths, a mud-covered and dripping Excalibur, as though it could not rest in this stretch of water that meandered into St Mary's Wharf, and the factory at which poor Bella had worked.

Further dragging by the police opposite the wharf itself, and a little way distant from the site of the discovery of the bicycle, revealed a service revolver holster, full of cartridges – some live, some blank.

The history of the bicycle proved easy to establish. It was a classy BSA bicycle made to special order, and could be identified by a serial number engraved on the saddle pin. That number had been carefully filed off. But what the person who had done so did not know was that the manufacturers always put the same number inside the tube of the front fork. When the bicycle was disassembled, there it was: number 103648.

Green bicycle 103648 had been ordered by a firm in Derby on behalf of their local agents, Messrs Orton Bros. It was a model *de luxe* gentleman's bicycle from the 1910 bicycle catalogue, and it was to be painted green with green handlebars. It was to have special fittings: a back-pedal brake and a disc on the handlebars to operate the gears. Ortons had sold it to a Mr Ronald Vivian

---

13   Statement of Ronald Light when first confronted by the police.

Light.

Light in May 1910. He had long left his Derby address, but it was not difficult to trace him to his mother in Leicester. By now – March 1920 – he had moved to take up a new appointment as junior mathematics and science master at Dean Close School in Cheltenham. It would seem that he was certainly at one time the owner of the green bicycle found in the canal. But that did not mean he murdered Bella Wright. There was still a long way to go.

Dean Close School had been opened in 1886 as a small public day and boarding school for boys, and was built on an evangelical Christian foundation. It thrived, and has grown into the vibrant school it is today, accumulating along the way its noteworthy alumni: the list is characterised by the diversity of the personalities and their achievements, as these lists always are – the Victorian poet James Elroy Flecker, the great twentieth century artist Francis Bacon, Brian Jones of the Rolling Stones, bishops, rugby players and film stars, all rubbing shoulders with a random irrelevance.

In 1920, the school was a small community still reeling from its losses in the war. 120 old boys who had fought after leaving school – imbued with the values of their class, honour, fair play, bravery, their hearts full of love of God and country – had died. A chapel was planned as their memorial, and it was subsequently built with funds raised from private subscriptions. Cautiously feeling its way back to normality, the school cannot have been best pleased by the arrival of two police officers to question the new mathematics master, for whom they had great hopes, in connection with a notorious murder. They had been particularly impressed with Mr Light, who had performed his duties with zeal and intelligence, and whose conduct was entirely satisfactory.

Superintendent Taylor, the more senior of the two policemen, told Ronald he was making enquiries about a green bicycle. 'What became of your green bicycle?' he asked him.

Ronald Light laid the first brick in the wall of circumstantial evidence built against him. 'I never had a green bicycle,' he said. It was the most disastrous lie; once told, there was no going back.

'You purchased one from Messrs Orton at Derby,' the police officer told him.

'No,' said Ronald Light, and then: 'Yes, I had one, but I sold it years ago. I don't know who to, as I have had so many.'

That was good enough for the police. He was taken to Cheltenham Police Station for further questioning.

At the police station, he elaborated. He had sold a number of bicycles, he said, one to a man named Bourne in Derby; one to a man in Leicester. It may well have been true. It might also have been true that he had sold the green

Introduction.

bicycle, and that someone else had thrown it into the canal.

Over the next few months, the police explored every conceivable avenue in their exhaustive investigations. They had now got a green bicycle, a gun holster, a bullet and a suspect to work with.

Eventually, they managed to trace the movements of the green bicycle, even if they were less certain about those of its owner: it had been regularly maintained by the same bicycle repairer in Leicester, Walter Franks, who had looked after it for eight or nine years and who knew the owner, Ronald Light, well. There was no problem of identification there. Franks could identify Mr Light easily. Franks had last serviced the bicycle in the spring of 1919.

After that, of course, there had been the bicycle's last visit to the repair shop, on the very day of Bella's death. But that had been at a different establishment, and the repairer, Harry Cox, had not known the owner. If Harry Cox could now identify Ronald Light as the man whose green bicycle he had repaired on 5 July 1919, it would mean that there was evidence of Light's still being in ownership of the bicycle on the day of the murder, and of his leaving Cox's premises at 2.00 pm. But what about later in the day?

There were people, in addition to Harry Cox, who had seen a rider on a green bicycle after 2.00 pm on 5 July – but could the police prove it was the same rider who rode it away from Harry Cox's shop that afternoon? There were the two young girls, Edith and Valeria, who said they had been pestered by a man on a green bicycle; there was a farmer called Tom Nourish who came forward with his recollection that, between about 7.00 and 7.30 that evening, he had seen a couple on bicycles; there was the wife of a carrier, a woman called Elizabeth Palmer, accompanying her husband on a delivery, who had seen at a distance a man and a girl on bicycles, and who subsequently saw Bella, whom she had then recognised, walking through her uncle's front gate, leaving a man waiting outside on his bicycle. And of course there was Bella's family: her uncle George Measures, her cousins Margaret and twelve year old Agnes, and Margaret's husband James. They had all seen Bella off at Gaulby, accompanied by a man on a green bicycle. But would they be able to identify that man as Ronald Light?

The police arranged identification parades, all rather haphazard affairs judged by the standards of today, all in different venues with different participants. The first of these, on 4 March, was held in Cheltenham immediately after Light was arrested. Harry Cox, the repairer, brought urgently from Leicester, identified Light as his customer on the day of the murder.

On 5 March, when a dazed Light arrived in Leicester in police custody, he was paraded in the police yard against the homely backdrop of the stable provided for the Chief Constable's horse. There were nine men, including the

Light.

accused, all in their dark suits – some buttoned, some waistcoated, in ties or bow ties, in varying types of hat. George Measures confidently picked out Light. Twelve year old Agnes did not.

The next morning, another parade was attempted: different men, yet somehow the same; the same anxious expressions, the same hats, but this time indoors in an office at the police station. Margaret and James Evans slowly inspected the line. James Evans picked out Ronald Light. Margaret did not. Nor did Thomas Nourish. Elizabeth Palmer was 'almost' sure that Light was the man she had seen.

It cannot have been very reassuring for the police. The two young girls who said they had been pestered now remained. The last parade took place in circumstances that would not now be allowed, in a room at Leicester Castle, on 10 March. Light had been taken before the magistrates and remanded in custody. A group of men were mustered to attend the castle that morning, and a photograph shows them lining up outside. Light was not among them; he joined them in a room after he had been formally remanded into police custody. The evidence does not tell us how the two girls themselves got to the room, but the circumstances did not preclude the possibility that Light's unique status might have become apparent to them.[14] They both identified Light as the man who had pestered them.

Identification evidence was all very well, and, having evolved in the 1890s, parades were by now a well-established way of eliciting that evidence, but no really rigorous procedure existed to ensure that they were fair to the accused; it was not until 1924, following a much earlier gross miscarriage of justice,[15] that an enquiry at last adjudicated on police practices with regard to identification

---

14   Echoes of Oscar Slater's unreliable identification in a New York corridor: 'While the witnesses Lambie, Barrowman and Adams were waiting with Inspector Pyper outside the Court-room before the examination commenced a dramatic incident occurred. Three men came along the corridor in which they were standing, passed them, and went into the Court; whereupon both of the girls simultaneously said to Mr Pyper that one of the three was the man they had seen on the night of the murder, Lambie's expression being, "I could nearly swear that is the man!" As this was their real recognition of Slater, the subsequent identification in the Court-room being only that of the man they had already recognised, the incident is of some importance. Slater was being conducted into Court by Messrs Chamberlain and Pinckney, Deputy United States Marshals, and it was contended by Mr Miller for the defence that he was obviously in the charge of those officials. He was not, however, handcuffed or otherwise branded as a prisoner, while his companions do not appear to have been in uniform, though one of them wore a badge which the witnesses said they did not notice, and the other was a very tall man. Both girls denied that they had been prepared to see Slater where they did.' (Roughead, xx-xxi.) Slater was wrongfully convicted of murder in 1909; William Roughead's *Trial of Oscar Slater* [NBT 10], from which this quotation is derived, followed in 1910. Slater remained in prison until 1928.

15   Adolf Beck [NBT 33], twice convicted of offences on the basis of mistaken identification evidence, and ultimately given a free pardon by the King in 1904.

Introduction.

parades. This bleak conclusion was then reached:

> Evidence as to identity based upon personal impressions, however *bona fide*, is perhaps of all classes of evidence the least to be relied upon, and therefore, unless supported by the facts, an unsafe basis for the verdict of a jury.

That assessment was still four years away, but it was the culmination of growing disquiet. In 1920, the police would have been well aware of the shaky ground on which they were basing a principal part of their case against Light.

Nonetheless, the murky picture of identification upon which the police had to rely was enough for a jury to be satisfied, if they were so minded, that Ronald Light had still owned the green bicycle on the day of Bella's death; that he had gone for a ride on it on that day; that he had been in Bella's company when she left her uncle's house between 8.30 and 8.45 pm; and that therefore he must have been in her company at least for some minutes thereafter, and prior to her being found dead at about 9.20 pm.

Mary Webb, the Lights' servant, was questioned as to the fate of the green bicycle after Ronald Light had had his late dinner on the night of the murder. It had remained in the back kitchen, she said, for three or four days, and then Mr Ronald had moved it to the box room at the top of the house. In December, he told her that he had sold it. The sinister fact was that Ronald Light had cycled about Leicester on his green bicycle until the day of the murder; and then was seen on it no more.

Given all that, Ronald Light had some explaining to do. Or had he?

Even leaving aside the uncertainties of identification evidence, there were some significant gaps, yawning wide, ready to be exploited by the clever defence counsel who would no doubt be instructed on Light's behalf by a family who were not short of a few guineas. There was no evidence whatever that placed Ronald Light in Bella Wright's company any later than (very approximately) thirty-five minutes before she was found dead; there was a gap between the conclusive evidence of Light's possession of the bicycle in 1919 and its eventual recovery from the canal in February 1920. And there was no evidence to link him to the bicycle's disposal.

Of course, they had the bullet which had been found at the scene of Bella's death, and the gun holster containing cartridges dredged out of the canal, although there was no connection between the two. Nor indeed, other than their close proximity in the canal, was there any link between bicycle and gun holster. The bullet was a .455, originally a black powder (or gunpowder) bullet adapted for use with cordite to increase its velocity, and one of the type used in army service revolvers. The bullets in the loaded cartridges found in the canal were of the same standard issue army type. No gun was found.

The police, desperately seeking something concrete to link Light to the crime, began to take the dogged first step of trying to establish whether Light had indeed owned a service revolver, and, if so, where it was. Exhaustive enquiries were made; letters and telegrams marked 'confidential' and then 'urgent' flew between the Director of Public Prosecutions and the War Office; the latter dispatched urgent orders for investigation to Buxton, the training centre for officers attended by Light at the outset of his service; to York, where the ordnance stores for service revolvers were situated; to the Newcastle depot from which revolvers had been dispatched to officers serving overseas; to Chatham, where the army weapon records were held. Light's batman, his commanding officer, and his army colleagues were traced and interrogated. It was all fruitless.

Yes, the police were told, in theory all officers had revolvers either issued to them or obtained by them with funds provided by the Army, though a shortage meant there was a possibility that they were sent abroad without one, or with one other than of service pattern, bought from a private firm; yes, they were all trained to use them. But no, there was no record of the particular weapon issued to Light, nor of any cheque issued to him to purchase one, nor of his training in firearms, nor any personal recollection from anyone that he had one in his possession any later than about 1915.[16]

The police were well aware that the ballistics evidence was equivocal. Among the welter of information provided in relation to the enquiries about the gun was an interesting observation made by a hurried official at the War Office in a memo to the Director of Public Prosecutions, and certainly never subsequently shared with the defence: 'It was only on a second examination that it was found that the woman had been shot ... a service revolver – which would make a large and obvious wound – could hardly have been used'.[17]

He was articulating just one of the mysteries which had begun to trouble the prosecution team. They were, they knew, vulnerable on the question of whether the nature of the injury to Bella's head was consistent with the bullet found. Surely, as the official implied, massive damage would have been caused by a revolver at close range? And there were other concerns: why had the bullet ended up resting a few feet from the body? Surely with no more resistance than a human head, it would have travelled on much further? Dr Williams had made a statement to the police saying that the wound he had examined was consistent with the bullet found at the scene, and the result of a revolver fired

16   See the evidence of Light's friend, Ethel Tunnicliffe, who tells a somewhat confused and certainly odd story that Light had sent to her a revolver for safekeeping, and that she had duly returned it to him.

17   TNA: PRO WO 339/52768.

Introduction.

at a range of about five feet. But even this was less useful than it ought to have been. Williams, as the defence would not hesitate to point out, was also the local doctor who had missed the injury altogether on first examination.

The police proposed to call a gunsmith who would say that the bullet found at the scene, six yards from Bella's body, and the bullets in the loaded cartridges in the canal were of the same type. In addition, he said, the damage and markings on the bullet found at the scene were consistent, in his opinion as an expert, with not only a mangling by a hoof but with its having ricocheted off a hard surface, either before or after going through Bella's head. If it had ricocheted before hitting her, it must have been fired from a distance. If, as Dr Williams said, it had been fired from five or six feet away, it could only have ricocheted afterwards. This put in question not only the extent of the wound, but also the position Bella was in when she was shot; at this stage, Dr Williams did not feel able to offer an opinion as to this. Both theories opened up a number of possibilities that might be exploited by the defence, and, all in all, the ballistics evidence cannot have instilled complete confidence in the prosecution.

Light's lies to the police, were, of course, helpful to their case; the one thing that was now crystal clear was that he had at some point owned the green bicycle subsequently found in the canal. Why, if he was an innocent man, had his immediate reaction been to deny it?

This, then, was the case for the prosecution; they could do no more, it seemed, in terms of investigation. Could they prove beyond a reasonable doubt to a jury of twelve men that the cumulative circumstantial evidence was so overwhelming as to prove that Ronald had shot Bella?

III.

'... your defence of Light seemed to me to be without a fault ... '[18]

The fullest transcript of the trial of Ronald Light yet reconstructed follows this introduction.[19] But reading the transcript of a trial is rather like reading a play with no stage directions as to the characters and surroundings: the dialogue is clear enough, but not what brings it to life.

18   Extract from a note sent by the trial judge, Mr Justice Horridge, to Edward Marshall Hall after Light's acquittal.

19   H. R. Wakefield published *The Green Bicycle Case* in 1930, reproducing the coverage of the trial as given by the *Leicester Post*. Wakefield had tried to track down a full and verbatim account of the case, but the official shorthand record taken in court 'was never transcribed, and the gentleman who took the note has since died' (Wakefield, 12). The transcript given in this volume is a composite of several newspaper sources, and nearly doubles the length of the transcript given in Wakefield's book.

Light.

A trial has a dramatic structure: it has real people, united by stress and stage fright, divided in their reactions to those emotions. It has professionals with huge workloads, reputations to build, scores to settle and livings to earn; and participants with images to preserve, consciences to placate, and secrets wholly unrelated to the facts of the case to conceal. It is bound by rules and conventions and rituals.

Trials carry their own stories. They are the forum in which victim and accused are linked in the defining aftermath of whatever event necessitated them, and in which the other main players, lawyers and judges, shoehorn the facts into the laws of evidence and criminal procedure and thereby fashion from the truths, lies, myths and legends of the original crime that special kind of truth that constitutes a verdict.

Read the transcript with all this in mind, and what is unspoken becomes just as important as the evidence given.

Counsel in the Green Bicycle Case arrived in Leicester to be greeted by a population and press with their emotions whipped up to fever pitch. None of the eminent barristers who had been instructed would have been particularly enthusiastic about the venue for the trial: Leicester Castle had housed the Assize court for centuries, and was highly picturesque with Norman arches and ancient beams. But it was notorious to the Bar for being far too small and extremely uncomfortable. Trials were conducted in what one onlooker described as a 'terrible physical intimacy'.[20] And, indeed, in a photograph of this trial, Light is squeezed into the dock between three burly warders, so close to not only his own counsel but to the prosecution team that he could have touched them, with judge and jury only a few cluttered feet away. Counsel's table was so small that papers were constantly sliding off it, and the seats were little more than ledges to lean against. The stellar personalities involved on both sides in this trial, whilst welcoming the spotlight of national publicity in which the case was to be heard, would certainly have resented the surroundings.

The team of barristers briefed to represent the prosecution was a formidable one. The recently appointed Attorney-General, Sir Gordon Hewart, K.C., was to lead. He was already a big name in Leicestershire as the Liberal member of parliament for Leicester East. Given the heavy workload entailed in the role of Attorney-General, it was rare for the incumbent to prosecute personally in any murder save those achieved through poisoning, which was regarded as a particularly heinous crime. Yet here he was, heading up the team to prosecute an obscure shooting in a country lane. It was an indication of the impact upon the authorities of public outrage at the crime; they did not want any mistakes to

---

20   A. E. Bowker 128 (Marshall Hall's Clerk).

Introduction.

be made in the presentation of the case against Light. They were going to do all they could to get the man in the dock.

In order to enable Sir Gordon to leave the trial to attend, when necessary, to his government duties, he was to be assisted by both Henry Maddocks, K.C., a highly experienced leader in the criminal courts, and by a rising star practising from chambers in Birmingham – Norman Birkett. Young Birkett had been called to the Bar six years previously. He was, later in his career, to become a highly regarded barrister, a judge at the Nuremberg trials of the Nazi war criminals after the Second World War, and a distinguished judge in the Court of Appeal. This was his first murder trial.

The talented legal battalion mustered by the Director of Public Prosecutions was a great reassurance to the Leicestershire police force, who also felt the huge public pressure for a conviction. 'It is most gratifying to hear of the splendid array of counsel you have secured,' the Chief Constable of Leicestershire wrote to the D.P.P.; 'undoubtedly the most complete justice will be done to our case.' He meant that they were bound to secure a conviction. That was what, despite the precarious nature of some of the evidence, everyone thought. It was said that Light stood in need of a miracle if he was not to hang for Bella's murder.

Light's miracle was embodied in the glamorous (and expensive) form of defence counsel Sir Edward Marshall Hall, K.C., the most famous barrister in England, and a man with an unparalleled reputation for saving his clients from the death penalty. And the fact is that it was Light's privileged background that was to give him a chance in this trial.

Public funding was by now available to enable an accused person to instruct defence lawyers, thanks to a public outcry in the early part of the century at the number of defendants who may have hanged because they could not afford proper representation. The 1903 Poor Prisoners Defence Act authorised a rudimentary form of what we call Legal Aid; £3 5s 6d was available for the lawyers; not only was it very modest, but it was only available to those who could show that it 'was desirable in the interests of justice ... having regard to the defence set up'.

This was hugely significant: it meant that, in order to qualify for public funding, an accused must reveal his defence in advance of the trial. If paying privately, however, he was perfectly entitled to keep mum as to his defence until the very last moment in the trial. The guidelines as to the interpretation of the statute indicate a pretty shameless erosion of the defendant's right to stay silent:[21]

---

21   The wheel has now come full circle; in modern times, all defendants are required to make known their defence in advance. No ambush defence is available to anyone.

Light.

> The Act was passed in the interest of innocent persons; and such would be advised in future not to 'reserve their defence', but to disclose it at once, so that it could be investigated. The prisoner would thus prevent the suggestion that he had kept back his defence so as to give the prosecution no opportunity of investigating it.[22]

As will be seen, the whole success of the Green Bicycle defence was its element of surprise. Ronald Light's money enabled him not only to 'buy' Marshall Hall but, just as precious, to buy ambush trial tactics. £3 5s 6d would not have achieved either. Without those two precious advantages, he would probably have hanged. There was indeed in those days the proverbial one law for the rich, and one for the poor.

Assisting Marshall Hall was 'junior' barrister George Wightman Powers. Powers was not a K.C., and therefore (despite his fifty-six years) was the junior in the case. He was to become more distinguished as a historian than as a lawyer; but, belonging to an old Leicestershire family brought up in the grandeur of the Manor House at Barwell, only about seventeen miles from Bella's home village, his local knowledge of the network of little roads which were central to the case would have been as invaluable to Marshall Hall as his status as a local man – a marked asset with a jury in those parochial days.

Famous for his showmanship, Marshall Hall always made a point of arriving in court at the very last moment. He knew the value of making an entrance. Despite his impossibly glamorous image, unknown to his admiring public, he suffered increasingly from varicose veins; and those seats in Leicester Castle were, for him, sheer torture. On the first day of Light's trial, he arrived fresh from the comforts of Leicester's most luxurious old coaching inn, the Bell, clutching ostentatiously to his chest a large cushion. In the future, it was to become one of his trademarks, like the perpetual cigar and the immaculately furled umbrella. And, as closely clutched to his chest as the cushion was, his defence. Not even his junior in the trial knew what line he was going to take until it began. Certainly the Attorney-General and his team were completely in the dark.

On the first day of the trial, 9 June 1920, in the cramped courtroom, in national newspapers and in living rooms across the nation, it was Marshall Hall who commanded attention. A starstruck young Norman Birkett, watching from prosecuting counsel's row the arrival of the defence team, wrote:

> I shall always remember the moment when Marshall Hall came into court at Leicester Castle. He brought with him a strange magnetic quality that made itself felt in every part of the court. The spectators stirred with excitement at the sight

22 TNA: PRO DPP 1/61.

Introduction.

of the man whose name was at that time a household word, and a faint murmur ran from floor to gallery. Marshall Hall came, of course, with all the prestige of the greatest criminal defender of the day, and every eye was fixed upon him. ... When he addressed the judge it was seen that to his great good looks and majestic bearing there had been added perhaps the greatest gift of all in the armoury of an advocate – a most beautiful speaking voice. He had in this case a terrible task before him.[23]

The prosecution team would have been well aware of the mythology surrounding Marshall Hall; it was frequently and increasingly resented by his opponents as an unfair advantage. Prosecuting counsel's pragmatic job of setting dispassionately before the jury the intricate facts upon which it would be invited to find a case beyond all reasonable doubt would have to be performed in a very engrossing manner indeed to counter Marshall Hall's legendarily spontaneous hypnotic advocacy.[24]

Painstakingly, prosecuting counsel embarked on opening the case. The fact that there were no provisions in the law in those days that required the defence to reveal anything at all at this stage – not the nature of the defence, not any admissions as to factual matters – made it a hard task. The prosecution had to prove every aspect, however small, of their case against the accused, with no idea of what did or did not really matter.

As a highly experienced prosecutor, Sir Gordon Hewart started not with the smartly dressed defendant in the dock upon whom all eyes had been fixed, but with the victim. The jury has to understand from the very outset that murders are about victims. The accused murderer, star of the show though he sometimes appears to be, has a mere bit-part. It is the story of the life lost that matters if a conviction is to be secured. So the Attorney-General drew, first of all, a picture, touching in its simplicity, of the attractive, hard working girl who kept company with a nice young man; and so the jury began to think of the life curtailed, the promise destroyed, the family desolate, the overwhelming imperative to nail her killer. The drama built: 'A conclusion you may think as quite irresistible is that that was a case of murder,' he thundered.

Marshall Hall, that consummate defender, would not have liked this ringing oratory at all, and he dealt with it in the traditional way – by creating a diversion. Indicating his client standing in the dock, as was then the invariable custom during the prosecution's opening speech, Marshall Hall addressed the judge; might his client sit down? The interruption, seeking to change the convention

---

23   Birkett 12.

24   For many other examples of this advocacy and an up-to-date analysis of its origins and power, see *Marshall Hall: A Law unto Himself* by Sally Smith (Wildy, Simmonds and Hill: 2016).

Light.

of the time, did what it was intended to do; it distracted the jury's attention from the Attorney-General, whilst underlining that Marshall Hall's client was a sensitive man under great stress. The judge, Mr Justice Horridge, was well aware of what Marshall Hall was up to. 'You may be seated,' he said to the defendant, and to Marshall Hall, reprovingly, 'I was going to say so when the Attorney-General was finished.'

When Sir Gordon Hewart resumed his speech, it took him a little time to get back into his stride, but he did so at last, working his way through a detailed account of Bella's last hours, of the man with the green bicycle who had been seen with her, and of the evidence linking that man and Ronald Light. Circumstantial it might be, but the coincidences of truth he pointed out were innumerable; if the jury examined what could be proved to be true, they would find it led to corroborative evidence of Light's guilt. But he had no real answer to what must have been the burning issue in the jurors' minds: what could possibly be the motive for the violent shooting of a girl who had not apparently been robbed or raped?

Sir Gordon was a courageous advocate; he did not shirk the apparent absence of motive. It was not for the jury to speculate, he told them; the prosecution had only to prove the deed was done, not the motive for it. That was correct in law, but, as Hewart well knew, human beings in jury boxes do not confine themselves to what the law tells them they ought to think about. So, having told them not to speculate, he did so himself: could it be revenge? Did the prisoner have his advances rejected? And he pointed out the tiny shred of evidence suggestive of a prior relationship between Bella and the man who had accompanied her when she left her uncle: 'Bella,' he was alleged to have said, 'you were gone a long time'. 'You will observe, of course' said Sir Gordon smoothly to the jury, just in case they had not, 'that he addressed her by her Christian name. He evidently knew her well enough to feel sure that she would not resent being so addressed.' It was an interesting angle. Surely more to the point was not whether he was familiar in addressing her, but the fact that he knew her name at all? Nonetheless, the unspoken question was the same; if the man had been Ronald Light, how was he going to get out of that one?

And so, painstakingly, doggedly, and, it must be said, pretty boringly for the jury, the prosecution embarked on the calling of all their witnesses and the cobbling together of the pieces of evidence that ultimately made up the devastating case against Ronald Light.

The detailed picture of the precise topography of the roads around Leicester, the history of the green bicycle from its manufacture to its ownership by Light, its emergence from the canal, the sightings of the man with Bella, the identification

Introduction.

of that man as Light: all these points slowly came into better focus. And so too did an astonishing phenomenon: Sir Edward Marshall Hall, the most famous cross examiner in England, was strangely quiet.

The public gallery and the press seats were full with spectators eager to hear the forensic fireworks, the displays of temperament, the baiting of the judge for which he was so famous; instead Sir Edward was almost desultory in his cross-examination of the first witnesses. A few questions of little moment of the County Surveyor who produced his plans, of Joseph Cowell and of Police Constable Hall, and the witnesses were stumbling from the box released from the long anticipated ordeal so quickly that they were dazed.

It was only when Edith Nunney – the first of the two little girls who said they had encountered Ronald Light earlier on the day of Bella Wright's death – was called into the witness box that Marshall Hall revealed a little of his hand. Her examination on behalf of the prosecution was begun by the junior member of the team, Norman Birkett; he elicited her address and then asked her if, on 5 July, she had been out cycling with her friend. This, of course was technically a leading question. Strictly speaking, he should have asked her an open question, such as, 'Do you remember a particular day last summer when you were out cycling?' and then, if she answered in the affirmative, 'Can you tell the court when it was?'

Marshall Hall leapt to his feet. His learned friend was not to lead the witness, he said. Although he was not proposing to cross-examine as to identity or the ownership of the bicycle, nothing whatsoever in this case was admitted. Having thus thoroughly confused everyone as to how he was going to conduct the defence, he sat down again.

The judge duly directed the jury that they must bear in mind that the date had been provided by the prosecution and not by Edith, and pointed out reprovingly to an abashed Birkett that the date must not be mentioned when Edith's friend was called into the witness box next. The smartly dressed schoolgirl then gave her evidence: a man on a green bicycle passed them, going in the opposite direction, and had smiled at them; he had turned round and followed them; when they stopped, they thought that he had tried to separate them by suggesting that one of them should take the lead. They refused, and he cycled away. The man she had picked out in the identification parade was that man, there, in the dock.

It might have been a relatively harmless little story, but its overtones were sinister. Marshall Hall knew that its danger lay in the germ of a sexual motive it provided for the prosecution. He proceeded to make mincemeat of poor Edith. By the time he sat down, he had underlined to the jury that the girl's statements had been made to the police nine months after the incident; and Edith had

Light.

said, 'Yes, sir,' to every question she had been asked. Yes, sir, she had read all about the green bicycle murder in the newspapers and she had heard everyone talking about it. Yes, sir, the policemen had asked her whether she had seen this particular man on 5 July. Yes, sir, the policeman had told her the date. Marshall Hall sat down quickly, and purring.

Edith's friend Valeria was made of slightly sterner stuff; she protested sturdily that the incident had occurred before she had heard all about the green bicycle. But Marshall Hall had undoubtedly established considerable doubt as to the reliability of the girls' accounts.

Similarly, Dr Williams was given short shrift; it was absurd, Marshall Hall suggested, to suppose that a bullet of the kind found, fired as Dr Williams said it had been from a few feet away, with the victim's head its only resistance, would only have travelled a few feet before coming to a halt. Crucially, Dr Williams agreed. His somewhat contrived theory, not rehearsed previously to the police or in the coroner's court, was that Bella might have been lying on the ground, and that the bullet, having passed through her head, bounced off the edge of the stony road and landed a few feet away. It was not particularly convincing in the light of his observation, only too apparent, that he had 'not much experience of gunshot wounds'. But nonetheless it was the only theory to emerge which fitted the evidence he gave of the angle of the trajectory of the bullet through the head – upwards, inwards and backwards – and the position a few feet away in which the bullet had landed; and to that extent it was inconvenient to the defence.

As a result, it was the gunsmith who at last aroused serious cross examination. Marshall Hall was a consummate shot, famous for his remarkable party piece of shooting off his wife's hat at garden parties. He had vast experience both personally and professionally of the niceties of ballistics, and had many friends in the gunsmith's trade – one of whom, it was said, he had informally consulted before the trial – and he fancied himself as an expert. He frequently chose, contrary to all the rules, not to call defence expert witnesses (who have what he regarded as a rather inconvenient duty to the court to give objective evidence), but to rely instead on the effectiveness of his cross-examination of the expert for the prosecution.

Dr Williams had scarcely been worth bothering with, but Henry Clarke, a gunsmith of Clarke and Sons with the appropriate address of Gallowtree Gate, Leicester, was called as an expert witness by the prosecution, and was an opponent worthy of Marshall Hall's attention. Clarke's function for the prosecution was specifically to prove that the bullet found by Bella's body was of .455 calibre, and of the type adapted for cordite powder cartridges for use with army service revolvers – the adaptation served enormously to increase the

Introduction.

velocity of the projectile. The bullet from the road was identical to those in the loaded cartridges found in the canal.

It sounded significant until Marshall Hall, in cross-examination, extracted the further information that Mr Clarke was unable to begin to estimate how many million cartridges and bullets had been made to an identical pattern; the bullet had been in standard army use ever since the Boer War. So much, was the unspoken message to the jury, for the astounding coincidence of the identical nature of the bullets.

Of far more importance, however, was the relationship between the nature of the wound and the bullet alleged to have inflicted it. The marks on the bullet indicated that it had passed through a rifled barrel, Mr Clarke agreed; the longer the barrel, the greater the velocity; he could not say whether it had been a revolver or a rifle. This, of course, was highly significant; in theory, at least, a rifle could have caused the damage just as effectively as a service revolver. Suppose, said Marshall Hall, the bullet had been fired from a rifle a considerable distance away, and had hit an obstacle such as a tree, and then the victim on the road – would it have ended up a few feet away from the body? 'It is possible,' Clarke replied cautiously. That was good enough to open up a whole new range of potential culprits, all unknown to anyone.

One of the skills of the good cross-examiner is knowing when to stop. Marshall Hall had sown a seed of doubt as to the very nature of the weapon used; lingering on the issue in the hope of fortifying his advantage would be an elementary mistake; it might have allowed Clarke to extricate himself. So Marshall Hall turned, without pause, to the nature of the injury – the very matter about which the prosecution already had some concerns. Nowadays, of course, with our sophisticated forensic laboratories and qualified forensic scientists, the evidence relating to Bella's injuries would be far more complex; but, nonetheless, however elaborately constructed or scientifically expressed, the defence point in the end was crudely simple: 'I suggest that the effect of a shot fired from four or five yards by a service revolver would be to almost blow the head right off,' said Marshall Hall. Clarke, having recovered himself, resisted this suggestion with spirit. It all depended, he insisted, on angle and velocity and how the bullet struck. It could, he said, echoing the doctor's theory, have passed through the victim's head at an upwards angle, struck the turf and been arrested where it was found. It was a damaging endorsement of Dr Williams, and Marshall Hall could only counter it with the unscientific pragmatism of a so-called 'jury point', designed to appeal to the less sophisticated responses of the juries of the time. 'Have you ever seen a human being who has been shot at a distance of within five yards with a service revolver?' he asked Clarke. 'No, sir,'

Light.

conceded Clarke, and Marshall Hall – who certainly hadn't either, but who was betting on the fact that more than one of his jury would have – rolled his eyes meaningfully in their direction. It was the best he could do; shortly thereafter, he subsided back onto his cushion.

The evidence was unclear, and it often suits defence counsel that it should be; in their closing submissions they can then speculate more creatively. But judges will sometimes step in and ensure the point is properly analysed. Mr Justice Horridge did so now:

'Do you see anything inconsistent in the condition of the bullet with its having passed through the head of the dead woman, and then having had its course arrested by the turf where it joins the metal at the edge of the road, and being found seventeen feet away?'

'No, my Lord,' replied Clarke.[25]

It was a neat encapsulation of the only plausible theory; it was a simple answer, and it must have been very irritating for Marshall Hall.

The prosecution team ground on with their parade of witnesses designed to link Light, the green bicycle and Bella. Light was satisfactorily identified in court by all those who had previously done so at the identification parades. His ownership of the bicycle was established; no objections were raised to any of the paperwork relating to its manufacture and retail history; bicycle shop employees and repairers gave unchallenged evidence as to both Light and his bicycle. The bargeman told of his finding; the police told of Light's denial of ownership, a clear lie in view of the evidence that had gone before. Still there was no real challenge from the defence.

Somehow, despite the strength of the case that was building, there was a sense that the whole court was interested only in reaching the case for the defence. It was just what Marshall Hall, the consummate jury psychologist, had intended, a masterly exploitation of the most precious card he held: ambush.

As the evidence progressed, it was apparent that the judge knew Marshall Hall's techniques well enough as to become increasingly jumpy. On two occasions, he intervened with questions of his own.

To PC Hall:

'Was the body identified by the mother the same body you found lying in the road?'

---

25 An interchange between Clarke and the judge that followed this is a good example of the dangers of relying on evidence in previous proceedings. On being asked whether, if the bullet had been shot from a few feet away, he would expect scorching to the skin where the bullet entered, Clarke said he would not. In the magistrates' court, he gave exactly contrary evidence ('If discharged within three or four yards, I should expect to find some blackening on the skin of the person at whom it was discharged'). As a matter of fact, no such scorching was found.

Introduction.

And to Dr Williams:
'What caused the death of Bella Wright?'
'Shock, following gunshot wounds.'
'So that the gunshot wound caused her death?'

Crashingly obvious the answers may have been, but their omission might have furnished Marshall Hall with the opportunity to submit that the case had not been fully proved.

They were both surprising oversights on the part of the prosecution. Even the judge commented on the omissions.

'I noticed that, my Lord, but I said nothing about it at the time,' said Marshall Hall, smugly. Both he and his opponent knew that he had no professional duty to point out any holes in the prosecution case, and he could exploit any weakness. The judge had spiked his guns.

Only one question put by Marshall Hall to Bella's uncle George Measures gave a hint of what was to come. He told the jury – as he had said throughout, since his very first statement – that he had heard the stranger with the bicycle address his niece when she emerged from his cottage: 'Bella, I thought you had gone the other way'. Was he a little hard of hearing? Marshall Hall asked in his irresistibly confidential way. Yes, Measures told him; a little deaf in one ear. It was the answer Marshall Hall had wanted. Didn't the man say, 'Hello, I thought you had gone the other way'? George Measures sturdily denied this suggestion, but the idea was planted in the jury's mind; Measures just might have misheard.

It was time for the defence to present the case for the accused. Nowadays, in the overwhelming majority of cases (increased in recent decades by legislation which allows comment to be made if he fails to do so), the defendant in a criminal trial is called to give evidence in his own defence. But in 1920 it was a relatively new procedure. The statute that permitted it was passed in 1898, only twenty-two years previously. For centuries before that, incredible as it seems to modern thought, no accused was permitted to do so.[26] The new rule had been sparingly applied as Bench and Bar grappled with its implications; should an accused person who went into the witness box and then lied be charged with perjury?[27] Should he be allowed to give an account in the witness box which he had not given previously? Would the jury condemn any accused person who did

---

26   The rationale for this derived from the argument that it is up to the prosecution to prove its case, and that the defendant, presumed innocent, has nothing to prove. It was also argued in those more religious times that a defendant might lie in the witness box, and that to ask him to give evidence was therefore to tempt him to put his immortal soul in jeopardy. Modernising jurists protested against these objections on the basis that the jury was deprived of a full explanation of the accused's conduct. After many attempts, the Criminal Evidence Act was passed.

27   This particular dilemma, often expressed by jurists, became highly pertinent later in the story.

Light.

not avail himself of the new right to give evidence, now he had it?

The answers to these questions were to evolve slowly, but the more practical consideration for a working defence counsel was whether his defendant had the personal qualities to appeal to a jury if they heard him. Those qualities have little to do with innocence. Was he quick-witted enough to follow the lead of his counsel's questions? Not to panic and stray off the path? Was he cool-headed enough to withstand cross-examination designed by clever, highly experienced men to catch him out? Could he ultimately be trusted with his own life in his hands? Light certainly thought that he had what it took.

> Will you please ask me to tell the jury in my own words exactly why I did not come forward? I shall say I was dreadfully worried, and for some days was quite dazed at such an unexpected blow, and could not think clearly. When I began to think, I could not make up my mind to come forward, and hesitated for days. I could not give the police any information whatever as to how the girl met her death. If the police and papers had only stated the known facts, and asked the cyclist to come forward, I shall [*sic*] have done so, but they jumped to wrong conclusions, and I was frightened when I saw I was wanted for murder. ... Let me do this in my own words.

So he wrote, during the trial, in a note to Marshall Hall.[28]

It was an admirably concise, articulate description of what he astutely recognised as his weakest point, and it augured well for his performance in the witness box.

In fact, Marshall Hall must have predicated the whole defence on calling Light and letting him do it 'in his own words'. At the end of the prosecution case, despite the inroads made into it by the defence, there were still far too many unanswered questions for any jury to acquit without hearing an explanation of the apparently admitted facts from the accused himself.

As, in his very quietest voice, without fanfare or flourish, Marshall Hall called his client into the witness box, they must both have felt they were skating on very thin ice indeed.

Along with all other counsel in the case and the judge himself, Marshall Hall well knew that, deep in the prosecution brief, concealed – so far – from the jury because it had to be unless very particular circumstances rendered it relevant, lay forensic dynamite. Ronald Light's background was not as exemplary as those defending him would have wished it to be. The police had been exhaustive in their inquiries into Light's personal life, and had uncovered information which, if put before a jury, might well have helped him along the road to the gallows.

---

28   Marjoribanks 403.

Introduction.

That is not to say that it was remotely relevant to the murder, and nothing may be given in evidence in a criminal trial which does not directly tend to the proof or disproof of the matter in issue. The prosecution could not call evidence as to an accused's bad character simply to show he was of low morals or criminal inclination; nor, under the statute that enabled him to go into the witness box and give evidence in his own defence, could they cross-examine him as to such matters. But like most rules of criminal evidence, there were exceptions to this: if the accused, personally or by his advocate, endeavoured to establish particular aspects of his own good character, then he was, in the eyes of the law, rendering himself open to cross-examination as to anything in his previous history which suggested otherwise.[29]

Any defendant, therefore, who has anything to hide has to feel his way across a treacherous no-man's-land stretching in front of him from the dubious safety of the witness box. He must endear himself to the jury while avoiding any positive assertions as to his character and history which might render him liable to cross-examination about things that he would prefer the jury not to know.

It is not hard to spot, once you know the rules: the tentative questions of defence counsel; the carefully-drawn outlines in the accused's personal history, without the background you would expect to be coloured in; the cautious, oblique answers of the accused. The Green Bicycle trial is a classic example of this.

It took place at a time when men were heroes, back from the war to end all wars, medalled and traumatised, in which they had risked their lives defending their country and the values of freedom. In the courts, defence counsel were using war records to get juries and judges on their side. Juries faced with delivering verdicts on ex-soldiers were reluctant to convict; and, if they did, judges were noted to be sentencing with greater leniency. This was despite strictures from the Court of Appeal that war service, however brave, was no more a mitigating factor than anything else, and certainly not an excuse for subsequent criminal behaviour. Counsel were not above exploiting these sensibilities for all they were worth; Marshall Hall had himself, in a trial shortly before Light's, described one defendant charged with the most disreputable offence as 'this grand old soldier, with the sands of time fast running out, standing in that dock with his head bowed, with all his great services to his country to look back upon'.[30] It had led to one of his best results.

---

29 This is not a legal textbook and the explanation will strike historians of our laws of evidence as simplistic. It is intended to encapsulate the basic difficulty that faced Light and Marshall Hall in view of Light's past. Those who require further detail should study the 1898 Criminal Evidence Act.

30 Smith 167.

Light.

And now here was Light, a public schoolboy, a qualified engineer, a young army officer, a public school master in those snobbish days when class was clearly delineated and respected, who had served his country in France amidst the worst of the carnage, who had been invalided out, deafened and shellshocked, and who had picked up the reins of civilian life with courage, now teaching the next generation of young men.[31] It was all there, and Marshall Hall would have been the first to see its dramatic value. And yet what do we hear about Light's background at the outset of his evidence?

'In 1915, did you enter the army?'

'Yes.'

And then:

'When did you first go to France?'

'In November 1915.'

'When did you come back from France first?'

'Either at the end of January 1916, or the beginning of February. ... The next time I went to France was in November 1917.'

Why do we hear nothing of Light's early history? Or of his war? The message to those in the know was resoundingly clear: Marshall Hall dared not go near it; a single assertion as to Light's good character might have revealed the facts known to the prosecution, hitherto unknown to the jury.

But they are known to us. In 1902, young Ronald, aged sixteen, had been expelled from Oakham School after a vague suggestion that he had been caught trying to lift a young girl's skirt over her head. There is no other detail to help us understand this better – was it the dysregulated curiosity of a young man in those sexually prohibitive days, or something much more sinister? – but to mention it would have been fatal in a case over which an unspoken sexual motive hovered palpably, completely unsubstantiated, yet very clear. The police who searched Light's home after his arrest all those years later had done their best to strengthen this flavour of sexual deviance: 'I think I shall be able to supply you with such evidence of the antecedents and character of the prisoner as will tend to suggest a motive for the commission of the crime,' wrote the Chief Constable to the Director of Public Prosecutions, and to that end Light's mother's house was searched.[32]

Found in the bedroom he had occupied since his teens, amidst the evocative lists of schoolboy possessions – birds' egg and stamp collections, an education certificate, and a letter from his mother – were seemingly more telling items; the police records disclose ominous descriptions of a parcel containing ladies

---

31   See Appendix VI.

32   TNA: PRO DPP 1/61.

Introduction.

underwear; plus some indecent prints and literature.[33] These were, in fact judgements influenced by the standards of the day; the parcel – addressed to a woman – was suggestive of no more than an illicit affair; the so-called obscene literature related to the purchase of 'preventatives', *i.e.* of contraceptive devices.

But one surprising fact did emerge; in October 1919, midway between Bella's death and his identification as the owner of the green bicycle, Light had been questioned by the police in relation to an allegation of sexual misconduct with an eight year old Leicester girl who lived across Victoria Park from Light's home. There are no details of the offence; he 'admitted' it and apologised, the police said. No charges were brought. No lawyer would say it had any relevance to the green bicycle murder; but what would a juror say? What would you say? Probably what the police thought: it was all beginning to look as though Ronald Light had a predilection. But not necessarily, or even probably, for murder.

In addition, however, to matters of sexual conduct, there were other dubious aspects of his history.

In 1914, Light had not left his job with the Midland Railway Company because of a burning desire to enlist, the natural assumption to be made given the chronology; in fact, he was dismissed. His employers had had their doubts about Light; a fire had been lit in a cupboard in odd circumstances; there were some indecent drawings on the walls in the lavatory; nothing that pointed conclusively to Light, but you did not need any evidence to sack a man in 1914, and so that is what they did.

And so Light had enlisted with the Royal Engineers and, after a stint of training in military engineering in November 1915, he went to France. At a time

---

33 TNA: PRO DPP 1/61. Light was also in possession of five military decorations to which he was not entitled. In Cheltenham, the police had discovered among Light's possessions a letter from a Mrs Annie E. M. Harper which referred to the 'Stretton Bicycle'. In 1911, a Mrs Annie Elizabeth Mary Harper lived with her husband George, a retired solicitor, at 19 Mecklenburg Street, Leicester, which crossed Highfield Street; Annie died at the same address in 1922 (although Mecklenburg Street had by that time been renamed Severn Street). She was by that time in her late sixties. George died at the same address, in 1923 in his late seventies. The coincidence of the Harper letter was investigated by Detective Superintendent Taylor of the Leicester County Police, who saw Mrs Harper at home. She explained that the letter 'had nothing to do with this case, and was the name of a bicycle firm related to her. Mrs Harper's maiden name was Stretton, and the firm was in Kidderminster.' Superintendent Bowley may have been less than impressed by this explanation, since he continued to believe that Mrs Harper would be called as a witness for the defence, but Chief Constable Edward Holmes demurred: 'She is a Leicester lady and a relation of hers brought out a bicycle to which he gave the name of "Stretton". This is doubtless what Mrs Harper had in her mind when she mentioned "the Stretton bicycle" in her letter to the prisoner.' In 1917, Bella Wright bought her bicycle – the only one she ever had, and the one she was riding on the evening of her death – from Messrs Harper & Sons, Leicester. Also found among Light's possessions at Cheltenham was a collection of 'small bore ammunition, small revolver ammunition', and a 'small revolver (taken from a schoolboy by headmaster and handed to Light)'. The ammunition belonged to the school; Light was 'in charge of [the] school armoury'.

Light.

when his country was desperate for men to fight, he lasted not much more than a couple of months before being sent home. He lacked the qualities required of an officer, said the Brigadier General; he was slow, he lacked initiative, he would not profit by the experience of his fellow subalterns, he could not organise working parties. He had, in short, none of the characteristics of his class and education; he might be the product of a public school, but he was not 'a good sort' who knew how to lead men.

He had protested loudly and disingenuously about this humiliation: 'I gave up a good position at the beginning of the war to do my share,' he wrote indignantly when appealing against his discharge.[34] But his plea was rejected and, by August 1916, he had drifted into haymaking on a small farm in Somerset with a story of sick leave from the army after a shrapnel wound. Here, he was 'strongly suspected of setting fire to some haystacks belonging to his employer'.[35] In September, he re-enlisted as a gunner with the Honourable Artillery Company, remaining in London in reserve when the bulk of the men went to France to fight.

There then followed an even less attractive incident. In May, two telegrams were sent from France containing orders from Lord Denbigh, the commanding officer of the regiment, to ready and then to mobilise the London reserve – they were to join the French contingent in the firing line. Each had been followed rapidly by telegrams rescinding these orders, and these telegrams, too, purported to have been sent by Lord Denbigh. An inquiry followed when Lord Denbigh demanded to know why his orders were not being obeyed. It transpired that Light had forged the countermands. It seemed that active duty in the trenches was not to his taste. He was court martialled – and his habit of wearing medals to which he was not entitled was mentioned, as was his improper possession of a book of military pass forms. He was sentenced to a year's detention in a military prison.

Having served no more than a third of his sentence, he was sent back to France again – this occurred, as he accurately stated in his evidence, in November 1917. In August 1918, three months before the war ended, he was sent home to England and the sanctuary of the Wharncliffe military hospital in Yorkshire, suffering from deafness and shellshock. And so ended his war. He topped the whole thing off by attempting to 'make love' – as the prosecution brief puts it – to a girl of the age of fifteen, who happened to be the daughter of an ambulance driver at Wharncliffe, and who had 'invited him home to tea'.

In front of a jury inculcated with patriotism, whose womenfolk had presented

34   TNA PRO WO 339/52768.
35   TNA: PRO DPP 1/61.

Introduction.

conscientious objectors with white feathers, who had lost a generation of their young men, this story of Light's war, even leaving aside any allegations of sexual misconduct, would probably have convicted him. It is a good example of the very reason for our restrictive laws of evidence. He was a dog with a bad name; but that did not mean he should hang.

An unknowing jury was to be presented with what, in the eyes of the law (if not in those of popular opinion), really mattered: the bare facts in question. And Light was no doubt very carefully warned to avoid giving any evidence himself that might entitle the prosecution to argue that he had 'put in' his character.

Together, Marshall Hall and his client embarked on one of those perfect question and answer sessions between counsel and witness which hit the right note at every query and every response, as satisfying to a listener as a rally in tennis, a musical duet or a *pas de deux*. In the hushed courtroom, jury and spectators listened, rapt with attention, their heads turning from one to the other of the two speakers; and together Marshall Hall and his client rowed Light out of trouble. Not one false move was made by either of them.

Light had had a service revolver, of course he had; he had taken it to France with him the second time he went, but had left the holster at home. The revolver he had relinquished with the rest of his kit at the casualty clearing station on his way home. He had been unfit for further service because of his shellshock. It was his holster that had been fished out of the canal. It was his bicycle too. It was indeed he who had been seen cycling with Bella, he who had ultimately ridden away from her uncle's home in her company. And actually, yes, he had thrown the bicycle and the holster into the canal in the October of 1919. Before he did so, he filed off the number so that he could not be identified as its owner. And then, yes, he was sorry to say, he had told lies to the police about the bicycle.

The prosecution team who had spent so many hours and called so many witnesses to prove all these facts listened incredulously as the admissions poured out of him; a bewildered jury looked at a mystified judge. Only Marshall Hall and Light remained supremely confident and, amongst the admissions, the audacious defence emerged like a repeating pattern in a patchwork: look at it one way and you see nothing but patches; look at it another and the repeating pattern dominates.

During his convalescence, Light told the jury, he had begun to go for rides in the country on his bicycle. On 5 July, he had gone out to run an errand and then for a ride in the country. He had not met Edith or Valeria on that or any other day. But riding along the upper road he came upon a young lady by the roadside with a bicycle. She asked him if he had a spanner. He didn't, but he dismounted and had a look at her bicycle. They had ridden on together, companionably,

Light.

naturally, he implied, until they reached a village which she told him was called Gaulby. She said she had a visit to pay, but she would only be ten minutes or so. He had taken that 'as a sort of suggestion' that he should wait for her. And so he had waited, and, when she did not reappear, he rode off up the hill and turned left, the road home to Leicester. He had been intending to cycle home, but he discovered that he had a puncture in his tyre. By the time he had repaired it, it was about 8.15 pm, hopelessly late for supper, and so he had ridden back a little way to see whether the girl he had left was still around. He had seen her coming out of the house at which he had left her. He had hailed her: 'Hello'. Emphatically not: 'Bella'.

Otherwise, it had all been as the witnesses said, and shortly thereafter – as the witnesses said – they had cycled off together in the direction of Leicester. His tyre went flat again; she cycled on whilst he pumped it up, and then he caught up with her. When they reached the division in the road that led right to the Upper Road to Leicester and left to the Via Devana, he had turned to the right, but she had dismounted and said that she must say goodbye. He thought that it was then about 8.40 pm.[36] He had pointed out that the road he had taken was the direct and quickest way to Leicester. 'I don't live there,' she said.

And so they parted, and Ronald Light had made his way home to his dried-up supper, pumping up his tyre every now and again, and ultimately giving up and pushing his bike until at last he arrived at about 10.00 pm.

The rest of his story was one of a dawning realisation that the dead girl who had triggered a manhunt was the same girl, and that the man sought was the man last seen with her, the man with the green bicycle: himself. He feared that no one would believe his story; he feared for his mother's anguish; he feared ultimately for his life. And so he had taken his steps of concealment, and told lies to the police. Why had he not spoken up immediately? Why had it taken him some months to discard the bicycle and holster in the canal? 'I did not make up my mind deliberately not to come forward. I was so astounded and frightened at this unexpected thing. I kept on hesitating, and in the end I drifted into doing nothing at all.'

It was a polished performance; or it was the truth. Or, of course, both. Whatever it was, it undoubtedly pulled the rug from under the feet of the prosecution; the stream of admissions left them with little material, and the cross-examination scarcely dented his story.

The closing speeches of counsel on both sides were exemplars of the art. No point that supported their respective cases was missed and, like all good barristers, they laboured the points that suited them and sought to skate over

---

36   This of course suggests that the two had left Measures's house at the earliest estimated time, 8.30 pm.

Introduction.

those that did not. In those days, the rule was that if any witness other than the defendant was called by the defence, the prosecution was granted a right of reply, thereby gaining the last word. By his strategy of calling no one but the defendant, Marshall Hall had secured the precious advantage of going last.

Mr Maddocks, and not the Attorney-General, made the closing speech for the prosecution. This was a murder, he began. This was not conceivably suicide or mistake. Sir Edward Marshall Hall's tentative suggestion that Bella might have been shot inadvertently by someone a long way off, taking a pot shot at the crow perhaps, with a rifle or revolver was so much nonsense. No one indulged in shooting crows or in rifle practice at that time of night. No, this was murder, and it was murder with a service revolver, at close range. Who was last seen with the girl? The man with the green bicycle, admitted to be Light, who had met her and hung about waiting for her. No one knew what had happened next; all the evidence relating to it was no more than the defendant's account. The jury must found their verdict on what was known; the meeting, the waiting about for her and then the proximity in time and place of the meeting with the defendant and with the girl's death. He emphasised the importance of the utterances overheard by Bella's family. The man who had said those things, he suggested, knew this girl; was expecting her to return to him; knew her intimately enough to reproach her for keeping him waiting. The jurors were men of the world, weren't they? It was a meaningless phrase, a barristerial nudge and a wink intended to flatter his listeners. As 'men of the world', didn't the circumstances suggest a motive? On the basis of Light's story, Bella had been shot a mile and about fifteen minutes after leaving him.[37] There were no other candidates for the role of her killer; how much more likely was it that he had made advances, been rejected, and shot her so she could not tell her story? And above all, of course, there were the accused's subsequent actions, 'all that a clever man could do' to cover his tracks and to mislead the police. Could the jury trust that clever, deliberate man now to be telling them the truth? If they could not, they must do their duty to society – and convict.

It was compelling stuff. It might even have won the day, had it not been for a masterly retrieval by Marshall Hall. Far from contesting what had been said, he began by endorsing it. It was indeed the jury's solemn duty to convict if they thought Light guilty. But then he reminded them of the shadow of the noose hanging over the courtroom. They held Light's life in their hands; he was not going to ask them for pity or sympathy for his client. And then he proceeded to do just that: the pathos of Light's isolation and his desire to protect his mother

---

37 Even putting the most favourable possible construction (from the prosecution's point of view) on the timings available to the prosecution counsel, it is hard to reach this conclusion.

Light.

lost nothing in Marshall Hall's speech, and nor did the speculative nature of the supposed motive. He, too, appealed to these men of the world. What was so odd about Light meeting a pretty girl and showing an interest? There was always, he pointed out, a sense of adventure – without any suggestion of immorality – when a man meets a charming girl. And then, striking a topical, chappish note: 'You know, gentlemen, you can give votes to women, but you cannot take away their femininity.'[38] The encounter was innocent enough, he suggested, and it was only because the prosecution were aware of the fatal flaw in their case – the lack of motive – that they had constructed this immoral fiction.

In a series of rhetorical questions, Marshall Hall gradually cracked the jury's confidence in the prosecution case. If not premeditated, why would a man be cycling down a country road with a revolver? If premeditated, it could only be because the killer knew his victim. Where was the evidence for that? The flimsy assumption that he said 'Bella,' when it could so easily have been 'Hello'? Predicated necessarily on the further assumption that, when Bella had told her uncle that the unknown man was 'a perfect stranger' to her, she must have been lying? Given the ballistics evidence, could the injury possibly have been caused by the bullet found a short distance away? Or indeed by a revolver? Light's concealment and lies showed great moral cowardice, but did that make him – a sick, shellshocked man – a murderer?

And then, lastly, his two trump cards. The burden of proof; it was up to the prosecution to prove that Light did it, not for Light to prove that he did not. And the standard of proof: beyond a reasonable doubt.

The speech took two hours, and when he finished it was into a deep and breathless silence.

It was clear from his summing-up that the judge was well aware of the mastery of the defence. Most of the evidence, he observed, owing to the peculiar course of the prosecution, was now irrelevant; the defendant had admitted it all. It was a fair summing-up, lingering on what were now the real issues: the nature of the relationship between Bella and Light, and Light's suspicious cover-up. And he left the jury with their dilemma. The conviction of an innocent man was a terrible thing. But it was a terrible thing if a crime like this went unpunished.

The jury was out for three hours and three minutes. Light waited in the corridor below the dock. Acquittal meant immediate freedom. Conviction meant that unimaginable further wait in terror; three clear Sundays, with no hanging on a Monday, and then that ritualised death. It is part of the mythology of capital

---

38 It was the hot topic of the moment: amidst huge controversy, the 1918 Representation of the People Act had been enacted in February of that year, enfranchising women over the age of thirty with certain property qualifications.

trials that jurors who are about to convict will not look at the dock where the man whom they are condemning stands waiting.

When Light was called back into the dock, he stared into the judge's face, and that of the jury foreman, trying to see his fate. They were, he said, fascinating in their immobility.[39]

The verdict was 'Not Guilty'.

IV.

'... the most fascinating murder mystery of the century ...'[40]

And so it was all over.

Marshall Hall returned to London and to the acclaim of the country – not to mention to his enormous fees, rumoured to be the lion's share of the astronomic £1000 that the defence had cost.[41] And back in his chambers, the green bicycle case banished from his mind, he would begin to prepare for what was to be his next great triumph, five months later: the trial of a solicitor, Harold Greenwood, for the murder of his wife.[42]

Through the avid crowds and frantic pressmen, police officers escorted Ronald Light out of Leicester Castle. He put on his cap and lit a cigarette, the first for some weeks; no man was allowed to smoke in prison until after conviction. Unobserved, he walked to Granby Street and boarded a tram bound for home in Highfield Street. It was only then that he realised that, released straight from the dock as he had been, his belongings had not been returned to him; he had no money on him. Fortunately, Leicester was a small place in those days: amongst the travellers on the tram was someone he knew. His acquaintance supplied him with the fare: threepence.[43]

Threepence took him home to mother. 'We said nothing,' he later said in a newspaper interview, 'precisely nothing'. And then: 'What can mothers say that is not too intimate for outsiders?'[44]

That weekend, the papers were full of his story, accompanied by pictures of his dog Togo, enthusiastically licking his face to welcome him home; of his mother dressed for the occasion, her hair in a bun, her white lace blouse, her cameo on a velvet ribbon around her neck; of Light himself, seated at

39   *Weekly Dispatch*, 13 June 1920.
40   Wakefield, 2.
41   *Star*, 12 June 1920.
42   See *Trial of Harold Greenwood* [NBT 52].
43   *Daily Mirror*, 14 June 1920.
44   *Weekly Dispatch*, 13 June 1920.

Light.

the table in his mother's claustrophobic dining room, answering his letters of congratulation. He hoped to go back to being a teacher, he told reporters, though he knew teachers must be beyond reproach and his lies to and concealment from the police might prevent that. Now free from the constraints of the witness box, a rather different man emerged, humble in a sanctimonious way, who told of his mental anguish as he fought for his country at the great retreat at Villers-Bretonneux in 1918, an anguish he said equalled only by that he felt as he stood in the dimly-lit corridor under the courtroom in Leicester Castle, waiting for the jury to deliver a verdict that might have seen him hanged.

There was one further contact with Marshall Hall, and it was a significant one. The first letter he wrote was to his advocate:

> I cannot find words to express how deeply grateful I am to you for your great and successful efforts on my behalf. It seems rather feeble to say 'Thank you' for saving my life ... Your speech to the jury was simply great, and practically obliterated any previous impressions they had obtained ... I shall always remember you with the deepest gratitude.

Marshall Hall received many letters of this kind from grateful defendants whose lives he had indeed saved. Some still exist, as do the replies. A warm and charming man, he wrote reassuring letters, frequently congratulating his client on the triumph of justice. His reply to Light is in marked contrast:

> Thank you for your letter, which I much appreciate. Quite apart from *the* matter which caused so much anxiety ... may I in all kindness and great sincerity express the hope that you will realise that life is a serious thing, and that work and self-denial are the only means to happiness. Please convey to your mother my sympathetic regards, and you will, I am sure, forgive me if I say that you can best show your gratitude to me by making her life happier in the future than I fear it has been in the past. I am indeed glad to have been of service to you, and through you to her.[45]

It is a very interesting response: Marshall Hall, that consummate psychologist and highly experienced advocate, had done his job with all his skill; but he clearly did not think much of his client.

The trial had ended on Friday 11 June and, after his weekend of newspaper interviews and what he tritely described as the 'sweet air of freedom'[46], Light visited Leicester Police Station on the following Monday to retrieve his

45 Marjoribanks, 407-408.
46 *Weekly Dispatch*, 13 June 1920.

Introduction.

belongings. There he was seen by Superintendent Bowley, the police officer who had been most closely involved with the case. And, later that same day, Superintendent Bowley made a statement. It was discovered many decades later in a police safe, and not reproduced in full until 2017.[47]

According to Bowley, he had told Light that he did not believe his story that he had left Bella at the point where their roads diverged ('knowing as I did of his fondness for women'), and after persistent questioning Light had told him that, having met Bella who was a stranger to him, he cycled with her. She asked him about the war, and he took his revolver out of his raincoat pocket to show it to her. He had fired off some shots in the afternoon for practice, Light said, and the revolver must have been fully cocked so that 'the least touch' would fire it. It went off, struck her accidentally and killed her. He had taken the steps of concealment as recounted in court, with the addition that he had thrown the revolver away separately into another part of the canal, and had never told his legal team the account he was now giving. This last statement was unsurprising: had Marshall Hall and the rest of the defence team known that story, they would have been obliged to run it in court. It would have been contrary to all the rules of the Bar – and consequently professional suicide – to conceal a defendant's account or to massage it in an attempt to secure an acquittal.

The story told by Light post-trial had, however, been foreshadowed in Marshall Hall's closing speech to the jury. If Light was lying, he said, why had he not made up a better story? Marshall Hall could himself come up with plenty: for instance, that he might have 'taken the revolver into the country to have a few stray shots; that he met a girl; that they were playing with what they believed were blank cartridges,' and that he had accidentally caused her death. There, said Marshall Hall, was the perfect defence, and 'there is not a man, woman or child who would not have accepted that story'.

There is a great deal of rhetoric in this submission, and it does not bear close analysis. It is hard to believe that any man or woman, or indeed many children, would not have questioned the plausibility of an experienced soldier letting off casual shots in the countryside, or so carelessly handling a service revolver that he allowed a death to occur. Even if accepted, it would have more probably led to a conviction and lengthy sentence for manslaughter than an acquittal on the basis of an accident. But it is certainly the case that Marshall Hall may well in his closing speech have inadvertently laid the foundations of Light's post-trial account.

The subsequent embellishments in the account which Light gave to Superintendent Bowley made the story even more implausible. Could Light

47   See Appendix VII.

Light.

really have been riding around on a bicycle through bumpy country lanes with a cocked revolver that the 'least touch' would cause to fire? And why in the first place were the two cyclists on the remote, indirect road home?

Unsurprisingly, given the decades that passed before it emerged from the depths of a safe owned by Leicestershire Constabulary, doubt has been cast on the authenticity of Superintendent Bowley's statement; but the records from the Director of Public Prosecution's office now kept in the National Archives make it almost certain that it is indeed an authentic document. In a series of memoranda,[48] it is clear that the Director of Public Prosecutions, in consultation with the Attorney-General, Sir Gordon Hewart, and with the Chief Constable of Leicestershire Police were considering the institution of perjury proceedings arising from the Green Bicycle trial. Against whom these proceedings were to be and the precise nature of them are unspecified; but the reference to 'the document' which was to be their basis, the fact that they occurred within days of the Bowley Statement being drafted, and the reference as to a different view being taken should 'precise information come to light as to the whereabouts of the weapon' make it clear beyond any sensible doubt that it was this post-trial statement that had triggered the memoranda.

That does not, of course, mean that it was true. It does not mean either that Light told the truth, or that Superintendent Bowley's account of what Light had said was true.

Why should the police officer have made up the account? Because he still had a strong conviction of Light's guilt? Then why not pin a full confession for murder on him? To propagate his personal view of what happened? It seems an unlikely course of action for a police officer who was, the evidence suggests, a decent man, and who had performed his duties with kindness and integrity.

Equally, why should Light have given an account only days after he had escaped the scaffold? And why should he have made it to a police officer who might, for all he knew, make what use of it he could? Because he needed to tell his truth to someone? Remembering his counsel's steer in his closing speech, in an attempt to lay to rest the still-turbulent speculation as to his guilt? For a bit of sport with a policeman who had hunted him and lost him? My guess would be the last. He was a funny chap, Light.

We do not know if further searches were made for the revolver as a result of what it is alleged that Light said. But, even if it had been found, the decision not to charge Light with perjury is predictable. The attempt to unravel the truth and lies in the context of the trial had been successful in the sense that, for Bella's family and the avid public, a kind of end-point had been reached, despite the not

48   TNA: PRO DPP 1/61.

Introduction.

guilty verdict. Light could never again, whatever was subsequently revealed, be tried again for Bella's death; the law prohibited it. A trial to determine whether his defence had been a lie (not necessarily whether the subsequent account was the truth) would have been highly problematical and, even if successful, a conviction for perjury carrying a maximum sentence of seven years' penal servitude would have been as likely to inflame popular opinion as to appease it.

The decision to let the statement rest in the safe at Leicester Police Station – and perhaps the gun in the canal – was probably the correct one. In the last analysis, it would not, to use the phrase beloved of authority, have been 'in the public interest' to feed the smouldering embers of speculation.

What is most fascinating about the Bowley Statement, however, is the resonance it possesses, despite the passing of what is now a century. Found only a few years ago, it seems to continue on with a story that will never rest – the green bicycle and its rider, the wheels still spinning on down the country roads of Leicestershire like some twenty-first century version of the headless horseman, the canal still holding secrets in its muddy depths, the public left guessing at each twist and revelation as time passes.

Ronald Light never did return to teaching; he lived his life in the shadows that shroud the controversially acquitted; reclusively at first, with only his mother for company. History does not tell us whether he ever took to heart Marshall Hall's strictures as to his future conduct towards her. Eventually changing his name, he moved to Kent, where he married a widow with one child and lived out his life, dying in 1975, aged eighty-nine. It was not until after his death that his family learned of his past.

Immediately after the trial, freed from the reporting restraints that applied while it was ongoing, the press had a field day. Even then, no one could so much as dare to hint that Light might have committed the crime. Damages awards for defamation were huge in those days, frightening off even the most aggressive of the newspapers. Even *John Bull*, a journal famous for its bellicosity, said this:

> Light is not guilty. That verdict is the right of no man or woman to question …
> The murderer therefore is still at large, rubbing shoulders with decent citizens.[49]

The second sentence of this somewhat alarmist report was, of course, correct. Bella's death was investigated in accordance with the forensic requirements of the time; Ronald Light was tried according to the appropriate rules of evidence;

---

49   *John Bull*, 19 June 1920. *John Bull* gets the prize for tight fistedness: during the hunt for the murderer, they had offered a £1000 reward for information leading to the apprehension of the murderer. The bargeman who had dredged up the bicycle tried to claim it. But the discovery of the bike had not led to the murderer, the newspaper decreed, and they gave Mr Whitehouse a measly £50 in consolation.

Light.

a jury whom we have no reason to suppose were idle or biased or stupid listened to the evidence and then acquitted him. That is where the law requires us to leave it; with the nearest that human beings can ever get to the certainty they crave.

But the trouble with human beings is that, though they insist that, in modern parlance, all they ask for is closure, in fact they want closure on their terms, their truth accepted as the 'true' truth. And so they go on rejecting the conclusions of those who come to different conclusions from their own and herald as 'the truth' the version that accords with their own beliefs.

Over the century that has elapsed since Bella died and a man was tried for her murder, layer upon layer of theories about the manner of her death have emerged and been adopted or rejected accordingly, each verdict based not only upon the evidence available at the time but on information (not of all of which can be dignified by the term 'evidence') that has subsequently become available; on advances in forensic science; on 'fresh looks' and 'different approaches' as another generation of armchair detectives becomes intrigued by the problems the case poses.

In the first book about the trial, published in 1930, the author H. R. Wakefield says that 'the Green Bicycle Case is largely a space-time problem. It is a question of minutes and yards.'[50] But there are two flaws to such an approach. The first is that those sternly precise calculations are based, like a building on sand, on the wholly inaccurate foundation of evidence which was riddled with inconsistencies – as all evidence is, or, with the passage of time, becomes. Some of the inaccuracies, of course, may be potentially significant, but most are the product of a hundred years of Chinese Whispers: multiple written statements deviating from one another, and oral evidence prepared for and later given in all the different hearings – at the inquest, at the committal proceedings, and at the trial – not to mention all the errors of reporting and transcription in the newspaper accounts. Since it is impossible to differentiate between innocent human inaccuracy and guilty subterfuge, on and on goes the endless and usually profitless speculation.

The second and perhaps even more important point is that these calculations all stem from the elaborately-detailed account of his cycle ride given by Light himself.

This second point is, in my view, one of the most striking aspects of the case. It is the point made forcibly in prosecuting counsel's closing speech. There is no corroboration (or supporting evidence) for Ronald Light's account from the moment he left Bella's uncle's house until the moment the family servant

50   Wakefield, 2.

Introduction.

Mary Webb says he arrived home. Prosecuting counsel contended that Light's policy of concealment (and unsaid, Marshall Hall's tactics in continuing that concealment) had played in this regard resoundingly in his favour. Had he told his story earlier – and if it was true – evidence could probably have been found: at the very least, for instance, from someone who had seen a man wheeling a broken bicycle towards Leicester on the relevant date at the relevant time.

Given the exhaustiveness and success of the police enquiries into the earlier part of the evening, this contention is probably correct. And, equally, those enquiries would have helped Light's defence – if it was true. If he was guilty, and his concealment was carried out for the very reason that thereby he would ensure a *lack* of evidence to support his defence, it was extraordinarily cleverly thought out. It could just as well be argued that in his (innocent) panic, he did his own defence unthinking harm. Given either his guilty cover-up (in which case his account of his movements must have been massaged to suit his defence), or his innocent cover up (in which case that same account would be influenced by a desire to exonerate himself), to rely on his account for fine deductions as to time and place becomes an unreliable method. Certainly, the fascinating books on the case have exhausted the speculative possibilities arising out of geography and chronology.[51]

Thanks to the lack of sophistication of the forensic science of the time and to the oddities of the doctor's original examination, the same speculation has arisen with regard to the ballistics and to the injury. It seems a remarkable coincidence that a few feet from a shot body in a country lane is found a bullet which could have been and yet was *not* the one that killed Bella. There appears to have been some agreement between doctor and gunsmith that the weapon and injury were consistent with the theory that Bella was on the ground at the time she was shot, but Marshall Hall greeted this proposition in his closing speech with derision. The idea, he said, that Bella had somehow been posed with the revolver above her head and her head between the revolver and the ground 'was a credit to (the doctor's) imagination'.

Such a position is, of course, an unlikely one if the proposition is that this was the encounter envisaged by the prosecution, in which a girl rejects a man's advances and the man shoots her in thwarted anger. It is not unlikely in the context of an exercise in humiliation and power; nor is it unlikely – indeed it is classic – in the context of a cold-blooded execution. But both these theories seem inconsistent with an encounter with a complete stranger. If Light shot Bella, and the evidence seems to point that way, and he did not do it accidentally, then it is

---

51   H. R. Wakefield, *The Green Bicycle Case*; C. Wendy East, *The Green Bicycle Murder*; Antony M. Brown, *The Green Bicycle Mystery*; and countless articles.

Light.

in their pasts that the truth might be found.

In the end, it really does seem that there is perhaps only one aspect of the case, linking both crime and trial, on which there is anything left to say. That is perhaps the most important issue of all: that of motive.

In this context, a little story told by Bella's mother hangs tantalisingly in the background, recounted by her in an early statement to the police. Twelve months prior to her death, or it may be longer, Bella had gone out for one of her cycle rides, and on her return had said to her mother, 'What do you think, I had an officer fall in love with me'. One can hear the triumph and the giggles, a good story to tell an admiring mother. Silly, of course, but flattering all the same.

'He got off [his motorbike],' she said, 'and asked me who I was and I told him I was a labouring man's daughter. He said what a nice girl I was and said by my nice ways and looks I ought to be in a nicer position than a labouring man's daughter.'

Her mother said what loving mothers say: have nothing to do with him. But did Bella do as she was told?

We are all fascinated by motive: lawyers exploit that fascination, and the law firmly dismisses its ultimate relevance.[52] But in this case it may just possibly be, above all else, the key. And the key only really turns comfortably if there had been some sort of prior relationship between the two of them.

Well, did he say, 'Bella'? Or did he say, 'Hello'? The jury is still out. And probably always will be.

---

52   A motive may of course be a circumstance of guilt, but its absence does not mean that a crime was not committed by the accused if the rest of the evidence points to it.

Introduction.

BIBLIOGRAPHY.

Birkett, N., *Six Great Advocates*
   (Penguin: Harmondsworth, 1961).

Bowker, E. A., *A Lifetime with the Law*
   (W. H. Allen & Co.: London, 1961).

Brown, A. M., *The Green Bicycle Mystery*
   (Mirror Books: London, 2017).

East, C. W., *The Green Bicycle Murder*
   (Alan Sutton: Stroud, 1993).

Marjoribanks, E., *The Life of Sir Edward Marshall Hall*
   (Gollancz: London, 1929).

Roughead, W., *Trial of Oscar Slater*
   (William Hodge & Co.: Edinburgh, 1915 [second edition]).

Smith, S., *Marshall Hall: A Law unto Himself*
   (Wildy, Simmonds and Hill: London, 2016).

Wakefield, H. R., *The Green Bicycle Case*
   (Philip Allan & Co.: London, 1930).

ARCHIVAL SOURCES.

FROM THE COLLECTION OF THE PUBLIC RECORD OFFICE:
   TNA: PRO ASSI 13/50.
   TNA: PRO DPP 1/61.
   TNA: PRO WO 339/52768.

Leading Dates in the Ronald Light Case.

19 October 1885	Ronald Vivian Light born at Leicester.
14 July 1897	Annie Bella Wright born at Melton Mowbray.
1906	Light graduates from university with a third-class degree in Engineering.
13 May 1910	Light buys a distinctive green bicycle, serial number 103648, from a cycle dealer in Derby.
27 February 1915	Light enlists with the Royal Engineers.
12 November 1915	Light is posted to France.
24 January 1916	Light is withdrawn from active service in France after seventy-three days.
1 July 1916	Light relinquishes his commission in the Royal Engineers.
2 August 1916	Light is formally Gazetted out of the service of the Royal Engineers.
September 1916	Light enlists as a gunner with the Honourable Artillery Company.
May (approx.) 1917	Bella Wright leaves domestic service for factory work.
June 1917	Bella Wright acquires a bicycle on hire-purchase from Messrs Harper & Sons.
24 July 1917	Light is tried by court-martial for forging a telegram, and is sentenced to twelve months' imprisonment with hard labour.
2 November 1917	Light is released from detention.
6 November 1917	Light is deployed to France.
24 August 1918	Light is removed from France and sent to Wharncliffe War Hospital, suffering from shellshock and deafness.
27 September 1918	Light is sent to a convalescent home.
18 October 1918	Light is returned to Wharncliffe.
22 October 1918	Light is discharged from Wharncliffe.
January / February 1919	Light is demobilised.
2 July 1919	Light takes his bicycle to be repaired by Harry Cox.
5 July 1919	Light collects his bicycle from Cox's shop. Murder of Bella Wright.
6 July 1919	Discovery of bullet near the location of the body.
8 July 1919	Inquest – first day.
25 July 1919	Inquest – second day.
8 August 1919	Inquest – third day. 'Murder by some person unknown.'

Light.

28 October 1919	Light is arrested on suspicion of improper conduct with a child. He admits the offence and apologises, but the girl's parents decline to press charges.
20 January 1920	Light moves to Cheltenham to teach at Dean Close School.
24 February 1920	The frame and front wheel of the green bicycle are discovered in the canal.
4 March 1920	Light is arrested and charged with the murder of Bella Wright.
5 March 1920	Magistrates' hearing – first day. Light remanded.
10 March 1920	Magistrates' hearing – second day.
12 March 1920	Rear wheel of green bicycle discovered in canal.
17 March 1920	Magistrates' hearing – third day.
19 March 1920	Holster and bullets discovered in canal.
23 March 1920	Magistrates' hearing – fourth day.
24 March 1920	Magistrates' hearing – fifth day. Light committed to Assizes.
29 April 1920	Gear wheel, crank and pedal of green bicycle discovered in canal.
30 April 1920	Left crank and pedal of green bicycle discovered in canal.
9 June 1920	Trial of Ronald Light – first day.
10 June 1920	Trial of Ronald Light – second day.
11 June 1920	Trial of Ronald Light – third day. Light acquitted of murder and discharged.
14 June 1920	Date of the Bowley Statement.
15 May 1975	Death of Ronald Vivian Light, aged eighty-nine.

Ronald Vivian Light

Author's collection

Annie Bella Wright

Author's collection

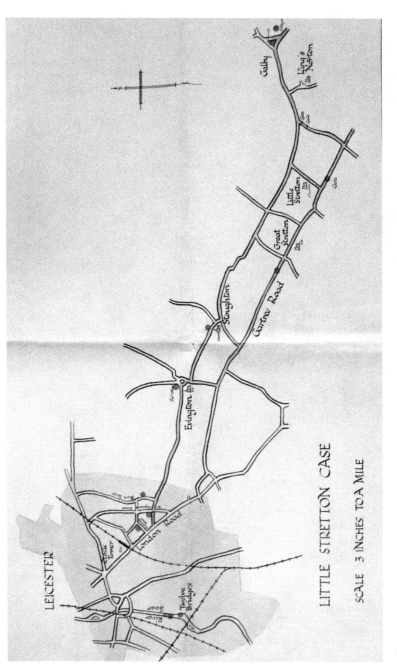

Map of Little Stretton and environs.

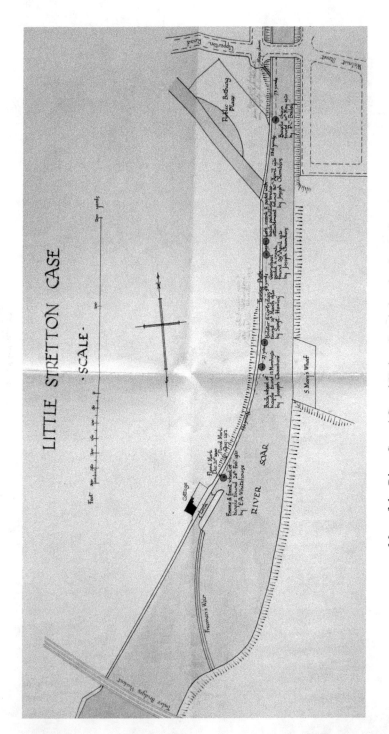

Map of the River Soar / Grand Union Canal showing items found.

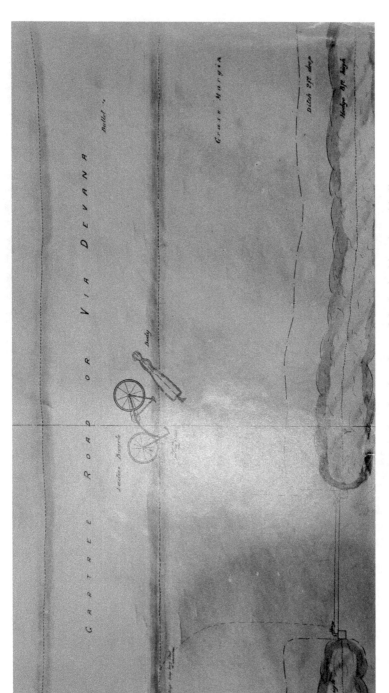

Contemoprary sketch showing locations of the body, bicycle and bullet.

B.S.A. Modèle de Luxe Gent's Bicycle.

SPECIFICATION

FRAME	Built with best selected butted steel tubing, D section back forks and stays; made in the following heights: 21-in., 23-in., 24-in., 25-in., 26-in., and 27-in.
FRONT FORKS	Special taper gauge steel blades, D section, fitted with solid steel machined-slotted ends, which allow of the front wheel being removed without straining the forks.
WHEELS	28-in. equal, constructed with best double butted steel spokes, Westwood or Wedgwood rims, highly polished and heavily nickel-plated, edges and centres enamelled and lined.
TYRES	Palmer heavy roadster or Dunlop special. 1½-in. with wired or beaded edges.
FITTINGS	B.S.A. throughout, light roadster pattern, with 7-in. cranks.
BACK HUB	Eadie two-speed coaster, 1½-in. chain line, with handlebar or top-tube control.
CHAIN	B.S.A. ½-in. pitch, tested to a strain of 2,000 lbs.
GEAR	48 teeth on bottom bracket wheel, and 16 or 18 teeth on hub wheel.
PEDALS	B.S.A. rubber or rat trap; size to order.
HANDLEBAR	B.S.A. standard upturned pattern, ⅞ × 18-in. fitted with best celluloid grips, and concealed oiler.
BRAKE	B.S.A. front rim brake, with rolling (or inverted) lever, specially curved to suit the design of the handlebar. Solid brazed clips and with B.S.A. patent detachable shoes.
SADDLE	Brooks' latest B 90/1 saddle, with plated springs.
GEAR CASE	B.S.A. special oil bath, detachable gear case.
MUDGUARDS	B.S.A. steel with plated stays and patent detachable ends.
FINISH	Enamelled with four coats of a rich shade of green on one coat of rust proof preparation, and neatly lined out with 22ct. leaf gold. The usual bright parts are heavily plated, and the finish is of the well-known B.S.A. high standard of quality.
	Equipped with best grade 15-in. celluloid inflator, plated clips, complete with tool bag, and the necessary B.S.A. spanners, to fit all nuts, cones, and cups.

NET CASH PRICES

Model No. 1	As per specification	£13 13 0
Model No. 1A	As per specification, but with B.S.A. Three-speed hub and two B.S.A. rolling (or inverted) lever brakes . . .	13 13 0

If fitted with "Roman" Aluminium Rims, 11/6 extra, net.

16

B.S.A. MODÈLE DE LUXE GENT'S BICYCLE

Bicycle catalogue description and illustration.

Top: Taken from the door of George Measures' cottage towards the church.
Bottom: Crossroads at entrance to the village of Gaultby.

© *The National Archives*

Top: Hedge and gate near where the body was found, taken from the meadow.
Bottom: Gartree Road, and gate near where body (indicated) was discovered.

LEICESTERSHIRE CONSTABULARY.

£5 REWARD.

At 9-20 p.m., 5th instant, the body of a woman, since identified as that of ANNIE BELLA WRIGHT, was found lying on the Burton Overy Road, Stretton Parva, with a bullet wound through the head, and her bicycle lying close by.

Shortly before the finding of the body the deceased left an adjacent village in company of a man of the following description :—

Age 35 to 40 years, height 5 ft. 7 in. to 5 ft. 9 in.; apparently usually clean shaven, but had not shaved for a few days, hair turning grey, broad full face, broad build, said to have squeaking voice and to speak in a low tone.

Dressed in light Rainproof Coat with green plaid lining, grey mixture jacket suit, grey cap, collar and tie, black boots, and wearing cycle clips.

Had bicycle of following description, *viz.* :—Gent's B.S.A., green enamelled frame, black mudguards, usual plated parts, up-turned handle bar, 3-speed gear, control lever on right of handle bar, lever front brake, back-pedalling brake worked from crank and of unusual pattern, open centre gear case, *Brook's* saddle with spiral springs of wire cable. The 3-speed control had recently been repaired with length of new cable.

Thorough enquiries are earnestly requested at all places where bicycles are repaired.

If met with the man should be detained, and any information either of the man or the bicycle wired or telephoned to E. HOLMES, Esq., CHIEF CONSTABLE OF COUNTY, LEICESTER, or to SUPT. L. BOWLEY, COUNTY POLICE STATION, LEICESTER.

County Constabulary Office,
Leicester, 7th July, 1919.

T. H. JEAYS & SONS, PRINTERS, 7 ST MARTINS, LEICESTER.

Police notice offering £5 reward.

Identification parade with Chief Constable's stable in the background.

Top: A police officer arriving holding the bicycle;
Sir Edward Marshall Hall at the trial.
Bottom: Ronald Light in the dock.

Author's collection

County Police Station,

Leicester.

14th June, 1920.

At about 11 a.m. this day, RONALD VIVIAN LIGHT (who was on 11th instant acquitted of the Murder of ANNIE BELLA WRIGHT, at Stretton Parva, on 5th July, 1919,) came to this Office to arrange for his property to be handed back to him. I talked with him for about an hour-and-a-quarter about his Trial and about the Murder generally. He and I were together in my Office with the door closed. I pointed out amongst other things that I could not swallow his story of his leaving the girl where and how he said he had done, knowing as I did, of his fondness for women and his past history in this respect. I returned to this subject time after time and told him that I did not believe he had wilfully shot her and that I never had believed that of him.

When Light was in my custody I had endeavoured to make him as comfortable as was possible, and had allowed him certain privileges which he missed when on remand at Prison. In consequence of this he was on good terms with me and said, "Well you are a good sport, if I tell you something can I depend upon your keeping it to yourself" ? I said, Yes, strictly. He said,- "Well I'll tell you, but mind it must be strictly confidential, no other person knows it and if you divulge it I shall, of course, say I never told you anything of the kind. He went on to say- I did shoot the girl but it was completely accidental, we were riding quietly along, I was telling her about the War and my experiences in France, I had my Revolver in my Raincoat pocket and we dismounted for her to look at it. I had fired off some shots in the afternoon for practice and I had no idea there was a loaded cartridge in it, we were both standing up by the sides of our bicycles, I think she had dismounted on the right of her machine and that the two bicycles were between us. I took the Revolver from my Coat pocket and was in the act of handing it to her, I am not sure whether she actually took hold of it or not, but her hand was out to take it when it went off. She fell and never stirred, I was horror struck, I did not know what to do, I knew she was dead, I did not touch her, I was frightened and altogether unnerved and I got on my bicycle

Page 1 of the Bowley Statement.

© *Leicestershire Police / Leicestershire & Rutland Records Office*

and rode away,I went by Great Glen,I saw some courting couples between Stretton and Glen and I slowed down somewhat so that I should not be unduly noticed,I thought that as no one knew me I should get clear away,and as time went on I thought it would never be found out. I cannot account for the shot unless it was that the Revolver was fully cocked,the least touch would fire it then. Mary Webb's evidence was quite true, and whenever the subject of the Murder was brought up I always said as little as possible and commenced of something else. I did not know the girl,I had never met her before that evening. What I said about her asking me for a Spanner was quite true I first saw her at the top of the hill,I screwed her bicycle up and we went down the hill then started to go up the next hill where Atkins saw us. I did not make any improper suggestion to her either on the way to Gaulby or after leaving there. I did not mention that at all,that might-and probably would,have happened later. If I had intended shooting her I should never have done it close up to the village,it was much more lonely along the road we had passed. I do not remember the two little girls,they must have mistaken me for someone else. I asked Light about the bullet- He said- I do not believe that the bullet found in the road is the one which was shot by the Revolver as it would have travelled much further,and from the position in which we were standing it could not have struck the ground,and if it had struck a tree it would have buried itself in the tree,and besides it would not have been found at that angle. It was, I think,in October that I threw the bicycle in the Canal.I unscrewed everything as far as I could before leaving home,I then walked with the machine to the Canal and got on the towing-path at Walnut Street Bridge,it would be about 10 O'clock when I got there. I first threw in the mudguards,then the gearcase,then the chain,then the Cranks & pedals and so on until I had thrown it all in,the holster was full of cartridges to sink it. I said- If you had left the Revolver in the holster that would have kept it down- Is that in there too? He said- No,I had it with me and it was loaded. I was in such a nervous state that if anyone had interfered with me I should have been guilty of murder,I should have shot him. I remember a man passing me as soon as I had got on the towing path,I pretended to be doing something at

Page 2 of the Bowley Statement.

© Leicestershire Police / Leicestershire & Rutland Records Office

my bicycle and he did not speak to me. I said- Where is the Revolver?
He replied- It is in the Canal but not there, I threw that and
another in near to Belgrave Gate. I said Did your Counsel know All
this? He said No, I told Mr.Powers I was not at Gaulby at all, and it
was not until later that I was persuaded to tell them part of the
truth. I told them the story I told in Court. I was asked about it
being an accident but I adhered to the story that I left the girl at
the two roads. I dared not admit the shot, I was afraid of a verdict
of Manslaughter. I said You ran a great risk. He said- I suppose I
did but I would rather have my neck stretched than do ten years in
prison. I asked Light to give permission to tell the Chief Constable
what he had told me. He declined to do so but eventually, after much
pressing, he said- You can do so after a while but not at present. I
said- Does your Mother know? He said My God no, I would not let my
mother know it for the world. No one on this earth knows it but us
two, and if you tell I shall say I never said anything of the kind.

L. Bowley.
Superintendent.

Page 3 of the Bowley Statement.

LEICESTERSHIRE ASSIZES, LEICESTER CASTLE

Wednesday 9 June to Friday 11 June 1920

Before Mr Justice Horridge.

The King

against

Ronald Vivian Light

for the

Wilful Murder

of

Annie Bella Wright.

Sir Gordon Hewart, K.C., M.P. (The Attorney-General),
Mr Henry Maddocks, K.C., M.P.,
and
Mr Norman Birkett
conducted the prosecution.

Sir Edward Marshall Hall, K.C.,
and
Mr George Wightman Powers
appeared for the defence.

First Day –
Wednesday 9 June 1920.

Probably no criminal case in modern times has aroused more public interest, and its importance was shown by the appearance in person of the Attorney-General (Sir Gordon Hewart, K.C., M.P.), to conduct the prosecution on behalf of the Crown, and by the engagement of Sir Edward Marshall Hall, K.C., to lead the defence.

Light is thirty-four years of age. He was described on the calendar as a civil engineer, while his alleged offence was recorded therein in the following unusually simple form:

Wilful murder of Annie Bella Wright.

A crowd of several hundred curious people had assembled on the little green mound in front of the Castle entrance before 10.00 am, waiting, with very moderate hopes, for a possible seat in the public gallery and, in the alternative, watching for something interesting to turn up. In animated fashion they discussed the arrival of the various persons who figure prominently in the trial.

When the court was opened just after 9.30, the queue of spectators entered the public gallery in orderly fashion, excellent order being maintained by a force of County Constabulary, under Inspector Hall. A force of city police was on duty in the precincts of the Castle, under Inspector Choyce.

The prisoner was driven to the Castle in the large van from the gaol at Welford Road. The vehicle was taken straight into the Castle yard, and the closing of the high gates behind it effectually prevented the public from getting that which so many had long waited for – a glimpse of Ronald Light. Some, however, did see the shadowy outline of the prisoner's face as he peered through the ventilators surmounting the doors at the back of the van.

The crowd witnessed successively the arrival of groups of witnesses, counsel and officials, including the under sheriff (Mr G. Rowlatt), the governor of the gaol (Mr Felmingham), the prison chaplain (the Rev. F. R. C. Payne), the chief constable of the county (Mr E. Holmes), the county coroner (Mr G. E. Bouskell), the clerk to the county magistrates (Mr E. G. B. Fowler), and others.

It was not until about 10.35 am that Mr Justice Horridge's carriage drove up and the buzz of conversation momentarily ceased while necks were craned in an effort to secure a good view of his Lordship, who was accompanied by his chaplain (the Rev. F. B. MacNutt) and the high

Light.

sheriff, Mr John Turner.

Numerous representatives of the press from all parts of the country – several of whom had to be accommodated in the public gallery, the seats available for the press in the well of the court being decidedly limited – were admitted to the court about 10.00 am. At the commencement of the case, the public gallery at the back of the court was by no means inconveniently crowded, there being, in fact, only a single line along the front of the gallery, about twenty people in all, and the majority of them ladies. A quarter of an hour later a section of the long queue of people who had been waiting outside for so long was admitted and permitted to stand at the back of the enclosure.

Considerable interest was taken in the preliminaries of the court, conducted by the Clerk of Assize, and following upon the calling of the jury, the trumpeters were heard heralding the approach of the judge (Sir Thomas Gardner Horridge), whose entry into the court immediately preceded the appearance of Ronald Light in the dock.

Light was looking paler and much more grave than he was at the magisterial proceedings, but there was about him a characteristic air of self-possession. He appeared to be absorbingly interested in the proceedings. He was dressed in a navy blue serge coat and grey waistcoat and a soft collar and tie. He was clean shaved, his hair very neatly brushed.

Resting his hands on the edge of the dock, he listened attentively while the Clerk of Assize asked him, 'Are you guilty or not guilty?' and replied in a firm voice, 'Not guilty'.

Mr JUSTICE HORRIDGE remarked that notice had been received of certain additional evidence as from 3 June, but that that evidence was only handed to him as he entered the court that day.

Mr JUSTICE HORRIDGE: I don't think that that is the way Treasury solicitors should treat a judge.

The ATTORNEY-GENERAL regretted the incident and assured his Lordship that it was purely an oversight and he was very sorry indeed.

Mr JUSTICE HORRIDGE: As I came into this court, I have a fresh body of evidence put into my hand that I have never seen before. It is not the first time I have had to complain of this sort of thing.

Opening Speech for the Prosecution

Attorney-General

The ATTORNEY-GENERAL, in opening the case, said that he appeared for the Crown with his learned friends Mr Maddocks, K.C., and Mr Birkett, and the prisoner was represented by Sir Edward Marshall Hall, K.C., and Mr Powers. The evidence that would be taken would

First Day – Wednesday 9 June 1920.

show that the murder was committed by Annie Bella Wright being shot through the head whilst on the main road at Little Stretton in the county of Leicester. Miss Wright at the time of her death was twenty-one years of age, was unmarried, and was living with her parents, who were labouring people, at a village called Stoughton, just outside the city of Leicester. Her family at one time lived in Leicester, where Miss Wright herself had been a domestic servant from the time she left school until the month of May 1917. In that month she went to work in a factory, and she continued to work up to the time of her death. She was described as a well-built girl of attractive appearance, and in the month of July last year she was employed by Messrs Bates and Co. at St Mary's Rubber Works in Leicester. It was her practice to go to and return from her work on her bicycle.

Miss Wright was, in local phraseology, 'keeping company' with a young man named Archibald Ward, a stoker in the Royal Navy, who expected to be demobilised in August 1919; and that young man had been with her early in July.

On 4 July, which was a Friday, the day before the one upon which she met with her death, Miss Wright had been working on the night shift at the rubber mills, and she returned to her home about eleven o'clock and went to bed. She got up at 4.00 pm, and at 5.00 pm she wrote some letters and went to the post office to get some stamps. On her return, she left at home her coat, in the pocket of which were afterwards found some stamps and loose change. She left her house again shortly after 6.30 on the Saturday evening, and was last seen alive by her mother a little before that time. On each occasion that she went out, she rode upon her bicycle, and at that time she was in good health and spirits.

A few hours later – about 9.20 the same night – her dead body was discovered on the Gartree Road at Little Stretton, about two and a quarter miles below the village of Gaulby. The road, which was downhill and could be easily ridden by a cyclist in a quarter of an hour or so, was right in the course of two gates separated by some little distance, and to get where she was found (coming from Gaulby), it would be necessary for her to pass through them and over the railway. It was not the direct or shortest way to her home.

It had been at 9.20 pm that the body of the young woman was found by a farmer named Cowell. It was lying partly upon the back and partly upon the left side, close to the grass edge on the left hand side of the road as one comes towards Leicester. Close beside her was her bicycle, which was also lying upon its left side. The road was rather a lonely one, and in July it was bordered by grass fields, and hedges more than eight feet in height. Close to where the body lay was a field gate, tied with rope, on

Light.

Attorney-
General
the left side, and a few yards from the body.

Mr Cowell, passing along the road, observed the body, and found that the young woman was dead but quite warm and bleeding from the nose. She was fully dressed – even her hat was on – but she was not wearing any gloves. Her head was lying in a pool of blood. Her clothing was decently arranged and there was no sign whatever of any struggle. He lifted her up and put her on the bank, placed her bicycle against the gate and went to fetch for the police.

A little later, Police Constable Hall arrived, and was followed by Dr Williams. By that time, it was dark, and the body had been placed in a milk cart. The doctor got into the milk cart and saw the body, and to all appearances death had been due to collapse and exhaustion. It looked simply like a case of death from natural causes. The body was removed to an empty cottage nearby for a more careful examination on the following day.

The police officer, however, PC Hall, to whom the greatest possible credit was due, was a man of considerable intelligence and thoughtfulness, and he went away and gave the case grave thought and earnest consideration. He was not at all satisfied that the affair was as simple as it appeared. The result of his deliberations was that at an early hour on the following morning – he thought it was about 6.00 – he went back to the place where the body had been found and searched the vicinity for a long time. His search was rewarded, for he found a bullet lying on the road about six yards away from where the body had lain. The bullet looked as though it had been trodden on or kicked by a horse's hoof. On the bicycle, there were some smears of blood, but the machine itself as a whole was not damaged.

Having discovered the bullet, PC Hall recalled Dr Williams to the cottage. The blood was then washed from the woman's face and a bullet wound was found below and behind the left ear, and a wound of exit just above the right cheek bone.[53] The injury to the girl's head was such an injury as would be made by the bullet which was found. There was no blackening as from gunpowder about the wound – a fact which indicated that the bullet was fired from a weapon held several feet away. Bullets make very slight punctures, and it is very easy for them to escape notice. There were no other signs or marks of violence upon the body and no signs of attempted outrage. At the inquest, which had been adjourned on two or three occasions, it was found that the poor girl's brain substance was injured, and that was the cause of death – no doubt, instantaneous death.

---

53 *Sic* in the newspaper sources. In fact, the doctor's testimony places the entry wound below the left eye, and the exit wound 'high up in the hair' on the right side.

First Day – Wednesday 9 June 1920.

These are the facts with reference to the discovery and condition of Miss Wright's body, and a conclusion you may think as quite irresistible is that that was quite a case of murder. One wonders what might have happened if it had not been for the vigilance and diligence of Police Constable Hall.

Sir EDWARD MARSHALL HALL, at this stage, asked if the prisoner might sit down.

Mr JUSTICE HORRIDGE: Yes, I was going to say so when the Attorney-General was finished. [*To the prisoner.*] You may be seated.

The PRISONER: [*who previously stood with his hands on the edge of the dock, in a quiet voice:*] Thank you, my Lord.

The ATTORNEY-GENERAL: The tragedy had appalled Leicester and Leicestershire. The question is, who was the murderer, and by what means was he evading detection? On the same tragic evening of 5 July, at about 5.30 pm, two little girls – aged twelve and fourteen respectively – were riding upon bicycles in the road leading away from Leicester. They were accosted by a certain man riding a bicycle. He was riding towards them, and as he passed them he smiled and addressed them. Having passed them, he turned round, followed them and subsequently overtook them. He asked them several questions, such as where they were going, and made an endeavour to separate them. The two young girls became alarmed, turned about and rode towards Leicester, and left the man standing by his bicycle near a farm gate upon the road. These girls will identify that man and tell the jury that he was carrying a raincoat, and further they will say that the bicycle he was riding was enamelled green.

Now pass on in your thoughts to the deceased girl at a time immediately preceding her death. The road which she took was the road very easily and obviously connected with the road upon which the two little girls had left the man with the green bicycle. A man named Atkins, who would be called, would tell them that about 7.00 that evening, he was walking along Stoughton Road – sometimes called the 'top' road – when he was passed by a young woman who was riding a bicycle, and by a male cyclist who was following her and shouting, 'Hi! Hi!' That was at a place distant about two miles from Gaulby, and it was in that direction that the woman and the man who was following her were riding. The cyclists joined up and rode off together towards the foot of the hill leading into Gaulby, where they dismounted and walked up the hill. About 7.30 pm, as a farmer was driving his beasts along the road towards Gaulby (about half a mile from the village), he was passed by a man and a woman, both on bicycles. A little later, when he reached the village himself, he found

Light.

that man waiting about near the finger-post. Further, a carrier named Palmer – and Mrs Palmer – would identify that man, and would tell them that he was carrying a raincoat.

Shortly after 7.30 pm, Miss Wright arrived at the house of her uncle, George Measures, in Gaulby.[54] A man with a green bicycle who had ridden with her into the village appeared to be waiting about outside the house. That man was seen by Measures; and by the girl's cousins, Mr and Mrs Evans, who were at the time visiting Mr and Mrs Measures. She sat in the house about an hour – until about 8.30 pm – but the man with the bicycle did not go away. Evidence would show that when she was finally ready to go, she found that the tyre of the front wheel of her bicycle required attention, and she and Mr and Mrs Evans went to the front gate and attended to the tyre. While Miss Wright and Mr Evans were at the front gate attending to the tyre of the front wheel of Miss Wright's machine, the man with the bicycle came up and said to Miss Wright, 'Bella, I thought you had gone the other road'. You will observe, of course, that he addressed her by her Christian name. He evidently knew her well enough to feel sure that she would not resent being so addressed.

The man remained while Mr Evans was adjusting Miss Wright's bicycle, and Mr Evans and the man with the green bicycle got into conversation about bicycles. Evans was something of a bicycle expert, and he noticed certain features about the green bicycle upon which he commented.

When Miss Wright's bicycle was ready, she and the man were seen to leave the village, pushing their bicycles, about 8.45 pm, and appeared to be on perfectly friendly terms. Both Measures and Mr Evans will identify the man who had the green bicycle. Thirty-five minutes later, at 9.20 pm, the farmer, Mr Cowell, came upon the dead body of the girl, two and a half miles out of Gaulby.

Who was the man with the green bicycle? Who was the man who got into conversation with the two young girls in the afternoon? Who was it that had overtaken Miss Wright as she rode towards Gaulby, rode with her, walked with her, waited for her, and came away from Gaulby with her? That man, whoever he was, was the man in whose company Miss Wright was last seen alive. The evidence that I have to submit to you will go to show that that man was the prisoner – Ronald Vivian Light – and that his was the hand that fired the revolver that took her life.

Who, and what manner of man, is the prisoner? Let me say a word or

---

54   Some sources indicate that the Attorney-General said, 'James Measures'. If so, this was a confusion with James Evans – Measures and Evans, who were consecutive witnesses, would give similar evidence – and is corrected here.

First Day – Wednesday 9 June 1920.

two upon that topic. He is now thirty-four years of age. He is the son of a former citizen of Leicester, and he is a man of some education. For some years he was in the service of the Midland Railway Company as a draughtsman, and in that capacity lived at Derby. He lived there in lodgings from November 1906 to August 1914. On 2 October 1914, he returned from Derby to Leicester, to his parents' house. Shortly afterwards, he gained, and again shortly afterwards resigned, a commission in the Royal Engineers. A little later, he joined the Honourable Artillery Company, and in February 1919 he was demobilised. From February 1919 until 20 January this year, he was living at home at Leicester – a person of no occupation. That is to say, he was living at home in Leicester for five months before this murder was committed, and for some six months after. On 20 January, he became and continued to be an assistant-master at a school in Cheltenham.

On 13 May 1910, while living at Derby, the prisoner bought a bicycle from Messrs Orton Bros., local agents of the Birmingham Small Arms Co. That bicycle was enamelled green, and was supplied with special fittings (notably in the back-pedal brake and a disc on the handlebars connected with the gearing mechanism) – characteristics which were perfectly obvious to anyone, and every person who had anything to do with that machine would be called to the court that day. The entries into the books would also be produced. The prisoner would be identified personally as the man who purchased that bicycle, and other people would be called who repaired the bicycle and tuned it up from time to time for him. He regularly rode the bicycle about Leicester – up to 5 July 1919.

Returning to the month of July 1919. On the Wednesday, Thursday and Friday preceding the tragedy, the prisoner took the green bicycle to Mr Cox, a bicycle repairer whose place of business was not very far from the house of the prisoner's mother in Highfield Street. Mr Cox would tell them that prisoner made to him this false statement: that his firm in London, being slack with work, had granted him a further month's holiday. He made a further false statement that he had come down to visit some friends in Leicester, whereas he had been living with his mother for some months. When he called and took the bicycle away, he was then wearing a raincoat. The cycle repairer noticed, as other witnesses had noticed, a squeakiness in Light's voice.

On Saturday 5 July, the prisoner told Mary Webb, a domestic servant at his mother's house, that he was going to get his bicycle from the repair shop. He did so, and, later, rode away, saying that he was going for a spin in the country. Between 4.00 and 4.30 that afternoon, the prisoner was at his mother's house for tea, and it was impressed upon him that he must

Light.

Attorney-
General

be home at 8.00 pm for a hot supper. He did not return until about 10.30 pm, and then he was wheeling his bicycle. He explained his lateness to the servant by saying that his bicycle had gone wrong again. He put the bicycle into the back kitchen for three or four days, and then removed it to the box-room at the top of the house. Mary Webb missed the bicycle in December, and never saw it again. Upon missing it, she asked the prisoner about it, and he said he had sold it.

You might think it a matter of no small importance in this case that, up to 5 July, the prisoner had not merely often, but regularly, ridden this green-enamelled bicycle; but after 5 July, never. I am not going to anticipate what may be the defence or defences to be put forward on behalf of the prisoner. One may imagine, as a matter of theory, that it might be said: 'Yes, but if there was talk about a man with a green bicycle, an innocent man who happened to have a green bicycle in his possession might become very uneasy, and, however foolishly and unexpediently, he might have taken steps to conceal it'. If that, indeed, be one of the arguments or suggestions to be urged on behalf of the prisoner, you will ask yourselves this question: 'Why did he begin so early in that matter?' He started on the Saturday night, when nobody, so far as the outside world was concerned, knew anything about a murder having been committed at all. Even the doctor who saw the body at that time thought that death was due to accidental circumstances, and it was not until the search by PC Hall and the washing of the body on the Sunday that it appeared to anyone a murder had been committed.

I have described to you how the prisoner acted with his bicycle on the Saturday night. What happened to the bicycle? On 8 July, Mr Cox, the cycle repairer, gave special information to the police concerning his repair of a green bicycle. Seven whole months went by, and, during the whole of that time, the prisoner was living in Leicester – up till 20 January.

Now, while the authorship of some crimes might remain a mystery, the coincidences of truth, as the jury knows, are innumerable. The more they examined that which was true, the more they found unexpectedly corroborative testimony. On 23 February this year, a bargeman named Whitehouse was proceeding with his barge along the canal near Leicester when his tow-rope sagged and dipped into the water.[55] On coming to the surface, the rope brought with it the frame of a bicycle, fished up from the canal with its front wheel attached. The parts of the machine fell back into the water, but the bargeman noted the spot, and on the following day

---

55 The *Leicester Mail*, 9 June 1920, gives the name of the bargeman, incorrectly, as 'White'. It is not clear whether this error was the Attorney-General's, or that of the journalist recording the Attorney-General's speech.

First Day – Wednesday 9 June 1920.

he returned and got a rope and recovered the frame and the wheel. He perceived that the wheel was enamelled green, and he handed his find to the police. The latter took the parts to Mr Cox, who identified them as parts of the bicycle which had been in his hands for repair. On 1 March, the police took the parts to a bicycle expert, Mr Saunders, who was able to say that they belonged to a B.S.A. bicycle.

That was one of the most significant pieces of evidence in the case. It was the practice to identify bicycles by numbers. The number on the saddle-pin of this machine had been filed off, but there was another place where the number was put by makers of bicycles, inside the tube of the front fork. When it was taken to pieces, the number was found there, and it was 103648. It was found by the B.S.A. that the machine had been ordered by a firm at Derby, who sold it to Messrs Orton, and the latter sold it to the prisoner. There are degrees of completeness in evidence, but on that part of the case, I put it to you, the evidence is wholly and perfectly complete. If you accept that evidence, then there cannot be a moment's doubt upon this point: that the portion of the bicycle fished up from the canal in February of this year was the bicycle which the prisoner bought in 1910, had used and had frequently repaired, and had ridden regularly until 5 July 1919.

It was difficult to find the prisoner, but he was found in a school at Cheltenham on 4 March. There he was visited by Superintendent Taylor and Sergeant Howe. Taylor referred to a green bicycle, and the prisoner said, 'I never had a green bicycle'. Taylor then asked, 'Did you not have one from Messrs Orton of Derby – a B.S.A. green one?' The prisoner again said, 'No'. Then, upon further reflection, he added, 'Yes, I had one, but I sold it years ago. I do not know who I sold it to. I have had so many bicycles.' Why these false statements? So far from having sold it years ago, he had it with him in Leicester, and was seen riding it up to 5 July. How came the prisoner to deny that he had a green bicycle?

He was taken to Cheltenham Police Station, and some three hours later made a statement to Superintendent Taylor: 'What is this stunt? I sold the machine before I left Derby.' He also said that he had had a Raleigh bicycle, and sold it in September 1919. In reply to the charge by the police, Light said, 'It is absurd'. Brought back to Leicester, he was identified by the dead girl's uncle, her cousin, and the two little girls who saw him on the road.

On 12 March, a man named Chambers, dragging the canal near Leicester, picked up the back wheel of a bicycle with the rim enamelled green. The police continued to drag the canal, and on 19 March a police sergeant fished up a revolver holster containing cartridges, both loaded and blank. The bullets of those cartridges were compared with the bullet

Light.

Attorney-
General
found by PC Hall, and were found to correspond, and they would be told that there was also correspondence between them and the wound in the head of the deceased girl, the evidence being that the wound could have been produced by a bullet of that kind. Did the prisoner have a service revolver? He did not appear to have one now. No service revolver had been found, but had he one? If they accepted the evidence that would be given, there could be no doubt that he had one at some time. The prisoner knew a young lady, Miss Tunnicliffe, at Derby, in 1915, and Light told her that he would send her a parcel, that she was not to open it, and that she was afterwards to hand it to him. She did this, and the parcel being opened in her presence, she would say that it contained a large service revolver. Light explained to her that he had been instructed in revolver practice at Buxton. The cartridges found were of the pre-1915 pattern.

The bicycle was apparently dismantled by the side of the canal, and the parts were dropped into the water at short intervals, 340 yards being the distance covered by them.

The prisoner's plea before the magistrates was: 'I am innocent. On the advice of my legal advisor, I reserve my defence.' The prisoner was committed for trial, and the dragging was continued. On 29 and 30 April, the gear wheel, cranks and pedals of a B.S.A. bicycle were also found in that part of the canal. They would be told by Mr Cox that they corresponded with the rest of the bicycle.

That, in the briefest outline, was the evidence to be given in the case. I have only two further observations to make. The jury might ask – it would not be an uncommon question – 'What is the motive that is suggested for this crime? Gain? Revenge?' Whatever it was, it is difficult – and it is not necessary – to prove any motive. Of course, if they had a case where a person had a clear motive – gain, revenge, or whatever it might be, directed to a particular individual – a clear proof of that motive was a circumstance of guilt, but it did not in the least follow that because the motive was not apparent that the crime was not what the rest of the evidence indicated. What was the motive? It was not difficult to conceive that there might have been a motive of a pretty obvious character. Suppose that the prisoner had made certain overtures to her and had been rebuffed. Suppose that in anger – or it might be with a desire of concealing that which he had attempted – he pointed that revolver at her head. Then it was not difficult to conceive a motive. The workings of the human mind were many and difficult to understand, and it was impossible to say with certainty what was the particular motive; but it was not for them to speculate as to the motive if they were satisfied that the deed was done.

No witness came forward and said, 'I saw the prisoner shoot this woman'. Crimes of that kind did not tend to be committed in the presence of an eye-witness. It might be said: 'Yes, but the evidence in this case is

First Day – Wednesday 9 June 1920.

what is called circumstantial evidence'. They heard and read remarks about circumstantial evidence as if it were evidence of a low degree of force. It might be that his Lordship, with his great experience in these matters, would direct them on that matter, but, subject always to his direction, may I mention this: that where a person comes forward and says, 'I saw it,' he might be mistaken – genuinely mistaken – and he may be dishonest. There is this about circumstantial evidence: it could be said that it is evidence of surrounding facts. It is the unexpected corroboration of unanticipated incidents, and if that evidence be such as unmistakeably to point in one direction, then, gentlemen, that class of evidence is not open to the criticism that it depends upon the credibility of this or that person.

The bicycle and the revolver holster had been thrown away. Why? Manifestly it was for purposes of concealment. The prisoner had had ample opportunities for reflection after the police had brought some of the facts to notice, but they had heard false statement after false statement – 'I never had a green bicycle' – 'I sold it years ago' – and others which would be present in the jury's mind.

If, when you have heard the evidence, you have any reasonable doubt – I do not say fantastic doubt, but reasonable doubt – as to whether this was the man whose hand fired that shot, why, of course you will not hesitate to act upon it. If, as reasonable men discharging your duty to your country and fulfilling the oaths you have taken, you are satisfied that this was the man, equally in that case you will not flinch, but will do that which you have undertaken – bring a true verdict in accordance with the evidence.

Evidence for the Prosecution

WILLIAM KEAY, sworn and examined.

Witness, the county architect and engineer, produced plans and tables of distances. On the plan he had indicated by red spots places with which the evidence was concerned – the principal points of importance in connection with the case. He produced also a detailed plan showing the exact places where the various articles were found.

[*His Lordship personally showed these plans to the jury, explaining in some detail the localities marked.*]

Cross-examined by Sir EDWARD MARSHALL HALL.

Witness said that the straight way home from Gaulby to Leicester would be by what was known as the 'upper' or 'top' road through

William Keay

Stoughton and Evington. He agreed that, just after passing the first house on the left hand side (which leads to King's Norton), there were two light gates. He would call them hurdle gates.

Mary Ann Wright

MARY ANN WRIGHT, sworn and examined by MR MADDOCKS.

Witness, the mother of the murdered girl, said she lived at Stoughton and her husband was a farm labourer. Her daughter was twenty-one years of age, and employed at St Mary's Mills, Leicester. On Saturday 5 July, she wrote two or three letters, had tea about 5.30 pm, and then set out on her bicycle in the direction of Evington post office. Witness did not see her alive again. On the following Monday, witness identified her body at a cottage in Little Stretton. She wore a light raincoat and also had an oilskin coat, which was handed to Superintendent Taylor the other week.

Joseph Cowell

JOSEPH COWELL, sworn and examined.

Witness, a farmer at Elms Farm, Stretton Parva, said that on Saturday 5 July, at about 8.00 pm, he left his house and went over a portion of the farm to the old Gartree Road, and came upon the body of a young woman lying on her back on the road near a field gate, about two miles from Gaulby. Her head was covered in blood, and a bicycle lay askew in the road, with the front wheel pointing towards Leicester. He placed the body, which was still warm, on the grass by the roadside and went for help. The dead girl's clothing was not disarranged in any way, and she was wearing her hat and raincoat. Witness sent someone to guard the body, and drove to PC Hall, also telephoning to Dr Williams of Billesdon. PC Hall cycled to the spot and witness went and fetched his float, in which the body was placed for removal. It was there when Dr Williams arrived and examined it. It was taken to an empty cottage close by.

Cross-examined by Sir EDWARD MARSHALL HALL.

Witness said the nearest house in Little Stretton would be about 220 yards from where the body was found.

Alfred Hall

Police Constable ALFRED HALL, sworn and examined by the ATTORNEY-GENERAL.

Witness spoke to being called by Mr Cowell to a spot on the Gartree Road, Little Stretton, where he saw the body of the deceased girl. He arrived about 10.30 pm.

Her clothes were not torn, and her hat was on her head. The left side of her face and hair was covered with blood but the right side had no blood on it; nor had her hands. A few splashes of blood were on her raincoat. A lady's bicycle was standing by a gate near. At that time, there did not

First Day – Wednesday 9 June 1920.

appear to be any reason to suspect a crime.

Witness had the body moved in the milk float to a cottage in Little
Stretton. Dr Williams saw the body in the float, and later examined it at
the cottage, when he found a small punctured wound under the left eye.
There was only an empty purse, a handkerchief and a box of matches on
the body.

WITNESS: After the doctor had left, I began to reflect. I decided to
visit the place the next morning.

At 6.00 am the following morning (Sunday), witness went back to the
scene and examined the bicycle and the road. On the cycle, stored at the
cottage, he found a few spots of blood on the right pedal. In the evening,
at 7.30, witness found the bullet [*produced*]. It was lying in the centre
of the metalled part of the road, about seventeen and a half feet from the
pool of blood. It was lying in a hoof mark, and was embedded in the earth.
It appeared to have been trodden on. He had had some experience of
firearms, and in his opinion the bullet was fired from a pistol or revolver.

Witness washed the blood from the left side of the girl's face and
discovered a bullet hole about one inch below the left eye. At that time,
witness did not find any other wound. About 8.40 pm, he pointed out to
Dr Williams the wound.

[*The circumstances of the medical re-examination and the inquests
were briefly referred to.*]

On 12 March of this year, witness was going along the towpath of the
canal in Leicester, near St Mary's Wharf, and he saw the back wheel of a
bicycle [*produced*] fished up.

The ATTORNEY-GENERAL explained to his Lordship that the canal
was really the canalised river.

Cross-examined by Sir EDWARD MARSHALL HALL.

Witness said he was led to believe that Dr Williams first formed the
impression that the girl had fallen off her bicycle and been killed. The
puncture which the doctor found was not the bullet hole which witness
found later. It was not till the blood was washed away that they found
the bullet hole. The puncture witness found in the girl's cheek was one in
which one could comfortably insert a lead pencil. The bullet was found
nearer to Gaulby than the place where the body was found.

A document bearing the date of 7 July and offering £5 reward for
information leading to the apprehension of the murderer was circulated
throughout the district on the Tuesday after the tragedy, and affixed at
the police stations.[56] In this a description was given of a green-enamelled

---

56 Wakefield (57) follows his source, the *Leicester Mercury*, in giving the date of the notice
as 17 July. This is corrected here.

Light.

bicycle.

Questioned as to a statement he made before the coroner that blood was found on an adjoining gate, witness explained that this was cleared up afterwards. At first, he thought that the blood marks on the gate had something to do with the murder, but it was evident afterwards, when a raven or a crow was found dead in a field close by, that the bird had been on the gate (witness had traced the marks of its claws on the gate) and that it had gorged itself to death with blood.

Re-examined by the ATTORNEY-GENERAL.

Witness said no notices were posted in his district before the evening of 7 July.

Mr JUSTICE HORRIDGE: I wish to say I entirely agree with all the Attorney-General has said in regard to the intelligence you have displayed in this case.

EDITH MURIEL NUNNEY, sworn and examined by Mr BIRKETT.

Mr BIRKETT put a question to witness, a smartly-dressed fourteen year old schoolgirl residing at 28 Evington Drive, asking her if on 5 July she was cycling with her friend, Valeria Caven, and Sir EDWARD MARSHALL HALL asked his learned friend not to lead the witness. Sir Edward intimated to his Lordship that the two girls were the only witnesses as to whom there would be any cross-examination. There would be no cross-examination as to identity or as to the ownership of the bicycle; the girls' part of the story was denied entirely, but he admitted nothing, of course. Sir Edward further pointed out that the two girls were not called upon to make statements until 9 March 1920 – statements of something said to have occurred on 5 July 1919.

Addressing the jury, his Lordship said they must remember that Mr Birkett had suggested the date to the witness, and must see that a date was not mentioned to the next witness.

Witness described how she and her friend, Valeria Caven, when cycling, met a man on the Stretton Road who smiled at them as they passed. He turned back, came after them and bade them, 'Good afternoon'. He cycled on with them until they came to a farmyard, where they dismounted.

WITNESS: The man told me to take the lead, but I said, 'No'. He then asked my friend to take the lead, but she would not go without me. The man then went hurriedly up the hill.

Witness stated that the bicycle the man was riding was a green one, with 'funny' handlebars. The man was wearing a light suit and carried a raincoat over his shoulder.

MR BIRKETT: Have you seen the man since? — Yes. I picked him

First Day – Wednesday 9 June 1920.

out of twelve men.

Do you see that man in court? — Yes, sir.

Where is he? — There, sir [*nodding in the direction of the dock*].

Cross-examined by Sir EDWARD MARSHALL HALL.

Did you hear about what was called 'The Green Bicycle Case'? — Yes, sir.

And I think you saw the photographs? — Yes, sir.[57]

You knew about this poor girl being found dead in the road? — Yes, sir.

You read it in the papers, I suppose? — Yes, sir.

You were asked whether you had seen this particular man on 5 July? — Yes.

They (the police) gave you a date? — Yes, sir.

Witness said she and Valeria had talked it over together. They were quite certain that the prisoner was the man they saw with the green bicycle on 5 July.[58]

Court adjourned for luncheon.

Up to the luncheon interval, the accused had followed the Attorney-General's statement and the evidence with obvious interest. Occasionally he leaned forward in the dock and placed his arms on the rails, supporting his head with his hands. Throughout PC Hall's depositions he assumed this position, only at times glancing around the court. He evinced considerable interest in Sir Edward Marshall Hall's cross-examination.

****

VALERIA CAVEN, sworn and examined.

Witness, aged twelve, said she was out cycling with her friend, Muriel Nunney, one Saturday in the summer – she did not think it was last summer – on the Stretton Road, when they met the prisoner, who was riding towards Leicester. He later caught them up and rode with them. They dismounted from their bicycles at the foot of a hill and the prisoner asked her friend to take the lead, but she would not. He then asked her

---

57   *Sic* Wakefield, *The Green Bicycle Case*, 59. The *Leicester Mail*, 9 June 1920, gives: 'Witness admitted that they had seen the account of the murder in the papers and a photograph of Light'.

58   *Sic* the *Leicester Mail*, 9 June 1920. Wakefield, following the *Leicester Daily Post*, gives: '[They] had quite made up their minds that it was on 5 July they met this man on a green bicycle'.

Valeria
Caven

to take the lead. Witness and her friend then turned their cycles and rode back to Leicester. The prisoner seemed to have something wrong with his machine, and stopped to attend to it.[59] He had a green bicycle and was wearing a light suit and carrying a mackintosh. Witness later identified the prisoner at the Castle. The incident she described took place before she heard of the Green Bicycle Murder Case.[60]

Edward
Williams

DR EDWARD KYNASTON WILLIAMS, sworn and examined by Mr MADDOCKS.

Witness, of Billesdon, told how, on 5 July at about 10.50 pm, he received a telephone message from the witness Cowell, and later went to the scene of the tragedy at the Gartree Road. He saw PC Hall in charge of a milk float in which was the body of the dead girl. He only made a casual examination, sufficient to satisfy himself that death had taken place. In his opinion, death had occurred within an hour and a half. The body was taken to a cottage, and he thought at that time the case was due to an accident.

The next day he met PC Hall, and, in consequence of what he was then told, he returned to the cottage and made a detailed examination. He saw that the face had been washed. He found a small punctured wound on the cheek under the left eye, and a larger one on the top of the head.

The small punctured wound would admit an ordinary lead pencil, and it passed upwards, inwards and backwards to another oval wound, one and a half inches long and half an inch wide, over the middle and upper right parietal bone. The exit wound was high up in the girl's hair. There was some dark discolouration around the face wound which at first he thought might be due to burning, but when he examined it afterwards under a magnifying glass he saw the natural down round the wound. In the wound were very minute fragments of metal; he took the skin away and extracted them.

On 7 July, he made a post mortem examination with another doctor. The body was well nourished, and there was no sign of bruising on the body or the arms. There were scratches on the left hand and wrist and left cheek, probably caused by gravel. He also found two small contusions near the right angle of the mouth, and the left eyelid and eyeball were injured. The wound through the head was such as might have been caused by the bullet produced, and the others were such as might have been caused through a fall from a bicycle.

59   The *Daily Telegraph*, 10 June 1920, gives: 'When they turned and left him, the prisoner pretended that there was something wrong with his machine'.
60   The *Daily Mail*, 10 June 1920, observed that Valeria 'had a curious trick of reaching her hand up behind her back and pulling her plaited hair to spur her memory'.

First Day – Wednesday 9 June 1920.

Cross-examined by Sir EDWARD MARSHALL HALL.

Witness thought it was about 10.45 pm when he got to Mr Cowell's house, but it might have been about 11.15 pm.[61]

Witness had not much experience of gunshot wounds. He produced the same pencil with its brass point-protector as he used before the magistrates to indicate the size of the entrance hole. Witness also produced the actual piece of skin from the girl's face, containing the hole and showing where the bullet entered, preserved in a bottle of formalin. It was examined by counsel and his Lordship. The clean cut entrance wound and the small exit hole were suggestive of high velocity.

Re-examined.

Witness said he thought the bullet was fired at a distance of not more than six or seven feet. He did not think that with a bullet of this size, travelling at a tremendous velocity, there was likely to be a larger exit hole. He did not know what distance a service revolver would throw a bullet, but he would not be surprised if it was more than half a mile.

Witness went on to express a theory of his own that the bullet was fired into the ground. In Leicestershire they got both hard and soft ground having stones in it against which a bullet could be arrested, and he thought the bullet would meet the soil, hit the hard ground underneath, and that it would have sufficient momentum to take it into the road.

Sir EDWARD MARSHALL HALL: Do you mean that? The wound was inward, backward and upward, in your own words. — Yes. I could produce an exactly similar wound in the chief constable's head as he sits down there, if he inclined his head a little.

Witness admitted that he told the coroner that he could not form an opinion as to the position of the woman when she was shot, but he had thought a good deal about it since. If a bullet was fired without any further resistance than the girl's head, it was absurd to suppose that it would be found only six yards away.

Sir EDWARD MARSHALL HALL: That theory is only tenable on the assumption that the woman was on the ground, or that her head was between the revolver and the ground.

MISS KATHLEEN POWER, sworn and examined.

Witness, employed at the Vicarage, Evington, said on 5 July 1919 she was employed at Evington post office, and while on her round met the deceased on a bicycle near the church. She bought some stamps from her.

---

61   Dr Williams stopped at Mr Cowell's house before going on to the scene of Bella
     Wright's death (see Appendix I), but this is not made clear by the incomplete transcript
     of his examination.

Light.

Kathleen Power	She gave witness some letters to post, and then rode towards her home.
Thomas Nourish	THOMAS EDWARD NOURISH, sworn and examined.

Witness, a farmer at Glebe Farm, Little Stretton, said he was driving beasts along the road from Stretton to Little Gaulby, he believed on Saturday 5 July, when a man and a girl passed him on cycles, going towards Gaulby, about a quarter of a mile distant. This was between 7.00 pm and 7.30 pm. After putting his beasts in the field, witness came back along the same road and saw a gentleman waiting there. He thought it was the same that passed him with the young lady. He was dressed in a grey suit and seemed about thirty-five, and wanted a shave. Witness was shown a picture of the girl which appeared in the *Leicester Daily Post* of 9 July, and said that was very like the girl he saw.

Elizabeth Palmer

Mrs ELIZABETH PALMER, sworn and examined by Mr MADDOCKS.

Witness, the wife of a carrier of Illston on the Hill, told the court that she was in her van near Gaulby on the evening of 5 July when she saw a man and woman riding cycles. They stopped, and she saw the girl dismount and go to Mr Measures's gate.

WITNESS: I had a good view of both.

Mr MADDOCKS: Will you look at the prisoner? [*Witness turned towards the dock.*]

Is that the man? — Yes, sir.

George Measures

GEORGE WILLIAM MEASURES, sworn and examined.

Witness, a roadman, said the dead girl was his niece.[62] She visited him on 5 July, and his son-in-law (James Evans) and Mrs Evans were also on a visit. She left her bicycle outside. He saw a man with a cycle standing near the house. When Bella was about to leave, witness heard the man say to her, 'Bella, you were gone a long time. I thought you had gone the other way.' The man accompanied the girl when she set off on her cycle. Witness noticed the man had not had a shave.

WITNESS: That's the man who was outside my house [*pointing to the prisoner*].

Cross-examined by Sir EDWARD MARSHALL HALL.

Did you ask your niece if she knew the man, and did she say, 'I do not know the man; he's a perfect stranger to me'? — Yes, sir.

Are you hard of hearing? — Yes: a bit deaf in one ear.

Didn't the man say, 'Hello, I thought you had gone the other way'? —

---

62   Measures was the husband of Bella's father's sister.

First Day – Wednesday 9 June 1920.

No. He said, 'Bella'.[63]

Did your niece tell you the man had overtaken her? — Yes, sir.

That he said he had come from Great Glen? — Yes.

And that he had asked her the name of the village? — Yes.

Re-examined by Mr MADDOCKS.

Witness said Bella remarked, 'I'll sit down a little while, and he will, perhaps, be gone'.

JAMES EVANS, sworn and examined.

Witness, a miner, son-in-law of the last witness, stated that he saw the deceased at her uncle's house on the evening of 5 July. He noticed a man walking up and down outside about fifty yards from the house. About 8.45 pm, Miss Wright got ready to go, and when witness was outside mending her cycle, he heard a man who had been walking up and down the road say to the deceased, 'Bella, you have been a long time. I thought you had gone the other way.'[64] Witness further said he had a conversation with the man about his bicycle, a B.S.A., which he said he had had for some time. Witness also noticed that the bicycle was pea-green, that it had a three-speed gear and a back-pedalling brake. The man, he also noticed, wanted a shave. He had a high-pitched, squeaky voice, more like a woman.

Mr MADDOCKS: Who was the man? — The prisoner.

The frame and other parts of the bicycle, including the back wheel and the handlebars, were produced, and witness said the exhibits were similar to the one prisoner had, except that the carrier was not, he thought, the same now, and the disc for the three-speed gear was missing from the handlebars.

---

63   In 1931, in Bodmin, Norman Birkett defended Sarah Ann Hearn on two charges of murder by arsenic poisoning. One of the alleged victims was Mrs Hearn's neighbour, Alice Thomas, whose husband, William Henry Thomas, would deliver newspapers and desserts to Mrs Hearn and her sister. One of the witnesses for the prosecution, a police sergeant named Frederick Trebilcock, testified that Mrs Hearn had made a revealing statement, *sotto voce*, during the copying of her initial statement at a police station in Torquay: 'Mr Thomas used to come to our house every day with the papers. Of course, that was only a blind.' In cross-examination, Birkett asked Trebilcock whether Mrs Hearn might really have said, 'Mr Thomas used to bring the papers every morning, and he was very kind'. Trebilcock denied the possibility. One wonders whether Birkett's mind had flashed back to Marshall Hall's defence of Ronald Light. Edgar Bowker, clerk to both Marshall Hall and Birkett, certainly spotted the coincidence between the lines of defence, and remarked on it in his book, *Behind the Bar* (200-201).

64   Some accounts vary the syntax, as for example in the report of the *Daily Express*, 10 June 1920: 'You were a long time, Bella'. The question of the placement of the name – at the start of the expression or at the end – substantially affects Marshall Hall's line of defence.

Light.

Cross-examined by Sir EDWARD MARSHALL HALL.

Witness said that he asked the girl who the man was, and she replied that he was a complete stranger to her.

Asked by his Lordship whether he thought Light said, 'Hello,' or, 'Bella,' to the deceased, witness asserted that it was 'Bella', and he was surprised at this.

Ethel
Tunnicliffe

ETHEL MARY TUNNICLIFFE, sworn and examined
by Mr BIRKETT.

Witness, of 218 St Thomas Road, Derby, was a tracer employed by the Midland Railway Company. She said she had known the prisoner since 1910 or 1911, and visited his mother at Leicester in 1912. She had been on cycle rides with the prisoner and corresponded with him. In Derby, he rode a green bicycle which he told her was of B.S.A. make. He left Derby in August or September 1914 to join the army. They continued to correspond.

About 1916, witness received a letter from Buxton or Newark in which prisoner said he was sending a parcel which she was not to open, but to take to his home at Leicester. Subsequently the parcel came, and she took it to Leicester. She saw the parcel opened at prisoner's home.

Mr BIRKETT: Who opened it? — Ronald opened it.

Witness said the parcel contained a revolver, larger than the heavy Colt revolver which counsel held up. She told the prisoner that if she had known what it was, she would not have brought it into his mother's house. Light gave her no explanation of why he had sent it.

In the middle of July last, witness was at the home of the prisoner in Leicester. The murder was discussed in prisoner's presence. His mother said what a terrible thing it was.

WITNESS: We asked him if he didn't think so, and he said, 'Yes'.

Mr JUSTICE HORRIDGE: Did you call it a murder? — Yes, sir.

Cross-examined by Sir EDWARD MARSHALL HALL.

Would you expect anybody to say the same thing? — Yes, certainly.

Mr JUSTICE HORRIDGE: That depends, of course, on their knowledge of the thing. — Yes.

Witness added that the papers at the time called it a murder, but she did not know the police were looking for a man.

Asked whether the prisoner did not ask her to keep the parcel for him, witness said she did not know. She thought the revolver was sent to her in 1915, but could not remember the date.[65]

---

65   The purpose of Marshall Hall's question was to illustrate a discrepancy between the evidence given by the witness during examination in chief – which was that the revolver

First Day – Wednesday 9 June 1920.

FREDERICK CHARLES MORRIS, sworn and examined.

Frederick Morris

Witness, a metal pattern-maker of Derby, said the prisoner came to lodge at his mother's house in St Giles Road in 1911.[66] He was then employed in the Midland Railway offices. In March 1914, they moved into a house in Hartington Street and prisoner accompanied them, and he remained until he left to go to Leicester, either just before or just after the war commenced. During the whole of the time he was lodging with them he had a three-speed green bicycle, and he took it away when he left. He saw it almost daily. It corresponded to the description given by the witness Evans, and he recognised the green bicycle frame and other parts handed up as exactly similar, except that the three-speed control was missing from the handlebar.

[*At this point the case was adjourned, a short discussion between the judge and Sir Edward Marshall Hall as to procedure indicating that in all probability the case would not be concluded until the next day.*]

Court adjourned.

****

---

was sent to her in about 1916 – and the evidence she gave at the police court, and signed into her deposition, which was that the revolver was sent to her ('I think ... in the summer of 1915'. (TNA: PRO ASSI 13/50.)

66   The 1911 census, taken on the night of 2-3 April, shows Light living at 53 Sale Street, Derby, apparently boarding (together with Michael Barrington-Ward, later Sir Michael Barrington-Ward, K.C.V.O., C.B.E., D.S.O., and – not itself listed on the census – a green bicycle, B.S.A.) at the property of Mr George Harry Burt. The Morrises' house was at 137 St Giles Road, a short walk to the south-west. The previous witness, Ethel Tunnicliffe, then aged nineteen, lived with her family at 55 St Giles Road.

Second Day – Thursday 10 June 1920

There was a remarkable scene at Leicester Castle this morning about the time the hearing was resumed of the trial of Ronald Light for the alleged murder of Annie Bella Wright last July.

Soon after the case had restarted, the crowd outside began to show signs of irritation at not being able to gain admission to the court, and, after many futile efforts to pass the police, a concerted rush was made for the doors. The mounted and foot police were able to cope with the situation, however. The doors were promptly barred, and the public were forced back to the grassy mound opposite the old building.

The jury overnight had been kept under lock and key at the Bell Hotel, except for a short period when they were taken for a drive in the country in a motor charabanc. Stringent precautions were taken to ensure that nobody should be able to speak to anyone in the party, and they were brought back to the court this morning in the safe custody of the two bailiffs.

Ronald Light had been taken to the Welford Road Gaol for the night.

Inside the court, every available seat was again occupied. Light, still looking smart and well-groomed in his blue suit with light waistcoat, seated himself in the dock and listened to the evidence in his favourite attitude, his elbows resting on the dock rim, and the forefinger of one of his clasped hands lightly touching his lips. Occasionally he leaned back in his seat for a time, but invariably he returned to the attitude described – strongly suggestive of a prayerful mood were it not that his bright eyes were constantly roving restlessly over the court. During the evidence of Miss Webb, he produced a piece of paper and a pencil and made notes.

The learned judge took his seat at ten o'clock. The jury had all answered to their names, and the prisoner, who was already in the dock, was observed to bow gravely as the judge acknowledged the salutation of the Bar.

It was noticeable, however, that the Attorney-General was absent, and that Mr Maddocks, K.C., was in charge of the prosecution.

At the outset, his Lordship, addressing Sir Edward Marshall Hall, remarked that there were one or two formal omissions which he desired to rectify.

Police Constable ALFRED HALL, recalled.

Alfred Hall

Mr JUSTICE HORRIDGE: Was the body identified by the mother the

Light.

same body you found lying in the road? — It was, my Lord.

Mr JUSTICE HORRIDGE: [*to Sir Edward Marshall Hall*] You will have noticed, perhaps, that the learned counsel for the Crown never asked the doctor the question as to what was the cause of death.

Sir EDWARD MARSHALL HALL: Yes, I noticed that, my Lord, but I said nothing about it at the time.

Mr JUSTICE HORRIDGE: Therefore I want the doctor back. The case for the Crown has got to be formally proved.

Mr BIRKETT said that it was probable that the doctor, who left early yesterday, had no knowledge of the fact that the court was sitting at 10.00 am.

Mr JUSTICE HORRIDGE: Most probable. Let me know as soon as he arrives.

JOSEPH ORTON, sworn and examined.

Witness, a partner in the firm of Orton Bros. cycle agents, of Friar Gate, Derby, said his firm were local agents for the Birmingham Small Arms Company, Redditch. He produced his ledger for the year 1910.

Replying to his Lordship, Sir EDWARD MARSHALL HALL said he was raising no objection to the production of business books as evidence.

Witness went on to prove the sale of a B.S.A. bicycle, number 103648, which was paid for by the prisoner on 13 May 1910.[67] He knew the prisoner at two addresses in Derby: 53 Sale Street, and 137 St Giles Road.

Cross-examined by Sir EDWARD MARSHALL HALL.

Witness said the standard colour of the B.S.A. bicycles at the time in question was black, but this particular machine was a Model de Luxe enamelled green.

Mr JUSTICE HORRIDGE: Was there any deviation from the standard pattern of any special feature? — The only special feature ordered for the bicycle – at the order of the prisoner – was the back-pedal rim brake.

ALBERT SIDNEY DAVIS, sworn and examined.

Witness, of Prospect Hill, Redditch, formerly a clerk in the B.S.A. bicycle works, produced an order book for 1910, and an entry on 3 May 1910 showing the sale of the green Model de Luxe bicycle numbered 103648 to Orton Bros., Derby. The machine differed in two respects from the bicycle described in the firm's catalogue for 1910 as 'B.S.A. Model de Luxe Gent's Bicycle'. There was a back-pedalling brake operating on

---

67 Wakefield, *The Green Bicycle Case*, 68-69, gives 'May 18th, 1910' – an error contradicting his source, the *Leicester Daily Post*.

Second Day – Thursday 10 June 1920.

the back wheel. The finish was all green, and the handlebars were painted green.

Albert Davis

SIDNEY GARFIELD, sworn and examined.

Sidney Garfield

Witness, of 106 Oakley Road, Redditch, assistant departmental manager in the B.S.A. works, said that, in June 1910, he was in charge of the despatching department. There was an entry in his book of the despatch of a bicycle to Messrs Orton Bros., Derby.

JOHN HENRY ATKINS, sworn and examined.

John Atkins

Witness, a farm labourer in the employ of William Parker, living at Little Stretton, who was unable to attend the court on Wednesday, said he was walking the 'top' road which leads from Stoughton to Gaulby between 7.00 and 7.30 on the night of 5 July. He met a lady and gentleman on bicycles. The lady was riding in front and the gentleman was coming up behind her. Witness heard him call out in a 'highish tone', but could not hear what he said, nor the lady's reply. They rode to the hill and then dismounted and pushed their machines up together. That would be about two miles from Gaulby. He noticed that the man appeared to be between thirty and thirty-five years of age, and the lady much younger.

MARY ELIZABETH WEBB, sworn and examined by Mr MADDOCKS.

Mary Webb

Witness, who lives with the mother of the prisoner at 54 Highfield Street, Leicester, told the court she had been in Mrs Light's employment for nearly eight years. Witness said that, by profession, the prisoner was a civil engineer. While Light was living at Derby, he used to come home by train at weekends. He came from Derby about October 1914, and remained at home until April 1915. Then (October 1914) he brought with him his luggage and a green bicycle with a three-speed gear controlled by a black disc on the upturned handlebars. At that time they were living at Granville Road, Leicester. In April 1915, the prisoner took a commission in the Army, and the bicycle was left at home in a box-room.

The prisoner returned home – they had removed to Highfield Street – about the end of January 1919, on demobilisation. He made use of his bicycle, and remained at home until January 1920. Before July of last year, he used to go out on his bicycle daily.

Mr JUSTICE HORRIDGE: Where was it kept then? — In the back kitchen, my Lord.

Mr MADDOCKS: After July 1919, did he use the bicycle at all? — Not to my knowledge.

Witness went on to say that, before July last year, the prisoner told her

Light.

he was helping a man to work up a business in Leicester. At that time, he used to go out about 9.30 in the mornings, going out again about 2.00 pm, and returning about 4.00 pm for tea; sometimes going out after tea. Supper was between seven and eight. The prisoner in the mornings and afternoons generally went out on his bicycle.

Mr MADDOCKS: Do you remember Mrs Light going to Rhyl in July last? — Yes, sir.

Do you remember Saturday 5 July? — I can't quite call it to mind, sir.

Witness further said she remembered the bicycle being taken for repairs before Mrs Light went to Rhyl on 8 July. Prisoner told witness he had taken it to a fresh man to be repaired.

Witness remembered Mr Light bringing the bicycle back from a repairer's on a Saturday, on which day he went out with his bicycle after tea and did not return till about 10.00 pm, despite the fact that a hot supper had been arranged for 8.00 pm. Witness let him in at the back gate. He had his bicycle with him.

Mr MADDOCKS: Did he look tired? — He looked tired and dusty, sir.

Did you say anything to him about being late? — I said to him, 'Why are you so late, Mr Ronald?' and he replied that his bicycle had broken down again, and he had had to walk.

Did he tell you where the bicycle had broken down? — No, he did not tell me anything about the bicycle or where it had broken down, or where he had been.

When he got in, what did he do? — He had his supper and went to bed.

Now, what became of the bicycle? — It remained in the back kitchen for some days. Then he took it up into the box-room.

Can you tell us when he took it up to the box-room? — That was while my mistress was at Rhyl.

Is the box-room a room at the top of the house? — Yes.

Can you tell us when the bicycle was brought down from the box-room? — As well as I remember, it was brought down just before Christmas.[68]

Mr JUSTICE HORRIDGE: Was it brought down by Mr Ronald? — By Mr Ronald.

Mr MADDOCKS: What did he do with it? — He took it out.

Mr JUSTICE HORRIDGE: What time of the day was it? — It was in the evening.

Mr MADDOCKS: Did he bring it back or not? — No, sir.

Did you ask him about the bicycle afterwards? — No, I did not ask him, but he told me some time afterwards that he had sold it.

68   The *Evening Standard*, 10 June 1920, noted that the witness was 'much distressed' at this point.

Second Day – Thursday 10 June 1920.

Witness [*examining the frame and handlebars of the green bicycle produced*] said the handlebars were of the same shape as those of the prisoner's bicycle, while the green on the frame was of the same shade and the carrier appeared the same.

Continuing her evidence, witness stated that the prisoner got his appointment at Cheltenham before Christmas 1919, and went there on 20 January 1920.

On Monday 7 July, the prisoner went out as usual in the morning, but not on his bicycle.

When did you first hear of the death of Miss Wright? — I think I heard of it on the evening of the day my mistress went away.

Did you say anything to Light about it? — I mentioned it to him the evening I heard of it.

What did you say to him? — I asked him if he had seen the papers, as there had been a dreadful murder.

What did he say? — He only replied, 'Oh'.

Witness said that they had a London morning paper every day, and occasionally a Leicester evening paper. About that time, the prisoner usually wore grey clothes, and he had several raincoats.

Mr MADDOCKS: Do you know what has become of the clothes the prisoner had last year? — There were certain clothes that were sold just before last Christmas.

Witness stated that after the prisoner came home in January 1919, she noticed that at times he was very deaf. As a rule, he shaved daily, but sometimes he would miss a day, and then he looked very dark on the upper lip and round the chin.

Cross-examined by Sir EDWARD MARSHALL HALL.

Witness said Mrs Light was at Rhyl about a fortnight. Witness had been nearly eight years in Mrs Light's service.

Sir EDWARD MARSHALL HALL: You tell us quite frankly that you cannot fix the Saturday? — Yes.

But he went out for a ride in the evening and came home tired and dusty? — Yes.

Had he the appearance of a man who had to walk and wheel a bicycle for a considerable distance? — [*No answer.*]

He was tired and dusty? — Yes.

I think before the magistrates you said the bicycle was in the back kitchen for several days? — Yes.

That was where it was usually kept? — Yes.

Witness agreed that from the time the prisoner joined up in 1915 until 1919 – all the time Light was in the Army – the bicycle was kept and

Light.

remained in the box-room. She only remembered one occasion when he brought it down, while he was on leave.

Sir EDWARD MARSHALL HALL: Had you seen the *Leicester Mail* for Tuesday 8 July? — No, sir.

Had you seen a Leicester evening paper on the Monday? — No, sir.

Re-examined by Mr MADDOCKS.

Witness said that both she and 'Mr Ronald' were out on the Sunday after the Saturday she had spoken of.

WITNESS: I missed the bicycle on the Monday morning, as far as I can remember.

Witness said that the prisoner was at home for some months when he was an officer, and he then used the bicycle.

By the court.

[*The judge, addressing the witness in kindly tones, said he knew what a great anxiety the matter must be for her, but in her evidence there were two inconsistencies, and he would like to ask her a question about them.*]

You said you went out on a Sunday. Was that the Sunday--? — I mean the Sunday of the week after he came home tired and dusty. That was the time I missed the bicycle.

Was it the first Sunday after Mrs Light went away that you missed it? — Yes, as far as I can remember.

Now, I want you to bring your mind back to the Sunday immediately after he came home late at night, and before your mistress went away. — Yes.

Can you tell me whether he went out on that Sunday? — He did not go out on Sundays at all, my Lord, as a rule.

Can you recall whether he went out on the Sunday? — I don't think he did.

So far as you can recall, this bicycle was never taken out again until he took it away just before Christmas? — It never went out, so far as I can tell.

Did he ever go to business again after your mistress went to Rhyl? — It was while my mistress was at Rhyl that he told me the man he had been helping had not been successful in his business, and had given up and left the town.

[*Sir EDWARD MARSHALL HALL, by the permission of the judge, asked a further question about the sale of the prisoner's clothing.*] Witness said Mrs Light sold some of her own and some of Mr Ronald's when she came home from Rhyl.

Mr MADDOCKS: And was Mr Ronald there when it was sold? — Yes.

Second Day – Thursday 10 June 1920.

Dr EDWARD KYNASTON WILLIAMS, recalled.

Edward
Williams

Mr JUSTICE HORRIDGE: A formal question was not put to you yesterday, doctor. What caused the death of Bella Wright? — Shock, following gunshot wounds.

So that the gunshot wound caused her death? — Yes, my Lord.

ENOCH ARTHUR WHITEHOUSE, sworn and examined.

Enoch
Whitehouse

Witness, of 123a Syston Street, Leicester, said that, on 23 February, nearing the New Lock, his tow-rope slackened down into the water and tightened, and a portion of a green bicycle was pulled up. The bicycle fell into the water again, and on the following day he dragged about the same spot and fished up the frame and front wheel produced. He took it on his boat, dried it and took it to Long Eaton, where he handed it to the police.

Cross-examined by Sir EDWARD MARSHALL HALL.

Another bicycle was found close by, wasn't it? — I don't know anything about it.

[*Joseph Chambers, witness, called into the witness box.*]

Joseph
Chambers

Mr JUSTICE HORRIDGE: Is this additional evidence, Mr Maddocks?

Mr MADDOCKS: No, my Lord. I have it in the depositions. You will probably not be troubled with the additional evidence at all.

Mr JUSTICE HORRIDGE: But I mean the batch of additional evidence that was put in my hands yesterday. Who looks after these things for the judge? Doesn't the Director of Public Prosecutions employ a proper agent at Leicester? I have had to complain of the same thing at Maidstone in a murder trial, and I have to complain of it here.[69] I think I have had to do so here before.

Mr MADDOCKS: This witness's statement is in my notes, my Lord.

Mr JUSTICE HORRIDGE: [*handing a bunch of documents down from the bench*] Well, here are the originals. I should like you to look at them. I should like to know who did this. It is of vital importance that the judge should have a copy of the depositions in the case. The prisoner was served very late – it was 3 June – with a copy of this additional evidence, but it was in existence. I came into court, and as I take my seat another bundle of evidence was handed to me.

Mr MADDOCKS: I am very sorry, my Lord. I will see that your views reach the proper quarter.

---

69   Perhaps an allusion to the February 1919 trial of George James Philpott for the murder of John Meaton, a boy of six, at Maidstone. Philpott was found to be guilty but insane, and was incarcerated in an asylum at his Majesty's pleasure.

Light.

Joseph
Chambers

JOSEPH CHAMBERS, sworn and examined.

Witness, of Highcross Street, a labourer employed by the Leicester Corporation, said he worked on the borough dredger. On 29 April, he was assisting to drag the canal and brought up a gear wheel, crank and pedal [*produced*]. It was fifty or sixty yards from the spot where the other parts of the bicycle were found. On 12 March previously, witness had found the rear wheel [*produced*]. On 30 April, witness fished up the left crank and pedal ten yards nearer Leicester than where he found the gear wheel. They were at different parts of the canal, but all near the towing path, and all nearer Leicester than the spot where the frame and front wheel of the bicycle were found.

Wallace
Healey

Police Sergeant WALLACE HEALEY, sworn and examined.

Witness, of the Leicestershire Police, gave evidence that, on 19 March, he was dragging the canal opposite St Mary's Wharf when he fished up a revolver holster [*produced*]. As it was fished up, some cartridges fell out of it, but twelve live cartridges and seven blank ones were left in it, and witness recovered ten live cartridges which had fallen into the water. They were near the towing path, close by the side of the water and about twenty-eight yards nearer Leicester than where the back wheel of the bicycle was found. Witness drew the attention of the jury to two scratched portions on the holster.

[*His Lordship drew the attention of counsel to the fact that there were certain comments in pencil on the plan which had been handed up to him, showing the places where the various finds were made in the canal, and, after having ascertained that the jury had not read these notes, said he could not understand the way in which the case had been placed before him, seeing the fact that it was controlled by the Director of Public Prosecutions.*]

Henry
Clarke

HENRY CLARKE, sworn and examined.

Witness, a partner in the firm of Clarke and Sons, gunsmiths, of Gallowtree Gate, Leicester, said he had examined the bullet [*produced*]. It was a bullet of .455 calibre, adapted for Army service cartridges for use in a revolver. The bullet was adapted for smokeless powder, and was originally a black powder bullet adapted for use with cordite powder in a rifle or revolver. Early in 1915, such bullets were in use in the service: the authorities used these with cordite, which enormously increased their velocity. Witness had extracted one bullet from one of the cartridges produced, and had examined it with the bullet produced by the police. They were identical. The latter was a black powder bullet adapted for cordite. The blank cartridges were loaded with powder only, and bore

Second Day – Thursday 10 June 1920.

the government mark. The .455 cartridge was issued for use with the service revolver.

Cross-examined by Sir EDWARD MARSHALL HALL.

Witness said he could not say, even approximately, how many thousand million similar cartridges and bullets were made that year. The bullet in question was the standard pattern for a .455 and had been so ever since the Boer War.

Sir EDWARD MARSHALL HALL: Looking at the bullet with a glass, do you find any marks upon the bullet which, in your opinion, indicate that it has passed through a rifled barrel? — Yes, sir. They are clearly shown.

Continuing, witness said the greater the length of the barrel, the greater the velocity of the bullet. What the length of the barrel through which the bullet passed would be, witness was unable to say.

The .455 service revolvers of the service pattern and cartridges were known as the Webley-Scott service pattern, but during the war they were also made by Colt, Smith and Wesson, and other firms. It was immediately after the Boer War that the cordite-loaded cartridges for the .455 revolvers were adopted, and the effect of cordite was enormously to increase the velocity of the bullet as compared with black powder. Even up to the armistice, cordite was issued in the Army for revolvers and rifles.

He had never seen a bullet that had been fired from between four hundred and five hundred yards, though he could say that the range of a bullet fired from a service revolver would be at least a thousand yards. He had only experimented at fifty or sixty yards, and at that distance the bullet would penetrate quite an inch of deal board, and probably a two-inch board. The entrance hole of a bullet was usually relatively small and the exit hole relatively large.

Sir EDWARD MARSHALL HALL: We are told that the exit wound in this poor girl's head was an oval wound, one and a half inches by half an inch. Is not that an unusually small exit wound to be made by a bullet of this size? — Taking into consideration the fact that the bullet was fifteen-sixteenths of an inch in length, no, sir.

Answering further questions, witness stated that the deflection of a bullet after contact with a hard substance varied in accordance with the velocity: a bullet travelling with great velocity was very little deflected when it struck anything. The exit hole in this case showed that the bullet had been deflected from its course, and from

Light.

its end-on position. The size of the exit showed that the velocity of the bullet when it entered the head had been very little diminished.

Replying to Mr Justice Horridge, witness pointed out there were three distinct marks upon the bullet: one, the cut, could not be caused by firing, but probably by being trodden on, and was apparently from a horse's hoof. There was another mark showing where the bullet went through some substance – probably the head – and a third mark showing where it came in contact with the metalled road. Witness agreed with Sir Edward Marshall Hall that the bullet was comparatively uninjured by meeting a hard substance in its flight.

Sir EDWARD MARSHALL HALL: If the bullet had been fired at a distance of six or seven feet from the metalled road, you would have expected to find the bullet in the condition this one is? — Yes, if it struck the road at an angle.

Would it not go on for several hundreds of yards? — Not if it went at an acute angle.

Further examined on this point, witness said if the bullet were deflected by the road, it might drop only a short distance away, and, if this happened, witness would not expect to find greater flattening of the bullet.

Sir EDWARD MARSHALL HALL: Have you ever seen a human being who has been shot at a distance of within five yards with a service revolver? — No, sir.

I suggest that the effect of a shot fired from four or five yards by a service revolver would be to almost blow the head right off – or at least the side of the face. — That would depend upon the angle at which it was fired, and the velocity, and upon how it struck, sir.

Pressed further on this point, witness said it depended also upon what part of the head was struck. Such a bullet could have been fired either from a revolver or a rifle, and if the bullet had been fired from a long distance, had struck a tree, been deflected, and then passed through somebody's head he would have expected to find the bullet only a short distance away.

Sir EDWARD MARSHALL HALL: Is it possible for the bullet fired from a rifle to ricochet and enter a person's head? — Quite.

The discharge of a cordite cartridge made a sharp, penetrating noise, audible in quiet surroundings for a very long distance.

Re-examined by Mr MADDOCKS.

Witness said a revolver barrel was rifled, and the rifling marks found on the bullet were consistent with its having been fired from either a revolver or a rifle. If the rifling of the revolver was badly worn, that would diminish the velocity and penetrating force of the bullet. If the

Second Day – Thursday 10 June 1920.

bullet had struck a hard surface and had ricocheted, witness would not have expected so clean a wound. The holster produced was one usually used with a service revolver.

Henry Clarke

By the court.

Mr JUSTICE HORRIDGE: Do you see anything inconsistent in the condition of the bullet with its having passed through the head of the dead woman, and then having had its course arrested by the turf where it joins the metal at the edge of the road, and being found seventeen feet away? — No, my Lord.

Sir EDWARD MARSHALL HALL: [*To the judge.*] Having put the question, would you kindly ask him if he would expect to find scorching round the place where the bullet entered the head?

[*At the request of Sir Edward Marshall Hall, his Lordship asked the witness whether he would expect to find scorching of the face if the bullet had been fired within six or seven feet of the victim. Witness replied in the negative.*]

Mr JUSTICE HORRIDGE: It is only in murder cases that I would permit counsel to cross-examine my questions.

Sir EDWARD MARSHALL HALL: I did not do so, my Lord.

WALTER FRANKS, sworn and examined.

Walter Franks

Witness, of 43 St Stephen's Road, Leicester, a cycle and motor agent and repairer, said he had known the prisoner for seven or eight years, and he repaired a green B.S.A. three-speed Model de Luxe cycle for him in the spring of 1919, when the tyres were repaired, a pair of black mudguards affixed, and the machine generally put in running order. He identified the frame and wheel produced as part of the machine he then repaired. The left crack and the pedal with the small adjustment for the back-pedalling brake were then produced, and witness explained the working of the back brake to the court. He described the new parts that had been found since the prisoner had been committed for trial as parts of the original machine. He had fitted the machine with black mudguards which were still missing, as were the gear case and parts of the back pedalling brake, the disc and the cable controlling the three-speed gear. It was a simple matter to remove the mudguards.

Cross-examined by Sir EDWARD MARSHALL HALL.

Witness agreed that when he saw the cycle, it appeared as if it had been stored away.

Light.

[*Before rising for luncheon, his Lordship, addressing Sir Edward Marshall Hall, said he thought it would be advisable to sit a little later this evening.*]

Sir EDWARD MARSHALL HALL: As late as you please, my Lord.

Mr JUSTICE HORRIDGE: I am really thinking of the jury. Of course, gentlemen, if you feel tired in any way and wish to rise, you must tell me.

A JUROR: I suppose we shall be here tomorrow, my Lord?

Mr JUSTICE HORRIDGE: It is in the hope that you may be able to get away altogether tomorrow that I am proposing to sit later this evening.

SEVERAL JURORS: Thank you, my Lord.

Court adjourned for luncheon.

****

Harry Cox

HARRY COX, sworn and examined by Mr BIRKETT.

Witness, of 214 Mere Road, Leicester, a cycle dealer and repairer, gave evidence that prisoner came to his shop on Wednesday 2 July and brought with him a green B.S.A. bicycle, asking for the three-speed gear to be adjusted and a patch put on the back wheel cover. He stated that he had been an officer in the Army, had had his month's leave, and, on going back to the firm he was with, they said he could have another week or two's holiday on full pay, so he had come to Leicester to visit some friends.[70] Witness broke the cable in adjusting the gear and had to put a fresh one in, and the prisoner took the bicycle away the next day. On Friday he came back for the cable to be shortened, and when he called for it on the Saturday he said he was fed up with messing about the town and was going to have a run in the country. The prisoner was wearing a raincoat and needed a shave badly. In consequence of reports in the paper he communicated with Superintendent Bowley.

He recognised, on the tyres of the bicycle produced, patches which he had put on, and the parts of the bicycle produced were similar to the machine he repaired for Light. In January,[71] he went to Cheltenham and picked out the prisoner from amongst other men as the man who brought

---

70 The *Daily Telegraph*, 10 June 1920, offers a slightly different story: 'Prisoner told him that previous to the war he worked for a London firm, and on going back after demobilisation was told to take a holiday, and that he had come to Leicester to see friends'.

71 *Sic* in the *Leicester Mail*, 10 June 1920. Of course, this identification did not take place until after the parts of the bicycle had been found in the canal – in February – by Whitehouse.

Second Day – Thursday 10 June 1920.

the green bicycle to him in the previous July.

The witness said the gear wheel produced had evidently been used in a gear case, and the left crank had been fitted to an old pattern back-pedalling brake.

Mr BIRKETT: Have you any idea how long it would take a man to dismantle the bicycle into the condition you now see it? — It would take a novice an hour at least.

The machine when it left your place on 5 July was in fairly good condition? — Yes.

Cross-examined by Sir EDWARD MARSHALL HALL.

It was weak about the tyres? — Yes, the back tyre was weak, sir.

Do you recall the conversation you had with him on that Tuesday about the firm in London? — That was on the Wednesday, sir.

Have you an exact recollection of the whole of it? — No, sir.

Are you quite sure it was he, and not some other customer, who told you about having a holiday from his firm in London? — Yes.

Witness denied that he had seen a description of a man and a green bicycle in the local press. He also denied that he had read in the papers that the girl had been shot by a bullet of large calibre.

WILLIAM EAST SAUNDERS, sworn and examined.

Witness, manager of the Champion cycle shop, Leicester, said that, on 1 March, he examined the frame and in the seat pillar lug – where the number of a cycle usually appeared – found it had been filed off. In the upper part of the front fork, witness found the number 103648.

Police Superintendent LEVI BOWLEY, sworn and examined.

Witness, of the Leicestershire Constabulary, said that, on 6 July last year, he received information as to the death of Annie Bella Wright. He saw the witness James Evans on 7 July. The following day, he interviewed the witness Cox. The first police bill, offering a reward and describing the man with the green bicycle, was dated 7 July, and circulated throughout England, Scotland and Wales on 8 July last year. The inquest was opened on 8 July, adjourned to 25 July, and concluded on 8 August. On 4 March this year, witness went to the prisoner's house.

Cross-examined by Sir EDWARD MARSHALL HALL.

Witness was cross-examined as to 'Exhibit 1', which consists of a copy of the *Leicester Mail* dated 8 July, and counsel read from it: 'Leicestershire young woman found shot'; 'Unknown acquaintance'.

Counsel referred to the statements which appeared. 'The girl has been

Light.

Levi Bowley

obviously murdered,' and 'The bullet in the possession of the police was fired from a pistol or revolver of large calibre,' and to the reward and the description of the man with the green bicycle.

Sir EDWARD MARSHALL HALL: Was the information that appeared in the paper supplied by you from your notes? — Not altogether!

Mr JUSTICE HORRIDGE: I thank you for that answer.

Mr MADDOCKS: What do you mean by that? — I mean that we asked the newspapers to give all the publicity possible in respect to the description of the man wanted, which would materially assist us in our investigations.

Herbert Taylor

Detective Superintendent HERBERT TAYLOR, sworn and examined.

Witness, of the Leicester County Police, said that, in company with Detective Sergeant Illes of the Gloucestershire Constabulary, he went at 9.30 on the morning of 4 March to Dean Close School, Cheltenham and told him he was making enquiries about a green bicycle because a girl had been shot. He asked Light what had become of the green bicycle. He said, 'I never had a green bicycle'. When witness told him that he had purchased one from Messrs Orton at Derby, he at first said, 'No,' and then added, 'Yes, I had one, but I sold it years ago. I don't know who to as I have had so many.' Witness told the prisoner that his answers were unsatisfactory, and when he told him that he would be removed to the Cheltenham Police Station, he said, 'All right'.

Three hours later, as witness was passing his room, the prisoner called him and said, 'I want to speak to you. What is this stunt about?' He went on to say that he sold a machine before he left Derby to a man named Bourne of 9 Wilmot Street, but he could not remember whether it was a B.S.A. because he had had so many. He had also sold an all-weather Raleigh, which he had bought off a dealer at Buxton, to an ex-officer in Leicester in September 1919.

Witness said, 'The man who has identified you is Mr Cox, and he said you were in his shop with the bicycle'.

Prisoner replied, 'I never was'. When formally charged with the crime, prisoner said, 'It is absurd'.

Harold Illes

Detective Sergeant HAROLD FRANK ILLES, sworn and examined.

Witness, of the Gloucestershire Police, said he was present at Cheltenham Police Station on 4 March when Cox identified the prisoner. When he escorted Light back to the charge-room, he said on the way, 'My word. That fellow had me spotted, all right.'

Second Day – Thursday 10 June 1920.

Mr MADDOCKS: That is the case for the Crown, my Lord.

Sir EDWARD MARSHALL HALL: I intend to put the prisoner into the box.

[*His Lordship intimated that there was one more question which should be answered before the Crown closed their case, and recalled Mr Clarke.*]

HENRY CLARKE, recalled.

Mr JUSTICE HORRIDGE: From the descriptions of the wounds on the body, do you think they could possibly have been self-inflicted? — I do not, my Lord.

By Sir EDWARD MARSHALL HALL.

Witness did not think that if the girl had been lying down at the time the bullet struck her, the exit wound would have been much larger.

Evidence for the Defence

Sir EDWARD MARSHALL HALL: [*in his quietest voice*] My Lord, I desire to call the prisoner.

RONALD VIVIAN LIGHT, sworn and examined by
Sir EDWARD MARSHALL HALL.

Prisoner stated, in answer to Sir Edward Marshall Hall, that his name was Ronald Vivian Light, and he was born on 19 October 1885.

Sir EDWARD MARSHALL HALL: In 1915, did you enter the Army? — Yes.

I want to ask you first of all about Miss Tunnicliffe's evidence. Will you tell my Lord and the jury the letter you wrote to her and what you sent her? — Well, my impressions about that are not very clear at all.

Had you a revolver in 1915? — Not in April 1915.

When did you first possess a revolver? — I first possessed a revolver in July 1915.

Where did you get it from? — I bought it from my commanding officer, Major Benton.

What sort of a revolver was it? — It was an ordinary service revolver. A Webley-Scott.

In November 1915 --? Have you seen the revolver produced here? Was it about the size of that?

Mr JUSTICE HORRIDGE: It is very difficult to ask questions like that. Get your points ready. I have to get them in my note.

Sir EDWARD MARSHALL HALL: I have got my object, my Lord, in the gunsmith's evidence.

Light.

Mr JUSTICE HORRIDGE: I don't want to stop you, but I can't have objects handed round the court like that.

Sir EDWARD MARSHALL HALL: [*to the prisoner*] Did you take that revolver to France with you? — Yes.

When did you first go to France? — In November 1915.

Had you in your possession a B.S.A. green-enamelled bicycle? — Yes.

We have heard the evidence, and you have seen the part of the bicycle here in court? — Yes.

Are they parts of your bicycle? — Yes.

Whilst you were away, was the bicycle left at your mother's home? — Yes.

Mr JUSTICE HORRIDGE: You had better say, 'Away in France,' because he had it at Derby.

Sir EDWARD MARSHALL HALL: When did you come back from France first? — Either at the end of January 1916, or the beginning of February.

How long were you in England when you came back from France the first time? — You mean, when did I go to France again?

Yes. — The next time I went to France was in November 1917.

What did you go there as? — A gunner in the Honourable Artillery.

When you went to France as a gunner in the Honourable Artillery Company, had you a revolver? — I took my revolver with me.

Were you allowed as a private to have a revolver, or not? — Well, one could not wear it, of course.

Mr JUSTICE HORRIDGE: You had a revolver.

Sir EDWARD MARSHALL HALL: How long were you in France when you went as a gunner in the H.A.C.? — From November 1917 till August 1918.

What happened to you in August 1918? — I left the battery, and I passed through the casualty clearing station at the base.

How did you come to be sent there? — I was sent there suffering from shellshock and deafness. I have been deaf ever since.

How long were you kept in the clearing station? — Only about twenty-four hours.

What became of you? — I went to the base.

Prisoner said that he remained at the base one or two days, and then he was sent across to England as a stretcher case.

Sir EDWARD MARSHALL HALL: As a stretcher case, what is sent with you? — Well, I came across in pyjamas and my sole possession was a 'dolly bag', as they call it.

What became of your revolver? — It was taken away from me with all my other kit, and left behind at Corby.

Second Day – Thursday 10 June 1920.

Have you ever seen that revolver since that time? — Never.

Was there any holster belonging to the revolver?

*Prisoner said there was a holster belonging to the revolver, which went
with him to France on the first occasion, but not on the second occasion.
It was sent home from the last camp he was in before he left England;
sent home with his kit.*

*Shown the holster fished out of the canal, prisoner said it was the
holster. He had no idea how the distinctive marks (scratches) on the
holster were caused. He had not caused them.*

*Continuing, prisoner said when he came home as a stretcher case he
went to Wharncliffe Hospital, Sheffield, and was kept there about one
and a half months, and then went to a convalescent camp at Worksop for
a month.*[72] *Thence he went to Ripon. He was out of hospital then. Ripon
was a command depot, and from there he rejoined a reserve unit, and
was demobilised at the end of January 1919. He then went home to his
mother's house.*

*From that time he had no employment, except for a short period.
The bicycle was at his mother's house when he returned home, and he
brought it down from the box-room and used it. The tyres had become
in a perished condition, partly rotted away. Prisoner generally repaired
them himself, and had a lot of trouble with them. On Wednesday 2 July,
he took his bicycle to be repaired at Cox's. He had no recollection of
telling Cox that he was on holiday at full pay from a firm in London.
What he did say was this: he told Cox he was having a holiday, by that
meaning that he was not in any employment.*

Sir EDWARD MARSHALL HALL: On the Saturday, did you tell Cox
you were going for a run in the country? — I cannot say. I may or may
not have done.

Did you, on the Saturday, go home to tea? — Yes.

What time did you have tea? — Shortly after 4.00 pm, as usual.

What time did you leave the house? — Somewhere about 5.30 pm.

How were you dressed? — I had an old suit on.

Somewhat similar in shape to that you are now wearing? — Yes, very
similar.

I will ask you just once: was there any pocket in that suit in which you
could have carried a service revolver? — Certainly not.

Had you in your possession at the time any revolver? — No.

Have you ever possessed any revolver except the one you bought from
your commanding officer? — No.

Had you any ammunition? — Yes, between thirty and forty.

---

72   Wakefield, *The Green Bicycle Case*, 89, gives 'a month and a quarter' – a misreading of
his source, corrected here.

Light.

Ronald Light

And were they .455, for the service revolver? — Yes.

And blank cartridges? — Yes.

And these produced here today were yours? — As far as I know.

After you left home at 5.30 pm, where did you go? — I went to some friends of mother's in West Avenue for a strap, which I did not get.

Continuing, prisoner said the house he visited was shut up when he got there. He then went for a ride into the country. It was about 5.45 pm when he left home. He passed through Oadby.[73] He did not know the district very well. He continued straight along the main road till he got to Great Glen. It would be between 6.00 pm and 6.30 pm when he got to Great Glen. Then he turned off the main road and rode towards Little Stretton.[74] He did not go anywhere near Evington on the outward journey.

Sir EDWARD MARSHALL HALL: Did you meet on that night either of the two little girls who gave evidence here? — No, I did not.

Continuing, prisoner said after he had reached Little Stretton, he turned on the first road to the left, back towards Leicester. He had got some way down this road when he looked at his watch and found it was about 6.45 pm. Then he decided, instead of riding straight home, he would go round by a rather longer route, as he did not want to get home too early.

Sir EDWARD MARSHALL HALL: Had you any fixed time in your mind as to the time you intended to return? — I intended then to get in between 8.00 pm and 8.30 pm.

Having made that decision, did you turn? — I turned into the road on the right.

That brings you into what is called the upper road? — Yes.

And in the upper road, did you see a young lady riding a bicycle? — Yes, after I had gone some distance down.

Which way was she riding? — As a matter of fact, when I saw her first she was standing by her bicycle at the roadside.

What was she doing to it? — She was bending over it.

Did you know her? — No.

Had you ever seen her before? — Never.

Did you speak to her? — She spoke to me.

---

73 Wakefield, *The Green Bicycle Case*, 91, gives 'passed through Gaulby', rejecting his source. However, Light must have said Oadby. He reports continuing 'along the main road' to Great Glen; there was no single road running straight between Gaulby and Great Glen, but there was between Oadby and Great Glen. Light had cycled a little over a mile due roughly south from his mother's house to West Avenue, and then set out south-east, away from the city, through Oadby and towards Great Glen (about five miles from West Avenue).

74 Roughly due north from Great Glen, and a little under two miles away.

Second Day – Thursday 10 June 1920.

Ronald Light

In answer to further questions, prisoner said he did not know the village of Gaulby by name, but he knew there was a village in that direction as he had ridden through it.

Sir EDWARD MARSHALL HALL: Tell my Lord and the jury in your own words what took place when this young lady spoke to you on this upper road. — As I got up to the young lady, she was stooping over her bicycle, and she looked up at my approach and asked me if I could lend her a spanner. I had no spanners with me, and I just looked at her bicycle. As far as I could see, from what she pointed out to me, there was a certain amount of play in her free wheel.[75] I could not do anything to it as I had no spanner. After that, we rode on together. We rode down a steep hill together, and up another, and when we came to the bottom of the one to go up, we dismounted and walked up the hill together. At the top, we got on our machines and rode on together.

Where did you eventually come? — We came to a village. I asked her the name of the village as we came to it, and she said it was Gaulby.

Did she tell you anything when you got there? — Yes. As we got there, she told me that she was going to see some friends there. She said, 'I shall only be ten minutes or a quarter of an hour,' so we rode on into the village together, and I went with her as far as the house where she was going.

Had anything been said one way or the other about waiting?[76] — Well, nothing in so many words.

Mr JUSTICE HORRIDGE: What do you mean by that? — Well, when she said she was going to see some friends, but that she was only going to be ten minutes or a quarter of an hour, I took that as a sort of suggestion that I should wait for her, and that we should continue our ride together afterwards.

Sir EDWARD MARSHALL HALL: How long did you wait? — As near as I can tell, about ten minutes or a quarter of an hour. I waited in the lane a little distance from the houses, between the house and the church, which formed an island in a triangle.

Having a quarter of an hour there, what did you do? — I walked my machine up the hill till I came to the church. Then I turned to the left towards Leicester.

A little further, is there a gateway there, and a finger-post? — Yes, I think the finger-post is at the apex of the triangle, and the gate at the other. I got on my bicycle, intending to go straight to Leicester, and found

---

75 One source – the *Evening Standard*, 11 June 1920 – has it that at this point Light added complaisantly, 'If you will let me have my bicycle, I can explain it better'.

76 The *Leicester Mercury*, 10 June 1920, gives: 'Had anything been said one way or the other about courting?'

Light.

the back tyre was flat.

What did you do? — I got off my machine and walked to the gate. I pumped the back tyre up to see if it would keep up, and then sat down on the gate. The tyre went down, so I had to mend it.

Shortly after you had seen the tyre, did you see someone?[77] — Yes, a man in a field, but I had no conversation with him.

How long did you stay at that gate pumping up and re-mending your tyre? — Just about an hour.

About what time would it be when you had finished mending your tyre? — About 8.15 pm. I knew I was late already. Before riding home to Leicester, I thought I'd ride round the triangle to see where this girl had got to in the interval.

Did you ride back towards the house? — Yes.

Did you see something? — I saw her just coming out of the house which I had seen her go in.

What sort of a road is it by Measures's cottage? — It's on a hill.[78]

Downwards or upwards? — Downwards.

You were riding a bicycle when you first saw her? — Yes.

What did you do? — Before I got to the cottage, I dismounted and walked to the gate.

Did you speak to the girl? — Yes. I said, 'Hello, you've been a long time. I thought you'd gone the other way.'

Did you know her name or her home? — No.

Did you call her Bella? — No.

When did you first know her name? — When I first read the accounts in the paper.

Do you remember the witness Evans doing something to her bike? — Yes.

Did you have a conversation with the witness? — Yes.

Except that you did not say 'Bella', Evans's evidence is fairly accurate? — Yes.

Prisoner continued that the evidence that the girl and he went away together was true.

Sir EDWARD MARSHALL HALL: When you got to the top of the hill, you would get into the upper road? — Yes, eventually.

Where did you get on your bicycles? — When we got to the top of the hill, near the church.

You know the turning that turns off to King's Norton on the left? — Yes. [*The prisoner was provided with a plan, and from it described the*

---

77   *Sic* in the only available source. More naturally: 'Shortly after you had seen the tyre deflate, did you see someone?'

78   Front Street, Gaulby.

Second Day – Thursday 10 June 1920.

point where they got on their bicycles.]

How far did you ride? — Well, when I got to the top – here [*indicating the plan*] – I found my tyre had gone down again, so I had to pump it up.

Further describing their directions from the plan, prisoner said they went from the north part of the triangle, in which the church stood, towards the top road. Before they got into the upper road or to the King's Norton turning, his tyre went down again.

Sir EDWARD MARSHALL HALL: Your tyre went flat? — Well, it did not go absolutely flat – it went soft – and I pumped it up quickly.

What did the girl do? — She rode very slowly ahead.

How long do you think you were? — Oh, only a minute and a half, or a couple of minutes.

Having pumped up your tyre, did you ride after her? — Yes.

How far had she gone? — Oh, not more than a couple of hundred yards.

Was there then some conversation between you with reference to tyres? — Yes.

Please tell us what it was about and why you remember it. — I told her that while she had been in the house, I had been repairing my tyre, and I said it had got in a very bad and porous state through having been laid by so long.

What did she say about tyres? — Well, she then told me the first thing I knew about her, and that was this: she said she never let her tyres get in such a state as she was employed at a tyre factory, and could get them at cost price.

Was that the first and only thing you ever knew about her? — Yes, it was the first thing.

Did you that night learn anything more about her? — Well, I did – at the last moment I left her.

You went along the upper road? — Yes.

Look at the plan. There is shown a turning to the left after the turning to King's Norton. — Yes.

If you went down that road, it would lead to the lower road? — Yes.

And if you kept straight on, it would take you to the upper road? — Yes.

When you came to the junction, did something happen? — Yes.

Tell me what happened. — As we came to the junction of the upper and lower roads, I turned to the right, and kept along the upper road.

Was there any conversation at that point? — Yes. As I turned to the right, she got off her bicycle.

Mr JUSTICE HORRIDGE: Yes? — I also got off my bicycle. She said, 'I must say goodbye to you here. I am going that way,' and she pointed to

Light.

the road on the left, through a gate. I said, 'But isn't this the shorter way to Leicester?' – meaning the road *I* was on.

Sir EDWARD MARSHALL HALL: What did she say to that? — She said, 'I don't live there'.

What did you say? — I said, 'Well, I must go this way because I am late already, and with this puncture I may have to walk part of the way home'.

Did you shake hands with her or anything of that kind? — No, we were standing some distance apart.

What time would this be? — Well, it would be about ten minutes after we left the house at Gaulby. I do not know the time.

What was she doing when you last saw her? — She was standing, just starting to move off with her bicycle.

Did you ever see her again after you parted at that corner?[79] — No, I never saw her again. I got on my machine and rode down the hill.

How long did it take you to get home? — Some time. I had to pump up my tyre several times. It kept going down every five minutes or so.

Eventually, what did you do? — It got so bad that I had to walk, and got home just before 10.00 pm.

Mr JUSTICE HORRIDGE: You agree the Saturday Mary Webb spoke of was the Saturday this girl was killed? — Yes, my Lord.

Sir EDWARD MARSHALL HALL: When did you first hear of the death at Little Stretton? — On the Tuesday.

Did you see the paper? — No, I saw the *Leicester Mercury*.

What did you learn? — That someone had been killed. I saw the description of the bicycle and the man, and came to the conclusion it must have been the girl I was with.

Sir EDWARD MARSHALL HALL: When did you first move the bicycle from the kitchen to the box-room? — I can't be sure. It was perhaps ten days or so after mother went to Rhyl.

You made the fatal mistake of not communicating with the police? — Yes.

Mr JUSTICE HORRIDGE: Did you tell a living soul? — I told no one.

Continuing, prisoner said he read in the paper that the bullet fired was a bullet of heavy calibre from a service revolver. He got to know that Cox had given a description of the bicycle and information.

Sir EDWARD MARSHALL HALL: Except that you could have told the police what you have told us, could you have given them any assistance as to the person who committed the crime? — No, or I should have done so.

---

79   Wakefield, *The Green Bicycle Case*, 98, gives 'at the Common', following his source. Surely 'at the corner' is to be preferred.

Second Day – Thursday 10 June 1920.

Did you, later on, read the account of the inquest? — Yes.

And did you see what was the finding of the coroner's jury? — Yes.

Did you do anything to the bicycle till Christmas time? — Yes. In October, I threw the bicycle away.

Mr JUSTICE HORRIDGE: Had you ever ridden it since that Saturday night? — No, my Lord.

Sir EDWARD MARSHALL HALL: Did you go out on the Sunday after the Saturday? — No, I don't think I did.

Has the puncture ever been repaired? — No, I don't think it was ever repaired.

Mr JUSTICE HORRIDGE: In the ordinary course, you would have had it repaired on the Monday and ridden it, would you not? — Well, I should have repaired it myself, but my mother was leaving the next day, and I was busy.

What time did your mother leave? — I think it was about 11.00 am.

What time did you see the evening paper? — It was about 6.00 pm, my Lord.

Sir EDWARD MARSHALL HALL: Before you threw the bicycle away, did you do anything to it? — Well, I took away a lot of the loose parts from it, and I loosened some of the nuts and bolts. Beside the bicycle in the box-room was the revolver holster and some cartridges, live and blank. I put the cartridges into the holster and threw it into the canal.

Sir EDWARD MARSHALL HALL: In March, the police came to you? — Yes.

And you made to them the false statement they have told us? — Yes.

Did you shoot this unfortunate girl? — Certainly not.

[*This concluded the prisoner's statement. Before the cross examination of the prisoner, Mr Maddocks, answering the judge, said he understood the Attorney-General would be unable to get back to Leicester for the remainder of the case.*]

Cross-examined by Mr MADDOCKS.

Mr Maddocks first cross-examined prisoner as to his Army career. Prisoner stated that he relinquished his commission about 1 July 1916, and, after going out as a gunner, he returned home in August 1918.

Mr MADDOCKS: In going out as a gunner, you would not be allowed to take a revolver with you? — Yes: we were not allowed to wear one openly, but I actually had one under my coat.

Mr JUSTICE HORRIDGE: That is not the question. If you were known to have a revolver as a gunner, would you be allowed to keep it? — Well, I really could not say, my Lord.

Further cross-examined, prisoner said he never underwent any training

Light.

*with a revolver, but he practised with one. Miss Tunnicliffe frequently
came with him when he went to do revolver practice at Buxton. To the
best of his remembrance, he did not write one letter (as suggested by
Miss Tunnicliffe), but two letters. The purport of these two letters was
that, as he could not get the revolver in the bag of a motorcycle on which
he was going over to see Miss Tunnicliffe, he sent it on to await his
arrival there. He was prevented from going to Derby, so he wrote her a
second letter asking her to come to Leicester and bring the parcel he had
sent to her by post with her.*

Mr MADDOCKS: What did you want a large service revolver for
while you were spending a weekend at Derby or Leicester? — I brought
it here because I wanted my father to see it.

Was your father going to Derby when you sent it there? — No, but I
was going to Derby on the Saturday, and coming on to Leicester by train
on Sunday.

Couldn't you have sent it to your father? — Well, I could have done so.

And why didn't you? — Because I happened to send it to Miss
Tunnicliffe instead.

Your might have addressed it to yourself at your father's house? —
Yes, I might have done that, but my father was away.

Then, if he were away, how could you show it to him? — Well, he was
only away for some time, and would come back some day.

*Further questioned regarding the revolver, prisoner said it was
probably in July [1915] that he bought the revolver from a Major Benton.*

Mr MADDOCKS: I suppose he has been killed? — No, I do not think
so.

Sir EDWARD MARSHALL HALL: I rather protest against the
assumption by my friend that Major Benton has been killed.

*Prisoner further said he bought the revolver from Major W. N. Benton,
141st Fortress Company, Royal Engineers, Buxton, and he thought he
gave £3 for it.*[80] *He had purchased the cartridges from the company's
stores at Buxton.*

Mr MADDOCKS: Did you take the revolver out with you to France
with the Honourable Artillery Company? — Yes.

That same revolver? — Yes.

When did you leave the holster at home? — When I went to France
the second time.

---

80   In July 1915 – the date of the sale of the gun – Norman William Benton (born Market
      Drayton, 14 March 1881) was a Captain and Adjutant in the Royal Engineers; his
      promotion to Major followed in 1916 or 1917. He was alive in 1920, but not called as
      a witness by the defence to substantiate the defendant's account. It is not known whether
      the transposition of his initials was a mistake made by the prisoner in giving his evidence,
      or a mistake by the reporter who recorded the prisoner's evidence for his newspaper.

Second Day – Thursday 10 June 1920.

**Ronald
Light**

In November 1917?[81] — That was when I went out.

Where did you carry the revolver? In your pocket? — I never had occasion to use it. I could not carry it in my pocket. I never tried.

Both with regard to the holster and the parts of the bicycle, there never has been the slightest doubt in your mind that they were all of them yours? — No doubt at all.

If you had said so at first, there was no mystery about the green bicycle? — None at all.

Did you hear some of the witnesses cross-examined at the police court about your identity with the cycle? — Yes.[82]

In answer to further questions, prisoner said that, after he was demobilised, he was assisting a man who was trying to build up an insurance business, but it failed. He used to go out, while he was with this man, every morning on his bicycle. He was with this man for about eight weeks in all, from the middle of April to the middle of June.

Mr MADDOCKS: Were you helping somebody up to 5 July? — No.

Prisoner asserted that after the middle of June he had nothing to do, though he used to go out practically daily. He had taken his bicycle to be repaired several times by Mr Franks. Mr Cox's was a little further away than Mr Franks's. It was not true that he told Mr Cox he was on a visit to friends at Leicester, or that he was employed by a London firm. He acknowledged that Cox's evidence was 'comparatively' true about his statement as to London, but he destroyed the context and spoiled the sense of everything he wanted to say. What he really meant was that he was on holiday and that he had been in London. He did not tell the cycle dealer his Leicester address, having no occasion to do so. If Mr Cox had asked him for his address, he would have given it to him. The cable of the cycle was in the canal.

Mr MADDOCKS: Which part did you throw it in? — I am sure I can't say. It was such a small thing.

Did you take the back-pedalling portion of the brake away from the frame and throw that in separately? — Yes.

Whereabouts did you throw that in? — It is somewhere in the canal between the parts you have marked on your plan.

Did you throw them in all on one occasion? — Yes, all on one night.

Was that a point particularly discussed between Evans and you? — Yes.

Mr JUSTICE HORRIDGE: Was the three-speed cable thrown in separately? — I don't exactly remember. It's such a small item.

81 Wakefield, *The Green Bicycle Case*, 103, gives 'November 1919' – an obvious error.
82 The *Leicester Mail*, 11 June 1920, amplifies this question slightly: 'He admitted that the parts of the bicycle and the holster were his, and that he knew it when he was before the magistrates'.

Light.

Mr MADDOCKS: Are the mudguards still in the canal? — I can't say, except that I put them there.

You have heard that these things are still missing? — Well, I put them in the canal.

Did you yourself file off the number of the cycle from the frame? — Yes.

When? — I did that shortly before I decided to throw it away.

When would that be? — The only way I have of recollecting that is that it was shortly after summer time had finished. That would be in October.

Did you file the number off at home? — Yes.

What did you do all this for, Mr Light, in October? — In view of this case, I wished to get rid of the machine.

Did Mary Webb ask you what had become of it? — I don't think Mary Webb asked me anything about it.

Did you tell her you had sold it? — I told my mother I had sold it.

May I take it that from 5 July up to the time you made away with this bicycle, no one had suggested you were the person who had committed the murder? — Well, from the first day I ever saw the accounts, every paper was saying the man who had ridden on this green bicycle had murdered the girl.

Many people knew you in Leicester as having ridden this green bicycle? — Well, I do not suppose many noticed my bicycle.

At any rate, nobody came to you and accused you of being the person? — No.

What made you do this in October, after July, August and September had passed? — I don't know.

Further questioned, prisoner said the revolver holster was second-hand when he had it, and there was no name upon it, as far as he was aware.

Coming to 5 July, prisoner denied that he was on the lower road, as described by the two little girls. Every word of what they said was untrue.

Mr JUSTICE HORRIDGE: Do we understand that their statement was untrue, whether it happened on that day or any other day? — I never saw these girls or spoke to them on any occasion.

[Mr Maddocks had not concluded his cross-examination when the court rose until 10.00 the next morning. In answer to the judge, Sir Edward Marshall Hall intimated that he had no other witnesses to call besides prisoner.]

Court adjourned.

****

Third Day –
Friday 11 June 1920

Public interest in the trial of Ronald Light for the murder of Annie Bella Wright at Little Stretton on 5 July 1919 reached fever heat this morning. The final stages of the trial are arousing a degree of interest unparalleled in the history of crime so far as Leicester is concerned. Everywhere today people are discussing the latest aspects of the evidence.

A large crowd gathered on the Castle Green to witness the arrival of Light in a Black Maria about 7.00 am, and remained to pick up what crumbs of information and excitement were going, in the absence of any real likelihood that they would be able to obtain entrance to the very restricted space for the public in the crowded court.

It was noticed that, as hinted yesterday, Sir Gordon Hewart was unable to attend for the closing stages of the trial. Mr Hugo Young, K.C., who was briefed in another case, occupied a seat among counsel.

Light appeared in the dock just before the judge arrived in court, and was directed to take his place in the witness box. He was still dressed in blue serge, with a soft collar and grey tie, and looked smart and self-possessed. His early answers to Mr Maddocks's questions were given very deliberately, usually after a short pause for reflection, accompanied by a nervous clearing of the throat and in so subdued a tone that the judge, after repeating one of his answers so as to make sure that the jurymen caught it, said to him, 'Do speak up so that we can hear you. It is in your own interest to do so.'

The prisoner was shown a plan of the locality in which the girl was found dead and asked by his Lordship if the arrows on the plan were those that he (the prisoner) had made as indicating the route he took before getting on the upper road. The prisoner replied, 'Yes, my Lord'.

His Lordship handed the plan to the jury, and afterwards asked that the distance should be obtained and supplied to him from the point where Light left the road to the point where the girl was found.

Mr Maddocks then resumed his cross-examination of the accused.

RONALD VIVIAN LIGHT, cross-examination resumed.

Ronald Light

Mr MADDOCKS: Before you left home that day, did you know there was to be a hot supper at 8.00 pm? — I don't recollect about hot supper. Supper time varied between 7.00 pm and 8.00 pm, and if I were going

Light.

out anywhere they would naturally tell me what time supper was.[83]

Pressed, prisoner said his mother, on the night of 5 July 1919, said they would be having supper about 8.00 pm, so far as he remembered.

Mr MADDOCKS: You had, when you left home, the intention of getting home about 8.00 pm? — About 8.00 pm.

Asked if he saw anyone when he went to the friends' house (before his ride into the country) who could state that they had seen him about 5.30 pm in Leicester, Light said Mary Webb could say so, as he left home about that time.

Mr MADDOCKS: How long have you lived in Leicester? — My parents have lived in Leicester all my life. I have been in the habit of coming here at odd times for many years.

Were you in the habit of taking bicycle rides on these occasions? — Not as a rule.

And in the early part of last year, when you had your bicycle daily, did you go many rides into the country? — No, I did not.

Counsel suggested that the prisoner knew the district well enough to correct the plan, and he replied that the only reason for that was that he was for half an hour mending his bicycle by the finger-post.

It was 6.45 pm when he turned up the road where the girl was. He had had no trouble with his bicycle up to then.

Mr MADDOCKS: What time did you begin to have trouble with your bicycle? — About 6.45 pm, by which time I had possibly ridden for seven or eight miles.

Cox had attended to your bicycle for the purpose of seeing that the inner tube was in order before you started? — No. There was a bad place on the outer cover which wanted attention.

Mr JUSTICE HORRIDGE: Cox had to repair a bad place on the outer cover.

As prisoner approached the girl, she looked up and asked for the loan of a spanner. Counsel asked several questions about the meeting with Bella Wright, but the prisoner did not deviate from the story he told yesterday.

Mr MADDOCKS: Can you mark on the plan the spot where she was mending her cycle? — Approximately. [*Prisoner marked the plan in pencil.*]

You had turned from Leicester direction into the upper road about half a mile before you saw Bella Wright? — Yes.

Where did you intend going? — I intended riding along through Gaulby, and just beyond the village there is a road to Houghton, where I

83 The *Leicester Mail*, 11 June 1920, gives: 'Most evenings his mother would tell him what time they were going to have supper'.

Third Day – Friday 11 June 1920.

could have got on the main road to Leicester.

Houghton on the Hill? — Yes.

Did you know the way to Houghton? — Yes.

Mr JUSTICE HORRIDGE: He said in his evidence-in-chief that he did not know the name of the village, but knew where it was.

Mr MADDOCKS: How long were you attending to the bicycle? — Two or three minutes, perhaps.[84]

Had you any tools? — No, except that I had a repair outfit and three small levers for getting off the tyre.

After you had satisfied yourself that nothing could be done, you rode together into Gaulby. — Yes.

Did you, in the course of the ride, tell her anything about yourself? — Yes. She asked me if I had come through Stoughton, and I told her I came through Great Glen.

Did you tell her you had come from Leicester? — No, I don't think so.

Did you tell her your name? — No.

Nor where you lived? — Of course not.

Nor what time you wanted to get home? — No, I don't think I mentioned it.

Nor where you were going? — No.

She told you nothing about herself? — No, not before she left me the first time.

Did you ask her how far she had ridden? — No.

Did you ask what journey she had come, or where she was going, or how long she had been riding? — No. It was no business of mine to ask such questions.

By the time you had got to Gaulby, it would be 7.15 pm? — It would be between 7.15 pm and 7.30 pm.

Was not that the time you ought to have been returning home if you were to be back home for supper at 8.00 pm? — At that time, I was not thinking of turning back. I was thinking of going on to Houghton.

Mr JUSTICE HORRIDGE: If you wished to get home at 8.00 pm, it was time to turn back? — I could have got home by 8.00 pm if I had ridden straight on by Houghton.

Mr MADDOCKS: How many miles was it from Houghton to home, by the shortest route? — Between seven and eight miles.

Had you gone by the shortest route, you would hardly have got home by 8.00 pm? — Probably a few minutes later. The shortest route was the one I ultimately took.

No arrangements, prisoner added, were made for him to wait or for

---

84   The reporter for the *Leicester* Mail, 11 June 1920, heard something quite different: 'The prisoner said he was trying to assist the girl for nearly fifteen minutes'.

Light.

*them to ride home together. Prisoner said he had no idea where the girl
wanted to go or where she lived.*

Mr MADDOCKS: For all you knew, she might have lived on the other
side of Gaulby? — Certainly, she might have done.

In that case, it would have been futile for you to wait for the purpose of
riding back with her? — Exactly, but from the fact that she had said she
would not be more than ten or fifteen minutes, I assumed that she would
probably be going back the way she came.

Did she say, just as she went into the house, that she would only be ten
or fifteen minutes? — Before we got to the village.

Were you so interested in the girl that you would wait and see her when
she came out of the house, for the purpose of accompanying her home?
— I was not.

Why didn't you go on to Houghton when you had mended your
bicycle? — Because it was then late, and I wanted to go back by the
shortest route.

Mr JUSTICE HORRIDGE: Why didn't you go back by the shortest
route, instead of going on waiting for her? — When I had finished
mending my machine, I rode round the triangle to see if I could see
anything of her, before going back the shortest route.

Mr MADDOCKS: Then, having mended your cycle, for some reason
the girl occurred to you, and you thought you would see where she had
gone? — I suppose so.

Then you came up and saw she was at the gate with some men, and you
stopped? — Yes, sir.

Did you say 'Bella' at all? — I never said the word 'Bella'.

[*Reading.*] 'You have been a long time. I thought you had gone the
other way.' Which way did you think she was going? — I thought she
might have gone the other way round the triangle, and I had missed her.

What did she say? — I don't believe she replied at all.

If no arrangement had been made for you to meet later on, don't you
think this was a funny way of putting it? — Well, the last words she said
to me were that she would be only a quarter of an hour.

*Further examined, prisoner said his bicycle was all right as they
walked up the hill together. At the gate junction of the roads, she left him
and rode on while he was pumping up his machine.*

Mr MADDOCKS: Was all she said, 'I must go this way'? — No.

What else did she say? — She said, 'I must say goodbye to you here.
I am going that way.'

Did you say anything to that, having waited some time for her? — I
said, 'Isn't this the shorter way to Leicester?'

What did she say to that? — She said, 'I don't live there'.

Third Day – Friday 11 June 1920.

Ronald Light

Continuing, prisoner said he knew that the turn the girl took led into the lower road, which also led to Leicester, but through other villages.

Mr MADDOCKS: Did you know that was quite a lonely road? — I should not say it was any lonelier than the road on which we had been riding.

Prisoner thought the distance from the point at which he left her to Measures's cottage would be about a mile.

Mr MADDOCKS: There are two gates at the entrance from the upper road, are there not? — I could not tell you.

When you were leaving her, you said, 'I must go this way, as I am late already,' and you went? — Yes.

Am I right in saying it would be 9.00 pm when you started your homeward journey on the upper road? — When I had finished repairing my bicycle, I looked at my watch: it was 8.15 pm. I then went down the village.

Now, about the time you left her at the gate? — I don't know. I am trying to tell you how I arrived at the time. It was 8.15 pm. After I had finished repairing my cycle, I looked at my watch. I went straight down into the village and I was there about ten minutes, and it probably took me five or ten minutes to ride from the village to the junction of these roads.

You heard Mr Evans and Mr Measures say it was about 8.45 pm when you left the house? — When I left her at the gate road, it would be about 8.40 pm.

I understand, then, that it took you an hour and twenty minutes to get home? — I got home rather before than after ten. It took me about an hour and ten minutes to get home.

Did you, in the course of your journey home, meet anybody? — After I came to Evington, I met a great number of people.

Did you come through Stoughton village? — Yes.

Did you see anybody there? — Well, I really can't say.

Were you walking your bicycle in Stoughton? — No, riding.

Between Stoughton and Evington, were you riding your cycle? — No.

And between Evington and Leicester? — No, I walked the bicycle the greater part of the way.

There were a great many people on the road? — Yes.

What was the matter with your cycle? — I had a slight puncture.

But you had a repairing outfit? — Yes. The puncture was very small, and I pumped the tyre up several times.

Mr MADDOCKS: Did you ever look at the tyre to see what the puncture was like, any time after you got home? — No.

Did you tell Mary Webb or your mother where you had been? — I

Light.

don't think so.

I understand on the Tuesday night you heard of the death of Bella Wright? — Yes.

Did you see the police notices asking for information concerning the man with the green bicycle? — I saw what was said in the newspapers, but I did not see the handbills.

Did you know that the police and everybody were anxious to find the person with the green bicycle? — Yes.

Why, Mr Light, didn't you give the information that it was you? — Because, at first, I was absolutely dazed about the whole thing. I did not think clearly about the matter, and I could not make up my mind what to do.

Did you see the *Leicester Daily Post* on 8 July? — Yes. [*Prisoner was handed a copy of the paper.*] No, that was not the account I first saw.

Prisoner was shown several cuttings from the local papers describing the murder and he told the court which was the account he had seen (a clipping from the Mercury *from Sir Edward Marshall Hall's notes). Mr Maddocks declared that the account prisoner said he had seen was the same as a previous one shown to him which he said he had not seen. To this prisoner replied, 'I don't think so'.*[85]

Mr MADDOCKS: Was this the first intimation you had of the death of Bella Wright? — Yes, certainly.

And was that the first knowledge that the name of the girl you had been with on the Saturday night was Bella Wright? — Yes.

Upon seeing that, why should you not at once have given information to the police that you were the man with the green bicycle who had been with the girl on that night, and explained your movements? — [*With 'traces of hesitation'.*] Because apparently everyone jumped to the conclusion that the man on the green bicycle had murdered the girl.

Mr JUSTICE HORRIDGE: Just attend to me for a minute. Don't you see that if you had gone to the police with the true story – if it were the true story – you would at once have put them off a false scent and put them on the track of the real murderer. You said yesterday that you could not have done any good by it. Don't you see that if you had gone to them

---

85 The *Leicester Mercury* and the *Leicester Daily Post* printed identical (except for errors) accounts of the trial of Ronald Light. The publication of the *Mercury*, which was an evening paper, preceded the publication of the *Daily Post*, which was a morning paper. Presumably, Light thought that the layout or other visual characteristics of the report carried by the *Daily Post* were unfamiliar to him, but he recognised the formatting of the *Mercury*. The articles may have been identical, but Light knew which one he had read, and the one he had read – if it was in the *Mercury* and identical to the one carried in the *Daily Post* – was printed on Monday 7 July, the day *before* the Tuesday evening on which, he claimed, he became aware of the death of Bella Wright.

Third Day – Friday 11 June 1920.

and had said, 'I was the man with the green bicycle, but I left the girl at the corner,' it would have put them on the right scent, possibly – or, at any rate, they could have made other enquiries. — I see it now, of course, my Lord.

You would have disabused them of the green bicycle. You would have said, 'I was the man with the green bicycle. I left the village with the girl, and I left the girl. Somebody else must have murdered her.' — [*In a quiet voice.*] My Lord, I did not make up my mind deliberately not to come forward. I was so astounded and frightened at this unexpected thing. I kept on hesitating, and in the end I drifted into not doing anything at all.

Even then, you could have gone to the police and said, 'Come and search my house. I have got no revolver. Come and search my raincoat, or my clothes. I have no pocket in which a revolver could have been put.' — [*Clearing throat.*] I feel that now. I could not think clearly of those things then, my Lord.

Mr MADDOCKS: And still more, the police could have ascertained whether a man wheeling a bicycle had been seen by anyone between Evington and Leicester. — I suppose they could.

And they could have examined the bicycle to see if it was true there was a puncture, couldn't they? — I think they could examine the bicycle now and they will find it punctured.

But they could have done it then? — Yes, but that bicycle has never been touched from that day to this.

You don't mean that? — By that, I mean I have repaired no puncture on the inner tube. It is there now.

Did you think yourself that your story, at the time, would not be believed? — I did not think so.

Mr JUSTICE HORRIDGE: Were you on affectionate terms with your mother? — Yes, my Lord.

In this difficulty – as to being innocent, having nothing to do with it and not knowing what to do – did you go to your mother for advice, or speak to about what to say about it? — No, my Lord, simply because my mother went away the morning before I read about it.

When did she come back? — A fortnight later.

Then, when she came back, did you go to her and tell her you were perfectly innocent? — No. One of the chief reasons why I did not come forward was that I did not want to hurt mother.

Did Mary Webb mention the murder to you? — I remember her mentioning it, but I do not think it was on the Tuesday. It was later.

Further questioned, prisoner said that when it was mentioned to him, he did not say he had been there, and that he was the man on the green bicycle.

Light.

Mr MADDOCKS: Why didn't you tell Mary Webb? — Because I had not made up my mind whether to come forward or not.

You would surely think that Mary Webb, your old servant, would, at any rate, believe you? — Certainly, she would.

Then why not have said to her, 'I was there on Saturday night'? — Because if I had told Mary Webb, I should have had to come forward and tell the whole story. If I had told anybody, I should have to have told everybody.

Does it come down to this: that, in your own mind, the facts that you alone knew have made it difficult for you to explain your own movements on that night – to be believed? — I really don't see what you mean.

In your own mind, were you afraid to tell of your journey and conversation and accompaniment of Bella Wright because you thought they would not believe you, and it pointed to you having something to do with her death? — No, I did not think that at all.

Mr JUSTICE HORRIDGE: You did not think it would be difficult to get people to believe you? — I did not think so.

Don't you see it is still more extraordinary, then, that you did not go and tell people? — Well, it meant unpleasant publicity, and that was what I shrank from. I failed to realise what a difficult position I was putting myself in.

It comes to this: in order to save yourself from unpleasant publicity, you were not prepared to go to the police and give them what would have been valuable information for the discovery of a very serious crime? — I could give no information whatever, my Lord, as to the cause of the death.

You could have given information to the police, saying, 'You are in the wrong about the green bicycle. It was not the man who rode the green bicycle.' Don't you see now that would have been of immense value to the police? — I see it now, my Lord.

Mr MADDOCKS: On the Tuesday you read the paper, did you know you had a revolver holster in your box-room? — Yes, sir.

Prisoner said he could not say whether Mary Webb knew he had a pistol holster. She might have known. It was true he was carrying a raincoat upon his shoulder.

Mr MADDOCKS: What has become of that raincoat? — I think it has been sold.

Mr JUSTICE HORRIDGE: Don't you know whether it has been sold or not? — Yes. It has been sold.

Why do you say you think so when you know perfectly well? Have you made any endeavour to get that coat back from the person to whom it was sold? — No.

Third Day – Friday 11 June 1920.

Mr MADDOCKS: Have the other clothes you were wearing on 5 July also been sold? — Yes. The jacket I was wearing has been sold.

And the other things? — I don't know.

Mr JUSTICE HORRIDGE: Have the trousers been sold? — I really don't know about the trousers. I was wearing an odd suit.

Whom were these things sold to? Was it a wardrobe dealer? — Yes, my Lord. I have always been in the habit --

Never mind about your habits now. You can tell me anything you like later, but now answer my questions, yes or no. Was this a wardrobe dealer in Leicester? — Yes.

What name? — Mrs Ridgway.[86]

On 11 July, did your mother write to you from Rhyl saying that she was interested in the cycle mystery?[87] — Yes.

Having received that letter from your mother, why didn't you either write or go to Rhyl, and tell her, or write her, that you had been at Stretton and were very worried about it? — Because, of all the people in the world, she was the last person I wanted to know about it. It was to save her worrying I did not come forward.

But she, of all persons, would accept your word? — Certainly.

Why shouldn't you have said to her, 'I was there. They may think it was me, but I left her at a certain road'? — She would have been greatly concerned. I knew what had happened and was greatly worried myself. She would naturally have been greatly worried, the same as I was.

Further examined, prisoner said he never rode the bicycle after 5 July, and he moved it up to the box-room.[88]

Mr MADDOCKS: Then you kept it in the box-room with only a puncture, which you could have mended yourself? — Yes.

By that time, you had made up your mind not to be identified with the green bicycle? — No, I cannot say that I had. I put it up in the box-room because I read about this case.

Mr JUSTICE HORRIDGE: Do you tell the jury that you wished to avoid identity? — I had no cause to ride it.

Do you tell the jury that you didn't put the bicycle in the box-room in order to prevent its being identified? — No, I put it there for that purpose.

Answer my question. Did you put the bicycle in the box-room in order to avoid identity with it? — Yes.

Ronald
Light

---

86   The 1911 census shows Sarah Ann Ridgway, a wardrobe dealer, wife of Tom, living at 34 St George Street, a fairly short walk north-west from Highfield Street.

87   The words used in the letter were apparently these: 'What is the news at home? We are interested in the cycle mystery.'

88   Wakefield, *The Green Bicycle Case*, 121, gives 'July 15th' – an error originating in his source, and corrected here.

Light.

Mr MADDOCKS: Was it dark when you took the bicycle to the canal?
— Yes.

*Prisoner said he had loosened the parts of the bicycle before he left
home, and filed off the number.*

Mr MADDOCKS: Was that done so that if a green bicycle was traced
as having been in your possession, you could deny that that green bicycle
was yours? — I don't quite follow what you mean.

What was your object in filing off the number? — Well, if that green
bicycle was found, I did not want it to be traced to me. I threw the bicycle
into the canal in pieces.

Mr JUSTICE HORRIDGE: At different places? — Yes.

*Further questioned, prisoner said he dropped in the holster with the
pieces of the bicycle. When Inspector Taylor visited him at Cheltenham,
he did not know that part of the green bicycle had been found.*

Mr MADDOCKS: And did you feel secure then – the identification
number having been removed – that it could not be traced to you? — I
thought so.

Is that the reason why you said to Superintendent Taylor, 'I never had
a green bicycle'? — I said the very first thing that came into my head.

Mr JUSTICE HORRIDGE: That is the first thing that happened to
come into your head? That you never had one? — Yes, my Lord.

*In answer to Mr Maddocks, prisoner said, when he was asked if he had
one from Orton's of Derby, it occurred to him that he might be identified.*

Mr MADDOCKS: You replied, 'Yes, but I sold it years ago'. What
made you say that? — Well, I had drifted into this policy of concealing
the fact that I had been out riding on that night, and I had to go on with it.

Mr MADDOCKS: Did you say that you were never in Mr Cox's, the
cycle repairer's shop? — I said that for the same reason.

Up to that day, you had been concealing the parts of a bicycle and your
identity, but your identity up to that moment had never been challenged,
had it? — No.

Did you, when you made those denials which you now admit to be
untrue, rely on the fact that you had so mutilated the bicycle that it could
not be traced? — No, I said anything to gain time until I could get some
advice.

You have heard the evidence at the police court in all its stages, and you
said nothing by way of statement? — I was prepared at the magistrates'
hearing to have made my statement, but I was advised not to do so.

Did it occur to you that it was better to wait and see if there was any
witness who had seen you on the --

*His Lordship here interrupted Mr Maddocks and said that he should
tell the jury that a man was at liberty to reserve his defence. He took the*

Third Day – Friday 11 June 1920.

view that when a man was once charged with a crime, he was entitled to say, 'I will wait until I come before my judge and jury'. The question of what he ought to do in the meantime was another matter.

Sir EDWARD MARSHALL HALL pointed out that the prisoner, after he had been identified, said to a police officer, 'My word, that man had me spotted'. He thought, in view of the presumption of the English law, that a man was innocent until proved guilty, a man was often well advised to take the attitude of reserving his defence.

Mr JUSTICE HORRIDGE: If a prisoner simply sits tight and says, 'I will wait until I am really tried before the judge and jury', I think he is often a very wise man. Personally, I shall not draw any inference from it, and the jury ought not to draw any inference either.

Mr MADDOCKS: Just one other question. Have you made an attempt to find out if there were people on the road between Evington and Leicester on 5 July who saw you wheeling your bicycle? — No, I made no attempt.

[Mr Maddocks closed his cross-examination just before 12.00 pm, prisoner having been in the witness box for some five hours in all.]

Re-examined by Sir EDWARD MARSHALL HALL.

Tell my Lord and the jury about your mother. Your father, I believe, died as the result of an accident? — Yes.[89]

Your mother has had a great deal of trouble within the last few years, then? — Yes.

You have been the cause of very great expense to her in one way and another? — Yes.

What is your mother's physical condition? — She has been under the doctor for many years with a bad heart.

Now, as regards yourself: you were, I think, invalided home suffering from shellshock in August 1918? — Yes.

Prisoner, answering further questions, said the shellshock he sustained upset his nervous system, and he had not been the same since.

Sir EDWARD MARSHALL HALL: Have you ever, to your knowledge, seen the spot where the body was found? — I do not remember that I have been along that road since I was a boy in school.

Further questioned, prisoner said he had no idea where the girl was going when he left her. He did not know in what direction she lived.

The holster was an officer's holster. A private would not be allowed to wear a holster with a revolver. He did not think, if a revolver were found in a private's haversack, it would necessarily be confiscated.

He went to the house he had mentioned in West Avenue and got a strap

Ronald Light

89   Several sources add the detail, 'by falling out of a window'. See Appendix V.

Light.

Ronald
Light

on the Monday. It was the house of Miss Shouler: 30 West Avenue.[90] *On the Monday, he helped his mother to pack, and went downtown for some things she required. Sometimes when he went downtown he used the bicycle, and sometimes he did not. He very seldom went out on Sundays. At this time he was advertising for employment, and answered a great number of advertisements.*

Sir EDWARD MARSHALL HALL: When this girl went into the house and said she would only be ten or fifteen minutes, you took that as an invitation to wait? — Yes.

If your bicycle tyre had not gone down, should you have waited longer? — No. I got on my bicycle, and I should have ridden home on it if my tyre had not gone down.

Mr JUSTICE HORRIDGE: When first you went as an officer, you took your revolver and holster both? — Yes.

Shown the holster, prisoner stated in answer to further questions by the judge that the revolver left a certain amount of space in the holster when it was in it – it was not a dead fit.

Mr JUSTICE HORRIDGE: When you went back to France, you took the revolver and not the holster. Was that because of the increased size of the holster with the revolver in it? — Yes, partly that, and partly because I did not want to carry the extra weight.

Did you take any cartridges with you abroad? — Yes.

Why did you leave the other cartridges behind? — I only wanted to take a few. I had not room for many, and I did not wish to take many.

How many cartridges had you out of those which you left at home? — The second time I went to France, I took hardly the thirty with me.

You waited, altogether, something between half an hour and an hour for this girl at the village, didn't you? — No.

You were half an hour repairing your tyre? — I waited a quarter of an hour in the village. I got on the bicycle to ride back to Leicester, I repaired the puncture on the outskirts of the village – making about half an hour – and rode back through the village.

You were in the village for half an hour? — Yes, but not waiting for

90   In 1911, Edith Hanwell Shouler, Margaret Phoebe Allen (a married sister of the other residents), Bertha Winifred Shouler, Irene Grace Shouler and George Henry Shouler – all siblings – lived at 19 Highfield Street, on the same road as Ronald Light's parents. By 1919, Bertha had died; in 1932, George died, and his address was recorded as 30 West Avenue when his probate was granted. Edith and Irene were similarly listed at 30 West Avenue when they died in 1936 and 1946 respectively. Margaret lived with her husband, Garibaldi Saunderson Allen, at the time of her death in 1936 (in fact, she died on 28 February 1936, and he died the following day, 29 February 1936). The Miss Shouler to whom Light referred was probably Edith, who, as the oldest of the siblings, was regarded as the head of the household in 1911, although Irene was probably also resident at 30 West Avenue in 1919.

Third Day – Friday 11 June 1920.

her.

Very well. Do you tell the jury that what you have told us was all that
transpired between you and the girl at the corner, where you parted? —
Certainly; well, we were speaking all the time.

I am asking you for all that passed between you about your parting.
Have you told us all that passed between you? — [*Prisoner, apparently
not following the question, was silent.*]

Have you told us all the conversation that passed between you about
your parting? — Oh, yes, that was all, my Lord, yes.

Did you hear any shots as you went along the upper road towards
home? — No, my Lord.

Can you tell me when you disposed of this raincoat, and of your own
coat? — Probably about Christmas, when my mother was selling a lot
of her things.

Why did you sell the raincoat? I suppose you would have use for one?
— Because it was a very old one and I kept it for cycling. It was my
oldest coat.

[*His Lordship intimated that he had no further questions, and prisoner
was escorted by the warders to the dock again. During his prolonged
cross-examination in the witness box, prisoner had handled a pencil,
only an occasional cough or a movement of the hands and shoulders
indicating that he acutely felt his position as the central figure in the
drama.*]

WILLIAM KEAY, recalled.

Witness, county architect and engineer, was recalled and stated that
from the gate junction to the prisoner's house by the upper road was
five miles, 1580 yards. By the Gartree Road, or lower road, the distance
between the same points was six miles, 1200 yards. From the gate
junction to the spot where the body was found was one mile, three
hundred yards.[91]

Closing Speech for the Prosecution.

Mr MADDOCKS rose to address the jury at 12.15 pm. In measured
tones and well-chosen sentences he rapidly reviewed the case from start
to finish. That the girl was murdered admitted of no doubt. There could
be no doubt, he said – it was abundantly clear – that at some moment
between 8.50 pm and 9.20 pm, she was shot by someone in possession
of a revolver of large calibre. It was impossible to believe that she took

---

91 The *Evening Standard*, 11 June 1920, adds: 'The judge then handed a telegram to
counsel, with the remark, "That is to show you the sort of thing a judge gets sent to him"'.

Light.

her own life. The further possibility of accident had also been raised by Sir Edward Marshall Hall in the course of his cross-examination, and he must deal with it.

Mr JUSTICE HORRIDGE interjected a remark that the suggestion as to an accident was that someone else might have fired a shot from a distance. He did not understand Sir Edward to raise it as a defence, but only as a possibility.

Mr MADDOCKS went on to say that it was not suggested that the prisoner had an accident with his revolver, and that as a result of that accident the girl met her death. It was suggested that someone else – at that time of night – might have been using a rifle or revolver and unintentionally had been shooting in the direction of the girl, and might have killed the girl directly or by a ricochet. The jury would have to say if there was any evidence of such a possibility, and in doing so they would have regard to the position in which the girl was found, and the nature of the wound. It was highly improbable that anybody should be indulging in rifle or revolver practice at that time of night, and, if they had, someone would have heard of it. Besides, a bullet coming from a distance would strike in a downward direction, and not upward as had been described. The idea of the bullet having ricocheted had been dealt with by the gunsmith.

Assuming they were satisfied so far, the question resolved itself into this: who fired that shot? A man with a green bicycle was seen in the company of the girl twenty-five minutes before her dead body was found. That man concealed his identity and concealed his machine, and the question was whether he was not responsible for her death.

> Gentlemen, there is no mystery now about the green bicycle. To one person there has never been any mystery about it. He knew that suspicion pointed to the owner of the green bicycle, and he knew what inference would be drawn from the circumstances known to the police in the absence of explanation. Yesterday he went into the box and admitted, 'I am the person with the green bicycle, but I didn't come forward because I was frightened'. It is my duty, gentlemen, to sift the evidence and to ask you whether you believe that statement at this late hour.

Mr Maddocks described the steps the prisoner took to conceal the bicycle and to obliterate all traces. He dismembered the cycle, and, knowing that someone might trace the machine by a number, he filed the number off. The jury could imagine him carefully scanning that bicycle! He knew special parts of the bicycle had been mentioned and he removed them, and they had not been found. To his silence he added the act of

Third Day – Friday 11 June 1920.

deception.

Step by step, the facts pointed one way, but difficulties and obstacles were placed in the way of those who were investigating the case. The prisoner had done all that a clever man could do to cover up his tracks, in case his silence had not been effective. It was his duty to say, in representing the Crown, that to his silence and his suspicious actions, the prisoner added a lie. He did not know on 24 March that the bicycle had been found, and when the police approached him he denied all knowledge of the bicycle, and he told a lie. 'I am not the man. I never had a green bicycle. I never bought one.' It was the word of the man who was to be judged that day. There was only one course open to him: one line of defence after his silence, concealment and lies had failed. That was to hope that there was no further evidence that could connect him with the case beyond the gate junction that he had mentioned. Until the prosecution knew – and that was only yesterday – how could they produce any evidence?[92]

If, at the time the body was discovered, the prisoner had come forward and told the police the story that he now said was true, the police could have made enquiries to see if anyone had been seen going in the direction he mentioned. They could probably have found somebody who saw a man wheeling a broken-down bicycle along the upper road towards Leicester that night, but he waited until such a course was impracticable, and now his whole story was entirely uncorroborated. Anything corroborative of the prisoner's story would have been of the utmost importance to the prosecution, in the way of showing them that he was not the guilty man. Unfortunately, the opportunity was gone. The prisoner had failed in his endeavour to cover up his traces; now he took the only other course open to him – to say that he knew nothing of the shooting of the girl, and was so bewildered and dazed that he did not know what to do. It was for the jury to say whether they believed his story.

Mr JUSTICE HORRIDGE pointed out that, whether the story of the prisoner was true or not, he should have to direct the jury that it was still the duty of the prosecution to make out beyond reasonable doubt that his was the hand that committed the crime.

Continuing, Mr MADDOCKS said the jury must be satisfied that the prisoner was the man. If they were satisfied that he kept his wonderful silence for a wrong motive, and told untruths for a wrong motive, and got rid of the bicycle with a wrong motive, then it would be strong evidence that he was the person who committed the murder. Was the prisoner's account one to be relied upon? Was he responsible for the girl's death? If

---

92 Not quite the apparently plaintive admission of failure that it at first appears, this observation was expressed rather more naturally by the judge during the summing up.

Light.

they were satisfied that the prisoner had been actuated by wrong motives in doing and abstaining from doing what he had done and what he had neglected to do, they were entitled to draw the inference that he was the man responsible for the death of the girl.

It was not for him to say whether the false statements the prisoner made, according to the evidence of Cox, meant that he anticipated anything. The evidence of the little girls corresponded completely with the description of the prisoner, and it was now established that he was upon the road they mentioned, about the time they said they met him.

Mr JUSTICE HORRIDGE questioned this point, and some discussion took place between counsel and his Lordship as to whether the Stretton Road and the Gartree Road were the same, and Mr Maddocks abandoned the point.

Mr MADDOCKS next proceeded to comment on the prisoner's evidence as to what happened in and about Gaulby. He said he had never seen the girl before, and who could give evidence to the contrary? The girl was dead! If he did know the girl, and had an appointment to meet her when she came back, then it was easy to imagine a motive. He had to admit that he waited about for nearly an hour, because he was seen. He drew special attention to the conversation which took place between the prisoner and the deceased girl outside the cottage at Gaulby, for it was that conversation which, in his opinion – and, as men of the world, he submitted, in that of the jury – could supply a motive. The witnesses Measures and Evans had agreed that the prisoner came up and addressed the deceased, saying 'Bella, what a long time you have been. I thought you had gone the other way.' It implied that he had expected her – that the prisoner and the dead girl were on such terms that he could call her 'Bella' – and that he felt he had a right to complain. He suggested that the only explanation of his conduct in waiting for her was that he knew her. He thought the inference might be drawn that, when the prisoner said they were perfect strangers, he was saying something which was not accurate.

For what happened after they went away from the village together, they could only have the evidence of the prisoner. According to him, after having waited for this girl all this time, not knowing where she was going, they parted on her saying she was going in a different direction.

The girl was shot; but as to how she was shot, it was all conjecture. Could they rely on the prisoner's statement? No one heard the sound of a shot, and prisoner said he did not hear one. Yet, at 8.40 pm, the girl was found dead, and Mr Cowell, who found the body, was proceeding slowly with his cattle, so that (if the prisoner's statement were to be believed) if a shot had been fired, it could not have been more than ten minutes or so

Third Day – Friday 11 June 1920.

before he found her.

This amounted to saying that, a quarter of an hour after the prisoner had left the girl, she was found shot with a heavy revolver cartridge. What a strange and terrible coincidence for the prisoner! The bullet was of a special kind, made for use with black powder, and adapted for use with cordite. Cartridges containing bullets of an exactly similar kind were now found to have been in the prisoner's possession. He said he had not a revolver. Had he not kept silence, inspection of the house would at once have shown he had not one, but that hope had gone, and they must now rely solely upon his word. Evidence had been given that the prisoner had asked a lady to take a parcel containing the revolver secretly home for him in 1915. Why this secrecy? With regard to the holster, prisoner gave an explanation as to why he kept it at home, and why he took the revolver away; it was for the jury to consider it with the greatest care. He would not have been allowed to wear the revolver in France; why should he take it? And if he did take it, why should he not have taken it in the only receptacle in which he could wear it?

Speculation as to how this terrible deed was done did not help the prosecution, and it did not help the prisoner. What happened that night would never be known. There was no sign of outrage, and the clothes were smoothed down properly and the body composed so much that the doctor, quite naturally, took it for an ordinary death, and no examination for outrage was made till the Tuesday, two days later. Whether the prisoner did or did not accompany her, or perhaps ride round and meet her; whether he had made overtures to her that had been repulsed; whether, in a moment of madness, he had produced his revolver to terrorise her; and whether he had shot her to save himself further consequences, so that it should not come out: no one could ever tell.

> If the prisoner is not the man, then somebody else did it, and that somebody has not been heard of. No suspicious character has been brought forward.

The prisoner was with the deceased girl between a quarter of an hour or twenty minutes before she was found in a spot a mile from where he said he left her. When he got home, he prepared them at home for the silence he was to maintain. Mr Maddocks commented on the neglect to repair the punctured bicycle on the Sunday, Monday or Tuesday morning. They might say that, before the news was made public that a green bicycle was connected with the case, he was preparing for the defence which he set up. The significance was overwhelming.

The prisoner had said that when he read the paper about the murder,

Light.

he was dazed. Why should he be so dazed? He could only be so for this reason: that if he gave the explanation he now gave, he would not be believed. From that moment onward his actions were entirely those of a guilty man, anxious to cover up the traces of his guilt and dissociate himself from the green bicycle. The prisoner, according to his statement, did not know where the spot of the murder actually was – it might have been miles away. Would not an innocent man go and inform the police that he left the girl only just outside the village? When all the prisoner's concealments had failed, it was only then that he came along and told the story he now told.

Mr Maddocks commented on the thoroughness with which the bicycle was broken up, and said this was not the work of an ordinary man, incapable of concocting a story, but of a very, very clever man, indeed, and a very deliberate man. Now the prisoner came into the box; there was nothing but his bare, uncorroborated word between him and a conviction. Could the jury accept his word? It was a calamity if an innocent man were convicted, but it was equally a calamity if a guilty man were allowed to go unpunished. Having regard to all the circumstances and looking at all the facts, if they jury thought they could not accept his story, they would be obliged to do their duty to society.

[At the conclusion of Mr Maddocks's address, the court adjourned for luncheon.]

Closing Speech for the Defence.

Sir EDWARD MARSHALL HALL solemnly observed to the jury that, however they might disguise it, there was no question that, shortly, into their hands would be put the life of a human being. He was not going to ask them for sympathy, or pity, or anything of that kind; he was merely going to deal with the case on the evidence, and if, after hearing what counsel and his Lordship had to say on it, they were satisfied beyond reasonable doubt that the hand of Ronald Light killed the girl Bella Wright on the night of 5 July, it was their duty to the community to find him guilty.

First of all, they had got to be satisfied that this girl was murdered. It was a somewhat curious fact in this case that even the super-ability of the Attorney-General was not able to present to them a definite theory with regard to the commission of this crime. The evidence of Cox was of importance only in one connection. The suggestion was that when the prisoner called on Cox on the Saturday for the purpose of getting his bicycle, he made a series of false statements to him in pursuance of other false statements, with the two-fold object of concealing his identity and

Third Day – Friday 11 June 1920.

putting anyone on a false track if enquiries were made as to his identity. That presupposed a premeditation at that time, and if Cox's evidence was of any value from that point of view, the theory for the prosecution must be that, going to Cox instead of Franks, the other repairer, he deliberately went to Cox in order that Franks, who knew him well, should not know what was being done with the bicycle.

If that were relevant at all to the charge, it meant that Light had made up his mind at that time to do some unlawful act which he was anxious to conceal, and if it is related to 'this job', it

> can only be, and must be, that on that Saturday morning he had made up his mind to murder Bella Wright. If this man had the criminal mind which the prosecution had to infer when they said that he went to Cox instead of Franks, and told him a pack of lies about his connection with London and his holiday in Leicester so as to cover up what he was about to commit, would he have acted subsequently as he had done?

What was a man doing with a revolver on the Stretton Road, unless he went out for the purpose of committing some crime? It could not be suggested that it was for the purpose of shooting some casual passer-by; that proposition was so ridiculous that it refuted itself.

Therefore the supposition must be that he deliberately covered up his tracks to create a false identification – to put people off his track – that he got possession of a revolver, and deliberately went out for the purpose of meeting this woman.

> Now, you see how important it is to do more than suggest that he knew the girl before? His evidence on it was positive: 'I did not know her'. What was the evidence with regard to her statement? 'I did not know him.' 'He is a perfect stranger to me.' Why was that evidence not to be accepted as much as other evidence that had been called?

> It is the uncontradicted and the uncontroverted evidence of the deceased girl and her friends, her uncle and her cousin Evans, and the prosecution must, for the purpose of the theory they were putting before the jury with regard to Light, ask them to believe that the girl was lying when she said that, and that she *did* know, and *had* known Light for some time. The only tittle of evidence that was the foundation for such a suggestion was the purport of a casual conversation between the prisoner and the girl when she came out of the house at Gaulby.

Light.

Edward
Marshall
Hall

One witness had said Light exclaimed 'Bella, you have been a long time,' and another witness said it was, 'You have been a long time, Bella'. Upon that thin and flimsy foundation, you are asked to find affirmatively that they were known to one another.

Why? Because the prosecution realised – the Attorney-General might say what he liked about the innumerable coincidences of truth – that the overwhelming difficulty in the case was the entire absence of motive, as between the prisoner and the woman. Had the jury any doubt in their minds that the dead girl was telling the truth when she said the man was a perfect stranger to her? Cross-examined as to whether it was not 'Hello' the man said, one witness had replied that he preferred his own version. They must consider very seriously before they said that this man murdered an innocent girl under the circumstances detailed.

The description of the man and his bicycle was accurate to the smallest detail. In a short jacket, one could not very well conceal a service revolver. If it be said it might have been in the pocket of his raincoat, surely people who observed with such nicety, exactness and minuteness would have seen there was weight in the raincoat. It was a curious and significant fact that not one of the witnesses who identified the prisoner could speak to anything about him resembling anything like so bulky an article as a service revolver. The description of him to the smallest details had been given, but it had not been mentioned.

Dealing with the theories as to how the wound was inflicted, counsel said they had got to have the revolver above the head, and the head between the revolver and the greensward. They had got to have the head almost posed for it.

It was a very difficult hypothesis to deal with. The doctor – and he might compliment him on his ingenuity, after having stated before the coroner and the magistrates that he could not possibly reconstruct the crime – had now evolved a theory which was a credit to his imagination, and did him a great deal of compliment.

You are asked to say that that bullet [*pointing to it*] caused the young woman's death. The witness Clarke gave the most absurd answer which has been given in a court of justice. We have had here a man calling himself a gunsmith, professing to be an expert, relied upon by a Government to whom expense was no object, saying you could have a lead bullet fired into the ground and it could bounce off a hard substance at right angles and drop several feet away. Are you satisfied that that bullet was the bullet that actually killed Bella Wright?

Third Day – Friday 11 June 1920.

If the jury thought there was any known law of dynamics by which one could fire a leaden bullet onto hard ground so as to make that bullet bounce up so as to fall back to the ground within a few feet of the spot, they might give some attention to it; but if that evidence was not reliable, they should do as he suggested and disregard the evidence. If his Lordship read the evidence, he hoped he would read it in section. If that was the sort of evidence the prosecution relied on, it was not very strong. They were told that a bullet fired from a service revolver would go at least a thousand yards. He suggested that that was a low estimate and he wanted them presently to take the medical exhibit and see if they thought it possible that the bullet produced could possibly have made the hole shown in the piece of skin, even if travelling nose on.

Sir Edward paid a high tribute to the police for the way in which they had taken the case in hand, and said it should be an example to all. Especially he should like to bear testimony to the absolutely fair way in which the identification had been carried out. He was very doubtful whether, when the doctor produced from his little black bag the rather gruesome specimen now before the court, the police knew anything of it. If he and his advisers had known of it, they would have had it submitted, by consent, to some great expert to see if the hole could have been caused by a .455 service bullet.

Sir Edward referred to a recent criminal case in which any doubt was set at rest by the superabundance of motive disclosed, and observed that, while in law it was not really necessary for there to be a motive, it was rather difficult to find that a person killed another of malice aforethought without having some motive in doing it.

Despite the law and the law-givers, here was a young woman of charm, not averse to adventure. She says she will not be away ten minutes, which Light interpreted as an invitation to wait. They ride together and eventually they part, the girl for her home and the man for his in Leicester; and although the Crown said motive was not a legal necessity to prove – which was quite right – the Crown, knowing the value of motive, had suggested that the motive might be found in some rebuff the prisoner received, and for that purpose also hoped to make out that the couple were known to each other before that evening. Here they had signally failed, because not only the prisoner but the dead girl had said they were strangers. She had told her uncle and Evans that she did not know the man who waited for her.

The Attorney-General had made some suggestion of an improper motive. That there was no immoral overture was absolutely, definitely and finally negatived by the medical evidence.

And then there was that pin of a flimsy nature, still intact on her blouse,

Light.

which would have been displaced in the slightest struggle.[93]

The clothing of the victim was not disarranged, and no suggestion of immorality had ever been made against the girl, for which he was very glad. This was one of the features of the case that must give solace to the parents of the girl – that she was modest and, whatever, the adventure may have been, there was no immorality. There was no sign of any struggle. If she had merely refused by word to kiss him, were they going to find that, for no other reason, this man pulled out a revolver and shot her dead? It was a little far-fetched to suggest that there had been improper overtures which would necessitate shooting. A man of that class would have done what he wanted first, and shot afterwards. He was glad that there was not a tittle of evidence on this point, because the memory of the poor girl remained unsullied by the evidence.

Although the Crown had said motive was not necessary, when they said he had brought a loaded revolver out with him, they surely did not mean to suggest that he meant to shoot the first woman he met. That was also why they tried to make out the couple were previously acquainted.

Sir Edward drew attention to the difference between English and continental criminal methods. The arms of the law never shifted. No accused person in a charge of murder ever had to prove his own innocence. In this country, every one of the jury must be satisfied of his guilt beyond reasonable doubt, and, unless they were all satisfied, the prisoner was entitled to an acquittal, even if they were not disposed to accept his story with absolute confidence.

> It is not for me to prove that she was shot accidentally, or that another man shot her. It is for the prosecution to prove that it was Light's hand that killed her.

It had been said that the prisoner took her to a lonely part of the road, but he brought her close to Little Stretton church and within two hundred yards of the houses.

> Is it not curious that, on this beautiful, still, moonlit night, not even the farmer who found the body while it was still warm heard the sound of a shot? Is it not curious that, with houses only two hundred yards away, no one heard that shot?

> Is it not also curious that the police have been unable to find anyone willing to say that Light and Bella Wright were acquainted?

---

93   This remark is given as per the *Empire News*, 13 June 1920. Note that Dr Williams, at the inquest, located the flimsy pin in Bella's hair, not on her blouse (see Appendix I).

Third Day – Friday 11 June 1920.

The resources of the police since the discovery of the crime had not been able to disclose a single person who could give the court one particle of evidence to say whether or not Bella Wright and Ronald Light knew each other in any sense. The jury could read between the lines and might think that, with the mother suffering from heart disease, very possibly he did not tell her what he knew for fear of disturbing her peace of mind.

Continuing, Sir Edward asked the jury to consider what would have happened had the prisoner immediately told his story to the police. He would have been detained immediately, and the only difference in his position would be that he had done nothing to deny his identity. It was true, and counsel for the Crown had said, that his conduct was consistent with the conduct of a guilty man, but that did not make him guilty. He assured the jury that never would this world get rid of the power of sex.[94] Here was a young man between thirty and thirty-five years old, who was met by a good-looking young lady on her bicycle. She speaks to him, and is obviously not displeased with his society. Much had been made of the fact that Light waited for the girl outside her uncle's cottage.

> But I ask you to remember that the power of sex attraction still dominates, and will continue to dominate the world, in spite of law and politics. Women may pretend to be more manly, and men may possibly become more effeminate, but you will never get rid of the power of sex. In these episodes there is always the possibility of adventure – without any suggestion of immorality – when a man meets a charming girl. Can his conduct in waiting for her be described as unnatural? Is it strange that sex attraction should dominate the world? Ask yourselves. You know, gentlemen, you can give votes to women, but you cannot take away their femininity; and you can take votes from men, but you cannot take away the unknown attraction – sex.

Then, if the prisoner had wanted to do away with the holster – well, knives and razors were cheap. Surely he could have cut the holster to ribbons and scattered the pieces throughout the street of Leicester, or thrown the pieces away in the street sewers, or something like that?

> Could he not have taken all these things down to the deep and flowing River Severn and despatched them there into the depths of obscurity to which they would be carried?

Then the evidence would have gone. He had not done that.

Edward Marshall Hall

---

94   The *Leicester Mail*, 11 June 1920, recorded this observation as referring to 'the problem of sex'.

Light.

Edward
Marshall
Hall

If counsel cared, he could suggest numerous defences. Another good one would be that he had taken a revolver into the country to have a few stray shots; that he met a girl; that they were playing with what they believed were blank cartridges – and he had some blank ones – and that a ball one had got into the barrel by accident, and had caused her death.

> There is not a man, woman or child who would not have accepted that story. There was the man's perfect defence if he wanted to invent a defence, and the defence – it would have provided there being nothing to connect him with those things – would have been positively cross-examination-proof.

But he had not to put forward any such thing. The onus was always, right up to the last moment, on the prosecution, and that they had failed to discharge.

> I admit that he showed the greatest cowardice, but you must not forget that he is a man who has undergone the awful ordeal of shellshock, an ordeal which reduces the strongest men to human wrecks and leaves them bereft of mental strength and nerve vitality.

It was not necessary for them to say they believed the whole of Light's evidence to acquit him. If they were not sure, he was entitled to acquittal. If, after they had heard his story, there remained in their minds some doubt, then he was entitled to acquittal. If the prisoner had told lies in certain parts of his story which could be tested, no doubt rebutting evidence would have been called. It was quite understandable that the man, not wanting to alarm his mother, should drift into a policy of concealment.

It was a vital factor of the case that the prisoner, after he knew that every detail of it was known, kept his tell-tale bicycle down in the kitchen for ten days, as shown by the evidence of witnesses for the Crown. Was that consistent with the prisoner having deliberately and premeditatedly murdered this girl? The prisoner was driven from a negative to a positive policy of active concealment, and he maintained this attitude to the police until the time when he was identified by Cox, and he said, 'That man had got me spotted'. From that point, there was no doubt of his identity. The stress that had been laid upon the alleged concealment of the revolver in 1915 was incomprehensible unless it was suggested that as long ago as that Light had in mind the murder of Bella Wright, of whose existence he had never heard. Otherwise it was of no moment in this case, except insofar as it showed the prisoner had a revolver – and

Third Day – Friday 11 June 1920.

this was not denied.

Mr JUSTICE HORRIDGE: [*Interrupting.*] Is that a camera being raised at the back of the court? Will the police bring that man round here?

[*The man was brought before the judge.*]

Mr JUSTICE HORRIDGE: Did you hold up that camera to take a photograph?

The MAN: I was hoping to do so, sir.

Mr JUSTICE HORRIDGE: You have no right to come into a court of justice with a camera.

The MAN: I had no idea it was not allowed, sir.

Mr JUSTICE HORRIDGE: Of course you knew it was not allowed. You are an extremely lucky man not to be sent to prison, and if you persist in that statement I shall be tempted to deal with you more severely. Go away, sir, and never do it again. No one is permitted to take a photograph in a court of justice.

Sir EDWARD MARSHALL HALL: [*To the jury, with a tremor in his voice.*] I have to remind you, gentlemen, that this is a matter of life and death. Unless the evidence leaves you with no doubt, you will remember that in the one scale, held by the finger of Justice, is what is called the presumption of innocence, which is the British judicial system's most valued feature. You will not hesitate to make use of that if there is any reasonable doubt in your mind.

[*The speech for the defence had lasted nearly two hours, and had been followed with breathless interest by the crowded court.*]

Summing Up.

Mr JUSTICE HORRIDGE, summing up immediately after Sir Edward Marshall Hall's able address to the jury for the defence, said they were all glad that the prisoner had the advantage, not only of skills, but, if he might say so, the discretion which had been exercised by counsel.

It was the duty of the prosecution to satisfy the jury beyond any reasonable doubt that it was the hand of the prisoner which caused the death of the unfortunate girl.

> That duty is of such a kind that it does not necessarily follow that, because you disbelieve the prisoner's story, you must find him guilty. The prosecution must satisfy you of his guilt.

No doubt, in considering the question whether or not he was guilty, the fact that he put up a story which they believed to be untrue – if they did believe it untrue – would be a large element for them to take into consideration in deciding the question.

Light.

Justice
Horridge

He did not propose to spend any time dealing with matters which, owing to the peculiar course which the prosecution had taken, had become irrelevant. Up to the time of the trial in that court, there was no knowledge on the part of the prosecution that the defence would admit that this man was the man who was last seen in the presence of the dead woman; nor was it known that it would be admitted that the green bicycle which was discovered lying at the bottom of the canal, and which he had broken up and placed there along with the holster and the cartridges, were his. The admission of those things in the box made it unnecessary for him to refer to the story of how those various matters were discovered.

The prisoner was the last person seen with the woman before she met her death, and, because he thought that part of the case was important, he read out the evidence of the roadman, Measures, and Evans, pointing out that the jury would have to ask themselves whether the prisoner knew the woman or not. They had heard evidence that the girl was a stranger to the prisoner, and that she said to her uncle that the man was a stranger. One must look at the probabilities of the story, and consider the circumstances under which the girl and man met. They had been in each other's company some considerable time; the man had been in the village for well onto an hour. He said he had no intention of waiting. Did the jury think he would be likely to be sent away by a conversation such as he had detailed? The jury had heard him ask the prisoner if he had told the court the whole conversation between himself and the girl, and prisoner replied that he had told all that passed. He reminded the jury of the insistence by the witnesses on the use of the word 'Bella', as being the way the prisoner addressed her.

Proceeding, his Lordship dealt with the prisoner's conduct after the tragedy – the disposal of the cycle – and asked:

> Is it a deception which, in your judgement, would have been practised by an innocent man? I don't want to influence you one bit, but I think that that question and the answer to it will largely help you to come to a conclusion in this case.

It was for the jury to consider, having regard to all the circumstances under which they had met, and under which they were cycling away together, whether they would be likely to part in the way he said they did.

Pointing out that the prisoner did not use his bicycle on the Monday or Tuesday after the tragedy, his Lordship asked the jury to put themselves into two positions. The prisoner was either an innocent man or he was guilty. If he was innocent, he knew he had been seen talking to this girl and coming away with her, and she willing, it appeared, to go with him. He had left this girl for her to go on her own way home. If he had gone

Third Day – Friday 11 June 1920.

to the police and told them, that would, at least, have shown them they were on the wrong scent. It was entirely for the jury to say whether it was credible that an innocent man should have behaved in that way. Then, on the other hand, let the jury put themselves into the man's place on the assumption that he was guilty.

> Do you think it is credible or possible that in such circumstances an innocent man should have behaved the way he did? He gave as his reason that he was dazed and did not know what to do. The other motive was the guilty motive. If his conduct was compatible with innocence, then you must give him the benefit of the doubt. The question you have to decide is whether that deception could have been practised by an innocent man, or whether it points the certain finger at a guilty man.

Having alluded to the possibilities of the bullet having been fired from a service revolver at close range, his Lordship advised the jury to put the minor incidents in the case out of their minds; not to trouble their heads about the two little girls on the road, or about the allegation that the prisoner made a false statement to Cox. He had certainly made false statements about which there was no dispute. It was said, and said truly, that no motive had been proved.

> You must always look carefully at a case where there is no motive. In the absence of a motive, the defence are entitled to say, 'Why should the prisoner go and kill another human being?' If you are satisfied he *did* kill that human being, then it doesn't matter tuppence whether there is a motive or not. If you are not satisfied, one of the things you look at is whether or not there is a motive behind it. In this case, no real motive has been suggested.

> It is now admitted that he was the last man seen in the company of the murdered girl before her death.

Did the jury think it likely that they would part in the manner the prisoner had said? Did they think it possible that an innocent man could have done what the prisoner said he had? If it were possible, though not probable, they ought to give him the benefit of the doubt. Did the jury think that the bullet found in the road was the one that caused the girl's death? Did they think the prisoner had a revolver out of which he fired the bullet? If they jury though there was grave doubt about it, they were entitled to consider the fact that there was no motive.

The prosecution had to make out their case beyond reasonable doubt. It was of supreme importance than an innocent man should not be

Light.

convicted, but it was also of supreme importance that a terrible crime of this kind, if brought home to the prisoner, should not be allowed to go unpunished.

[*That was the conclusion of his Lordship's summing up, and the jury retired, taking with them the bullet and the skin exhibit showing the bullet hole.*

It was about 4.35 pm when Mr Justice Horridge concluded his summing up. When the jury had been absent three hours, they were recalled into court.]

Mr JUSTICE HORRIDGE: Are you agreed upon your verdict?

The FOREMAN: We wish to know --

Mr JUSTICE HORRIDGE: [*Interrupting.*] I do not wish to know the secrets of your room, gentlemen. I just want an answer to my question. Are you agreed upon your verdict.

[*The foreman remarked that they wished to have another ten or fifteen minutes' deliberation, and then he thought they would have arrived at a unanimous verdict.*]

Mr JUSTICE HORRIDGE: Certainly, gentlemen.

[*The jurymen again retired, but were back again in three minutes. Their names having been called out and answered, the Clerk of Assize put the formal question to them.*]

Verdict.

The CLERK OF ASSIZE: Are you agreed upon your verdict, gentlemen?

The FOREMAN: We are, sir.

The CLERK OF ASSIZE: Do you find the prisoner guilty or not guilty?

The FOREMAN: Not guilty.

The CLERK OF ASSIZE: You say that he was not guilty, and that is the verdict of you all?

The FOREMAN: Yes, sir.

Mr JUSTICE HORRIDGE: The prisoner may be discharged.

The verdict was delivered in clear tones so that everyone in the hushed court could plainly hear. The murmur of excited conversation was drowned in cheers which were silenced by the court ushers.

During the hubbub, it was observed that the foreman of the jury desired to say something. The noise was instantly stopped, and the foreman then expressed the jury's great appreciation of his Lordship's consideration to them during the hearing of the case, and also thanked the high sheriff and the under sheriff and all the officers for having made such excellent

Third Day – Friday 11 June 1920.

arrangements for their comfort.

Mr JUSTICE HORRIDGE: Thank you, gentlemen.

The excitement of the public then held sway once more. Congratulations were shouted to Light and hands waved to him as he left the dock. He chatted with the warders who had kept watch over him for three days, and inadvertently put on his cap.

Cool and calm all through the trial, he was still composed, but it was impossible to mistake his air of jubilation on the happy termination of the ordeal through which he had passed. People wormed their way from the public gallery along the narrow passages of the court either to shake him by the hand or pat him on the back. Whichever way he turned, he found people eager to show their pleasure at his release, and it was some time before he could make his way out of the court.

A dense crowd of excited people remained outside the court for some time in anticipation of seeing the acquitted man, and whenever anybody left the Castle they made a great rush to the point of exit.

They were disappointed, however, for Detective Superintendent Taylor and Inspector Hall escorted him safely out of the building by a back entrance.

Appendices.

APPENDIX I

The Inquest.

___

First Day – Tuesday 8 July 1919.[95]

Since the discovery of the terrible tragedy at Little Stretton on Saturday night last, the usual quietude of that small village has been very much disturbed, and yesterday, after it had become known that the Coroner would open the inquest that afternoon on the body of the twenty-one year old woman, Annie Bella Wright, found lying on the Burton Overy road, with a bullet wound through her head, the villagers once again earnestly returned to discussing the mystery, seeking to find a possible explanation. At various spots in the village, little groups of people assembled, and were particularly drawn to outside the house where the body lay.

The inquiry was conducted by Mr George. E. Bouskell, Coroner for the southern division of the county, at the residence of Mr J. Cowell, farmer, Elms Farm, Stretton Parva. A jury of nine was empanelled, and Mr Walter Allen was appointed foreman. The Chief Constable for the county (Mr E. Holmes) and Supt. L. Bowley were present.

The Coroner, addressing the jury after the body had been viewed at the little cottage a stone's throw away, said the deceased girl was twenty-one years old. She lived at Stoughton and worked at Leicester. He had no doubt they had seen in the press the circumstances under which the unfortunate girl had met with her death, and according to the particulars which the police had obtained, it appeared that she was found last Saturday night, about twenty minutes past nine, by Mr Joseph Cowell, of Stretton, who lived in that house, lying on the road which leads from Stretton to Burton Overy, at a distance of about 200 yards from what is called Stretton turn. She was lying on the road, her bicycle close by her side, and in a pool of blood. Mr Cowell at once went for the police, and the body was subsequently removed by the latter to the empty house where the jury had seen it. A doctor was then sent for.

From an examination of the body by Dr Williams it was ascertained that the unfortunate girl had undoubtedly met her death from a bullet wound in the head. He (the Coroner) did not think it was necessary to go into further details that day,

___

95 Composite account: *Leicester Daily Post, Leicester Mail, Leicester Mercury,* 9 July 1919; *Leicester Journal,* 11 July 1919.

Light.

and, although no revolver or gun was found, the jury would no doubt gather, on the face of it, that it looked like a case of wilful murder against somebody.

There was certain information he could give to the jury, but he did not think it desirable to do so at present, because there was more evidence than he proposed to go into that day: he would go into the whole question at a future date. He proposed to call as a witness the mother of the poor girl, and a witness who would speak as to the finding of the body, and then to adjourn the inquiry to a time to be fixed later. The Coroner added that the Chief Constable told him a bullet had been found on the road within a short distance of the spot where the body lay.

MARY ANN WRIGHT, sworn.

The first witness was the mother of the deceased, and she was allowed to sit whilst giving evidence.[96] She gave her name as Mary Ann Wright, the wife of Kenus Wright, a farm labourer, living at Stoughton, and explained that next Monday would have been her daughter's twenty-second birthday. She identified the body as being that of her daughter, Annie Bella Wright, who was single, and who lived at home with them The deceased was employed by Messrs Bates, St Mary's Mills, Aylestone, Leicester, her work being that of a rubber hand, and she used to cycle to and from Leicester. She left off work at ten o'clock on Friday night last, and did not go on Saturdays, and would not go back to business again until Monday morning.

The CORONER: What time did she go out on Saturday? — Between six and seven in the evening. She left home to catch the post at Evington. That was the last time I saw her alive.

The CORONER: Was she as a matter of fact engaged to be married, or was she walking out with a young man? — She was not engaged to anyone, but she had been walking out with a young man, but he is away. The young man is a sailor stationed, I believe, at Portsmouth.

She was walking out, but not actually engaged to be married? — No.

The CHIEF CONSTABLE: You told the Coroner that she was going to the post office at Evington. Can you tell us whether to your knowledge she had letters to post? — She was writing letters on Saturday afternoon, and I saw them in her coat pocket when she left.

The CHIEF CONSTABLE: And the Evington post office would be her nearest post office? — Yes, it would.

JOSEPH COWELL, sworn.[97]

96   The *Leicester Mail*, 9 July 1919, described Mrs Wright as 'typical of the wife of a farm labourer'.
97   The *Leicester Mail*, 9 July 1919, said that 'Mr Cowell's evidence of the discovery of the crime was quietly told'.

Appendix I.

Joseph Cowell, farmer, Elms Farm, Stretton Parva, stated that on Saturday evening last, about 9.20, he was driving a herd of cows along the Burton Overy road in the direction of Stretton Parva, and in the distance, about 400 yards away, he saw something on the road which he at first took to be either a horse rug or a bag, or something which might have fallen from a trap. He went to the spot, about 200 yards from the turning to Stretton, and saw that it was the body of a girl, together with a bicycle lying by her side.

The CORONER: In what position?

Witness replied that the bicycle was lying with the front wheel towards Stretton Parva.

The CORONER: The girl; what was her position? — Lying on the road on her left side, with her head towards the centre of the road, and her feet would be towards the hedge.

What did you do? — I at once went to her, and found that she was bleeding very much.

From where? — I considered the nose; there was a lot of bleeding from her nose.

And mouth? — Well, I cannot say that.

Was there a pool of blood close to her body? — A very large one.

I believe you picked the body up and placed it on the grass? — When I picked her up, her head fell back, and I found she was dead.[98]

Then did you place her on the turf by the side of the road? — On the grass, out of the way of the traffic.

Witness added that he went home and told his wife of what he had seen, and he asked her to get someone to look after it whilst he went up to the field and caught a horse to ride to the police. In reply to the Coroner, witness said that whilst he was going for the police, he believed his man, named Alec Naylor, and another named Deacon watched by the body. After the arrival of P.C. A. Hall, the body was removed to an unoccupied cottage in the village, and he telephoned for Dr Williams of Billesdon.[99]

Asked if he could identify the body as the one he helped to remove, witness said

98   This part of Cowell's testimony is given as it appears in the *Leicester Daily Post*, 9 July 1919. The *Leicester Mail*, 9 July 1919, said that 'he picked her up with the idea of bringing her to his home, but her head fell back, and he then felt certain she was dead'. His deposition, signed at the end of his testimony to the inquest, gives: 'Her head fell back and I felt certain she was dead' (TNA: PRO ASSI 13/50).

99   This sequence of events is described with slight variations in the various newspaper accounts. The account given in the *Leicester Journal*, 11 July 1919, gives: 'After witness had informed P.C. Alfred Hall at Great Glen he telephoned for Dr Williams. He then returned to the scene, and afterwards helped to remove the body to an empty cottage in the village.' The account given in the *Leicester Mail*, 9 July 1919, gives: 'The police came at once, and he [Cowell] telephoned to Dr Williams, of Billesdon. Witness, returning home, helped to remove the body to an unoccupied cottage in the village.' Cowell put his signature to a version of his testimony in which he telephoned for Dr Williams *before* notifying P.C. Hall (TNA: PRO ASSI 13/50).

Light.

he had not seen it since Saturday night.

On the instructions of the Coroner, the inquest proceedings were stayed while the witness left the room with a police constable to view the body, and on his return he stated that he could identify it as the one he helped to remove on Saturday night.

Replying to the Coroner, the Chief Constable said he had no questions to ask the witness.

The Coroner said that as Mr Cowell would be recalled at the next inquiry, and the jury would then have an opportunity of putting any questions should they desire to do so.

The CHIEF CONSTABLE: The only remark I have to make about Mr Cowell is that he seems to have made every possible endeavour to render every assistance to the police. I cannot imagine anyone under such tragic circumstances who could have behaved better.

The CORONER: I quite agree.

*

The inquest was adjourned until Friday 25 July, and in order that more accommodation might be available, it was decided to continue at the village hall, Glen Magna.

The jury were formally bound over to appear.

Second Day – Friday 25 July 1919.[100]

The inquest was resumed at the village hall, Great Glen, today, on the victim of the Stretton murder, Annie Bella Wright, the twenty-one year old girl whose home was at Stoughton.

The district coroner, Mr G. E. Bouskell, again conducted the inquiry.

The Chief Constable of the county, Mr E. Holmes, was present, with Supt. Bowley and Det. Supt. Taylor, and the case was followed carefully by the two Scotland Yard officers who have come over to conduct the hunt for the murderer, Chief Det. Inspector Hawkins, and Det. Sergt. Stephens. Comparatively little interest was taken in today's proceedings by the public. The girl's father and mother were present at the commencement.

Dr EDWARD KYNASTON WILLIAMS, sworn.

Dr Williams, surgeon, of Billesdon, said he received a message by telephone,

---

100   Composite account: *Leicester Mail, Leicester Mercury*, 25 July 1919; *Leicester Daily Post*, 26 July 1919; *Leicester Advertiser*, 2 August 1919.

Appendix I.

at 10.30 pm on Saturday 5 July, to go to Stretton Parva. He believed the communication was from Mr Cowell of Stretton Parva, and, as far as he could recollect, it was to the effect that he had found a woman lying dead on the road. Witness went to the village in his motor car, first calling at Mr Cowell's house. It was then about 11.15 pm. There he was directed to where the body lay, and went to the spot on Gartree Lane, Stretton, on the road to Gaulby.[101] When he got about 200 yards from the Stretton Lane corner, going towards Gaulby, he saw several people standing nearby, and a vehicle which he thought was a milk float at the side of the road. The milk float was the property of Mr Cowell. He was then told that the body had been placed in the milk float, and witness got in and satisfied himself by cursory examination that the girl was dead.

The body was quite warm, and he estimated that death could not have taken place more than two hours previously.

The CORONER: What about the blood? — I did not see much blood until she was taken into the house.

The witness directed that the body should be taken to Little Stretton.

The CORONER: Then when the body was taken into the house did you have an examination? — I looked round where the body was found while they were taking it. I looked round the road from where the body had been removed. I saw a large patch of blood and a very small one.[102] Then I went back in the car to the cottage where the body was. I just looked at her; we did not make any detailed examination at all.

Who was there? Was P.C. Hall? —Yes, and several other people.

You then, again, examined the body? — I only just looked at the body. I did not make any detailed examination.

To go back to the telephone message you received. Was not something said on the telephone about a bicycle? That a girl had been found with a bicycle lying beside her? — I really don't know. I would not like to swear that anything was said about a bicycle. I think perhaps there was.

Turning to Mr Cowell, who sat at the other end of the room, the doctor asked if that was so or not.

Mr Cowell said he thought it ought to be left to the Coroner to ask questions.

The Coroner said he thought in a case of this kind it would be better, perhaps, because at present one could not tell where it would lead.

The CORONER: Let me put the question this way. When did you first hear anything about the bicycle? When you went that night to the road from Mr

---

101   Dr Williams apparently said 'Gartree Lane', but must have meant 'Gartree Road'.

102   This part of Dr Williams's testimony is given as per the account in the *Leicester Mercury*, 25 July 1919. The *Leicester Mail*, 25 July 1919, gives: 'several small ones'. His deposition gives: 'one large patch of blood & several smaller ones' (TNA: PRO ASSI 13/50).

Light.

Cowell's house? — Yes.

When was it first brought to your notice? — When I arrived at the place.

When you got to the lane and saw the body in the milk float, was anything then said about a bicycle? — Yes, someone did say something about it.

Who told you? — I don't know, but someone told me that a girl had been found with a bicycle. I didn't go there taking a note of anything that anybody said to me.

No, I only ask you to the best of your recollection. — I only know that somebody told me that a girl had been found there with her bicycle.

Did that somebody tell you that before or after you made the cursory examination? — Before, I imagine.

What did they tell you? — I really don't know the exact words. But one doesn't take a mental note of what is said or who said it in cases like this.

Yes, but you ought to. I am only putting these questions in fairness to yourself. You realise the importance: that you made a cursory examination in the float, and a second one in the cottage, and walked away from the cottage without any suspicion in your mind, with the impression that there was no question of foul play. The reason for that would be, naturally, that the girl had been found with a bicycle by her side, and that it was an ordinary bicycle accident. Did someone tell you she had fallen off the bicycle? — I was told that the girl had been found with a bicycle.

With a bicycle by her side? — Yes, I think so.

You went to the cottage with P.C. Hall? What was the reason you made no detailed examination? — Yes. There was no light – it was very dark – and I made no detailed examination, as I had not been led to suppose there was any foul play.

Did you treat it simply as injuries, the result of a bicycle accident? — I did, then.

At that time? — Yes.

You had no suspicion of foul play? — No.

That was all you did that night? — Yes.

Replying to further questions, witness went on to say that while walking in the country on the Sunday evening he saw P.C. Hall, who was cycling to Billesdon to get witness's written statement, but he told the officer that he could not do that, as he knew nothing about the case yet. In consequence of what the officer said, witness went to Little Stretton again, and made a more detailed examination, for which he had the head, face and neck washed. He then found a punctured wound in the left cheek bone, one inch behind and half an inch below the level of left eye. He probed the wound, and found it passing backwards, inwards and upwards. It passed through the brain to a wound of exit over the middle and upper front of the right brow.[103] At its entrance the wound would just about admit an

---

103   The location of the exit wound is given here as per the account printed in the *Leicester Mail*, 25 July 1919.

Appendix I.

ordinary lead pencil. He carried the examination no further at that time.

At this juncture the Chief Constable produced a bullet and handed it to the Coroner.

The CORONER: [*showing the bullet to witness*] Might the wound have been caused by that bullet? — Yes, it might.

On the next day, in conjunction with Dr Phillips of Kibworth, you made a post mortem examination? — Yes.

Witness, giving the result of the post mortem examination, stated that the body was well nourished. He thought it was important to say that the deceased girl's skin was peculiarly fair and white. He proceeded to explain that he proposed to give evidence which would include to some extent past of what he found on the Sunday night.

The Coroner refused to permit that, saying he wanted to keep the two examinations distinct and would turn back to his notes and add anything that was necessary.

The statement by the doctor that the girl's face was covered with blood and the hair saturated was inserted in his evidence as to Sunday evening. There was also blood in the nose and mouth, but not in the ears.

Proceeding, the witness said that when he made the post mortem examination with Dr Phillips, he noticed, externally, that there was a circumscribed bruise over the left cheek bone about the size of a two-shilling piece. In the centre was a small punctured wound as previously described. There were two small contusions below the right angle of the mouth, a contused cut through the left upper eyelid with discolouration of the eyeball, and a cut on the left cornea. There were scratches on the left hand and wrist, and also on the cheek. These were probably caused by gravel.

The Coroner asked questions as to the other organs of the body, and elicited the fact that the girl was not *virgo intacta*, but there was no evidence that she was suffering from venereal disease. There were no other bruises or marks of violence. Internally, the brain substance was shattered, and there was a small round hole in the base of the skull through which a lead pencil would pass. There was an oval-shaped hole, one and a half inches by half an inch, in the skull.

The Coroner referred to the discolouration of the left cheek, and the witness stated that he had carefully dissected portions of the skin from the discoloured part round the wound, including the bruise, and found deeply embedded in it minute particles of gravel and also minute particles of metal, which would have some influence on the distance from which the shot was fired. In his opinion, the bullet could not have been fired from more than four or five feet away, although

---

The account in the *Leicester Mercury* gives: 'at the right side of the back of the head'. Dr Williams's deposition describes 'a wound of exit over the middle and upper third of the right parietal bone' (TNA: PRO ASSI 13/50).

Light.

he found no evidence of discolouration caused by gunpowder burning.

The CORONER: Have you formed any opinion as to the probability of her position when shot? — The shot must have been fired in an upward direction.

Do you think she was riding a bicycle when shot? — You cannot say.

In all probability she was shot while in an erect position.[104] However, there were many possibilities, and he could not form an actual opinion. The actual cause of death was shock following a gunshot wound, and death was practically instantaneous.

The CHIEF CONSTABLE: You said the effect of the wound would be instantaneous death? — Yes.

And whatever the position of the body, whether she was on her bicycle or standing, what would happen when she was shot? — She would fall like a log.[105]

Are all the bruises you found, and the scratches on the hand, consistent with, and might all have been caused by, a fall after she had been shot? — Yes, it might easily have happened.

Did you see anything in your examination which would suggest that anyone had attempted to assault her? — No.

No evidence that anyone had even attempted to assault her, and that she had resisted? — No. Her clothes were not disarranged. She was wearing a bow in her hair, like girls do, which was only fastened by a flimsy little pin which would surely have been torn off in any struggle. It was intact.

You have already said about the whiteness of the skin. Would any rough handling of her have left its mark? — Yes, certainly.

And all the conditions that you found did not indicate that there had been any recent assault? — That is so.

You say the distance of the wound at which the shot was fired would not be more than four or five feet? — Yes.

That, of course, would be slightly in front of the body? — Yes.

May I suggest that all her injuries were consistent with the shot having been fired from the front left hand side, from a lower point than she was at? — Yes. That is quite certain, because the bullet took a perfectly straight course through the brain.

You have been told that the bullet was found seventeen and a half feet in the rear of the spot where the deceased lay, and, having some knowledge of guns, did you not feel surprised, having regard to the velocity at which the bullet must have entered, that it should not have travelled a greater distance after its exit? — Yes.

---

104   This statement is as given in the *Leicester Mail*, 25 July 1919. The *Leicester Mercury*, 25 July 1919, gives: 'Witness added that the girl might have been standing'.

105   This somewhat brutal but distinctly rustic description is given in the *Leicester Mercury*, 25 July 1919. The *Leicester Mail*, 25 July 1919, gives: 'She would fall in a heap at once'.

Appendix I.

It was a fairly large bullet and would need a strong charge to drive it. The fact that the bullet did not travel further might suggest that she was shot as she was on the ground.

Dr EDGAR VAUGHAN PHILLIPS, sworn.

Dr Phillips, of Kibworth, bore out the evidence of the last witness as to the post mortem examination, saying he wished to emphasise the fact that there could have been no struggle of any kind just prior to the shot being fired, or her skin would have been injured – there would have been much bruising, bearing in mind the nature of deceased's skin. There was no evidence at all of any recent intercourse.

*

The Coroner intimated that he did not propose to carry the case any further today. There was additional evidence which he would have to call, but at the present moment he did not intend to do so. So far as the police were concerned, an adjournment for a fortnight would be satisfactory. He would adjourn the hearing for a fortnight, fixing 9 August at 11.00 am for the resumption of the inquest.[106]

Before the court dispersed, the Chief Constable, Mr E. E. Holmes, stated that he would like to say, in the presence of the press, that the police had evidence in respect to the death of the girl which established in their minds the absolute certainty that the man they wanted – although, of course, he would not say the man who committed the murder – was the man who was seen to go away with the girl from Gaulby within an hour from the time she was found dead. This was the man who, on Wednesday, Thursday and Friday previous to the tragedy – three consecutive mornings, and on the afternoon of the Saturday – visited a shop in Leicester with respect to the repair of his bicycle, and they were satisfied that he was riding that bicycle at the time he left Gaulby with the girl, within an hour of her being found dead. The common sense conclusion which they had formed from that knowledge – and they were satisfied about it – was that that man at that time must have been living in or near the district in which the bicycle shop was situated, to which he resorted to have his bicycle repaired.

If he was so residing or lodging, whichever it might be, they could not help thinking that somebody knew something about him. He had offered £20 reward for information with respect to the bicycle or the man, and nobody had responded, and he would again ask the press to appeal to the public. There must of necessity be some common sense people. The man called at the cycle shop on the Wednesday, Thursday and Friday morning, and took the cycle away about two o'clock on Saturday, after it had been repaired. As a matter of fact, he took it

---

106   *Sic* in *Leicester Mail*, 25 July 1919. The third day of the inquest was in fact held on 8 August 1919.

Light.

away on the Friday, but returned it to have something further done to the machine. It was clear that the man was living near at the time, although it might have been only temporary. The assumption was that the man must have been near the place on four days, and someone must know something about him. That somebody ought to come forward and give information, and he appealed to them in the interests of justice to do so. That girl was going along a country road enjoying herself in an innocent way and she was deprived of her life. One would hope that all law-abiding people who wished to protect themselves would be ready to give information – not only for their sake, but for others'.

Continuing, the Chief Constable stated that Chief Inspector Hawkins, of Scotland Yard, who was inquiring into the case, desired him to point out that when the man visited the bicycle shop, he gave an account of himself which they had no reason to believe was not a true account. He told the cycle repairer that he was a demobilised officer and that on coming back from the war he had been to rejoin his firm in London, but they had no vacancy for him at the moment, and pending the time of them having something for him to do, he came to Leicester to visit friends. He told that story at a time when so far as was known there was no need for him to say anything else than what was true. People who wanted protection should assist the police in their efforts to trace the man. He would like to thank the press for all their efforts, and he was very grateful for the way in which they had kept the matter before the public.

Third Day – Friday 8 August 1919.[107]

Today, for the third time, Mr G. E. Bouskell and a jury sat to investigate the cause of the death of Annie Bella Wright, who, on the evening of Saturday 5 July, was found dead on the highway near Little Stretton. The inquiry, which was opened on Tuesday 8 July, and adjourned to the village hall, Great Glen, Friday 25 July, was resumed this morning at the village hall, Great Glen.

GEORGE WILLIAM MEASURES, sworn.

George William Measures, a roadman of Gaulby, said the deceased was his niece. On Saturday 5 July, the girl came to his house on a bicycle, arriving about 7.15 in the evening. She left her machine just outside his cottage gate, and stayed chatting in the house until about 8.30. Witness's wife was not at home. Directly after her arrival a carrier named Charles Palmer called at the house to deliver groceries. Witness went to the door and saw a man about forty or fifty yards up the road. He was a stout-built man, and was a stranger to the witness. Strangers

---

107   Composite account: *Leicester Mail*, *Leicester Mercury*, 8 August 1919 and 9 August 1919; *Leicester Daily Post*, 9 August 1919; Leicester *Journal*, 15 July 1919.

Appendix I.

were not frequent in Gaulby.

The CORONER: Had you ever seen that man before? — Never before, sir.

It was simply because he was a stranger you noticed him? — Yes, sir. I asked Palmer if he had brought the man. At that time I had not noticed the man's bicycle. Palmer said, 'No, he is quite a stranger to me'.[108]

Was there anything peculiar about the man's appearance to cause you to notice him? — I did not know him in the least. I thought the man was lurking about, and I did not altogether like his appearance.[109] In some way I associated the man with Bella's visit to me. I did not like his looks much.

Bella has not been over to see you for some little time? — About a fortnight after Easter.

Did she come alone? — She brought a sailor boy. They stopped and had tea with me.

What sort of terms were they on? — They seemed on the best of terms. They gave me the impression they were sweethearts.

Continuing, Measures said that on Saturday 5 July, after he left Palmer and went into the house, he remarked to Bella that there was a strange man up the road, and added that the carrier did not know him. He had in his mind that the stranger he saw came over with the deceased.

The CORONER: Did she make any reply? — She said, 'He overtook me, and said he came from Great Glen. He wanted to know the name of this village (Gaulby).'

What happened next? — About eight o'clock, I went to the door and saw the same man walking up and down the village street. I said to Bella, 'That man is walking up and down the street now'. Bella had just got up, ready to go, and she said, 'I'll sit down for a few minutes, and perhaps he will be gone'. She waited about fifteen minutes and then got up to go. She went out to her bicycle, and I remained on the doorstep.

Did you see this man then? — Yes. He came down the street pushing his bicycle, and stood against Bella. I was standing at the door, about three yards away.

What did he say? — I know he said, 'Bella'.

Did he not say more than that? Think now. Did he not say to the girl, 'I thought you had gone the other way'? — I think he did say something like that.

Did you hear Bella make any reply? — I don't think she answered him.

When this man came nearer to you, did you alter your opinion of him? — I did not like his looks at all.

---

108 The *Leicester Mercury*, 8 August 1919, adds that Palmer described the strange man coming into the village behind him.

109 The *Leicester Mercury*, 8 August 1919, gives Measures's description of the man's behaviour as 'lurching about' – a possible mishearing by the journalist, or a misapplication of vocabulary by Measures.

Light.

Did you like him less than at first? — Yes.

Why? — Well, I thought if it was anybody that Bella had known, she would have asked him in.

What age did you think he was? — Something between thirty-five and forty.

Did the fact that he was between thirty-five and forty create any suspicion on your part? — Well, I said to myself, 'I didn't think Bella would have taken up with a man like that'.[110]

At this stage the Coroner asked the representatives of the press to leave the court while certain questions were put to the witness. No explanation was given of this unusual proceeding. After the lapse of about ten minutes, the press representatives were readmitted, and the public inquiry was resumed.

Measures, continuing his evidence, said he did not hear the strange man say 'Bella' more than once. Before they left, Bella came into the house for a spanner, but he did not remember saying anything to her. He did not see any more of her or the man.

The CORONER: Did you say anything to Bella while she was in your house about not liking the looks of the strange man? — Yes. When she said she would sit down, and that perhaps he would go, I told her, 'He is a strange man, and I don't like the looks of him'.

Did she say, 'I'll try to give him the slip'? — I think she did say that.

Did she appear to be nervous? — No.

Did she say it in a fearful and trembling way, or in a joking way? — In a joking way, and laughing.

Did you think he was a stranger to Bella? — Yes.

Do you think so now? — Yes, I do. The man would hear Mr Evans [witness's son-in-law] call the girl 'Bella', and would know her name from that.[111]

By the FOREMAN OF THE JURY: He had no conversation with the strange man. Bella said the man was a stranger to her.

The Chief Constable elicited from the witness that when Bella came to the house Mrs Evans went outside with her. The word 'Bella' was used several times before the stranger used it.

The CHIEF CONSTABLE: Are you clear whether the village the man referred to was Gaulby, or some other village? — I cannot say.

Proceeding, witness, in answer further to the Chief Constable, said that the girl was carrying gorse when she arrived at his home, which he presumed she had obtained from a bush on the direct road from Stoughton to Gaulby. The strange

---

110 The *Leicester Mercury*, 8 August 1919, gives: 'Well, I did not think she would want a man that age'.
111 The *Leicester Mercury*, 8 August 1919, adds: 'She was not a girl who would resent being called "Bella" by a stranger'.

Appendix I.

man had no gorse. When the deceased arrived, his married daughter (Mrs Evans) and her husband went to the gate. He heard Mrs Evans call the deceased 'Bella', and the man might have got her name that way. He was in doubt as to whether his niece was referring to Gaulby as being the village the man asked her about. Witness formed the impression that Bella did not wish to go with him.

The CHIEF CONSTABLE: Do you now think that Bella was telling the truth when she said the man was a stranger to her? — Yes.

Should you know the man again? — I think so. I noticed no peculiar feature.

By the CORONER: When the girl went away with the man, witness did not think the girl was afraid to go with him. Witness did not notice whether the man had a squeakish, effeminate voice, although he heard him speaking. The place where the body was found was about two miles from his house.

This concluded the witness's evidence, he having been before the court an hour and a quarter. He was permitted to leave the village, having to attend the funeral of his son in the afternoon.[112]

MARGARET LOUISA EVANS, sworn.

A young woman, Margaret Louisa Evans, wife of James Evans, a collier, of 6 Grove Terrace, Maltby, near Rotherham, was next called. She said the last witness was her father. On 5 July, she and her husband were visiting her father at Gaulby. The deceased girl, on her arrival at the house, about 7.15, called witness downstairs, and they all talked together. Witness remembered her father going to the door and saying on his return that a strange man was in the street, adding, 'He must be waiting for you, Bella'. Bella replied, 'I don't know him. He has overtaken me on the way, and told me he came from Great Glen and wanted to know the way to some place.' She also said she would wait a few minutes to see if he went. She was then about to go. Witness's husband also remarked on the man's presence. Her father said, 'He looks old enough to be your father', and Bella laughed, but said nothing. Witness remembered her father saying, 'I don't like the look of that man, Bella. I should make the best of my way home.'

The CORONER: Did Bella ever get up from her chair to look at the man? — No, not while I was there.

Did you see the strange man up the street? — I saw him walking towards the cottage. He came straight up to Bella and said, 'You've been a long time. I thought you had gone another way.' Bella made no reply to that; she blushed a little, and seemed a little confused. She gave me the impression that she did not want to have anything to do with him. They were there a few minutes, and stood talking with the others. When Bella came into the house for the spanner, my father made the remark to her about her getting home as soon as she could, and she said she would; she would soon be home.

112   Apparently the funeral of Henry Measures, son of George Measures by his first wife, Sarah.

Light.

Did you ask Bella if she really knew the man? — Yes, and she replied, 'I do not know him. He is a perfect stranger to me.'[113]

What impression did you form of him? — That he was a rude man. He stared at me in a rude way.

He didn't look like a straight man? — No, he did not look like a suitable man to be out with my cousin. Before they went away I formed the impression that Bella did know him.[114] I still think that, though she may not have done so. We came to the conclusion she must have known him. They went away together smiling, just as though they knew one another. I said when she had gone that I would 'pull her leg' about it when she came on Sunday.

You think you will be able to know the man again? — Yes. He would, I should say, be quite forty. His hair was dark, but was turning grey. He was of a pale complexion, and looked as if he worked indoors or down a coal mine.[115] Certainly he did not look like one who worked in the open air. He was a broad-built man, of big, full face, and had dark eyes. His nose was on the large size. I believe I could pick him out of fifty or sixty men. He spoke unlike a Leicestershire man; but quickly, like a Londoner. He had a Cockney twang. He wore a grey suit and a grey cap. He carried a Mackintosh, rolled up, over his shoulder, and tied with string; it had a pronounced green check lining.

By the CHIEF CONSTABLE: The deceased was at the house about an hour. There was no communication between Bella and the man before the latter came down to the gate. From what the man said, witness had the idea the girl wanted to avoid him, and that the man knew that she wished to avoid him.

JOSEPH COWELL, recalled.

Joseph Cowell, the Stretton farmer, who discovered the girl's body was recalled, and the Coroner asked him what telephone message he gave to Dr Williams.

The WITNESS: I told him I had found a girl who had fallen from her bicycle at Little Stretton, and she was dead.

Further queried, witness said he saw a man and woman at 8.30 cycling near the spot where the tragedy occurred. He made the discovery at 9.20. He was three fields away, but he did not associate these persons with the crime.

By the CHIEF CONSTABLE: Had the couple been the deceased and the man, he would have expected to hear a shot fired. This he did not hear.

---

113 The *Leicester Mercury*, 8 August 1919, adds: 'When the deceased came back into the cottage to get a spanner, he did not follow her in, but stood at the door and looked in'.

114 The *Leicester Mercury*, 8 August 1919, adds: 'and she said as much to her husband. She was judging partly from the way they went up the street together.'

115 The *Leicester Mercury*, 8 August 1919, adds: 'It struck her afterwards that he was just like a collier in complexion'.

Appendix I.

By the FOREMAN OF THE JURY: The head of the deceased was lying in a large pool of blood when he found the body.

HARRY COX, sworn.

Harry Cox, cycle dealer, carrying on business at 214 Mere Road, Leicester, said that on Tuesday 8 July he went to the County Police Office and explained that, after reading a description of a bicycle in the local newspapers, he thought he could give them some information about the machine. He said that on Wednesday 2 July a man came into his shop with a bicycle and said, 'I want my three-speed adjusting', and, after looking at the machine, witness told him he could get it done by the next day. In adjusting it, he broke the cable. When the man came into the shop first, he started talking; they had a conversation of half an hour. The man said he was glad to be demobilised; he had had a month's leave, which had not yet expired, and on going to his firm they told him they were not very busy, and he could have a week or two's holiday on full pay; he therefore thought he would come down to Leicester and visit some friends.

The CORONER: Did he happen to say in what district these friends were living? — No, sir; but it would not be likely to be far away, because the bicycle was not rideable when he first brought it, and he would not have pushed it from the other end of the city.

Did you form any opinion as to where he came from? Do you think he was a Leicester man? — No, sir, he was not; he was a Londoner.

You are sure of that? — I am certain, sir.

Continuing, witness stated that the man spoke very quickly, and with a squeaking, Cockney voice. He imagined that he would be from thirty-five to forty years of age; he was from 5 feet 8 inches to 5 feet 9 inches high, and had a sallow complexion.[116] Witness put him down as a man who worked in a factory – a warehouseman. He did not look like a stoker or a real manual worker. He was a wide awake fellow. His nose was on the long side. His hair was dark and turning grey. He was clean shaven, but very dark on the chin and upper lip. His face was a full, broad one. The first time he called at the shop he was wearing grey flannel trousers and a light grey sports coat with a soft felt alpine hat.

The man called at his shop between ten and eleven the next morning, and witness told him that in adjusting the three-speed, he broke the cable. The man said, 'Put me a new one on'. Witness told him it would be ready on Friday. On this occasion he was in the shop for about five minutes, and so far as he could remember was dressed in the same manner as the day previous. The man called on Friday morning, about eleven o'clock, and took the bicycle away. He returned about

---

116   Cox's deposition, signed by him at the conclusion of his testimony to the inquest, gives: 'about 5 ft 7 in to 5 ft 8 in height'.

Light.

4.00 pm, and asked to have another inch taken out of the cable so that he could adjust it himself. On the Saturday he called between 1.30 and 2.00 pm, and was then wearing a raincoat nearly the colour of a khaki drill suit. Before taking the machine away, he said he was 'fed up' with 'messing about' the town, and that he was going for a ride in the country. He rode off in the direction of Old Evington village.

The CORONER: Did he tell you he was a demobilised officer? — Yes, sir, and I thought he must be, too. He said he was working for a firm in London.

Can you swear to the description of the bicycle? — All but the mudguards. They might have been black or green. He told me he was the owner of a B.S.A. motor-bicycle before the war. He seemed to be a fellow with a lot of money.

By the FOREMAN OF THE JURY: The man gave no indication as to where he was living. When he came to the shop, he came from the St Peter's Road end. It was a B.S.A. model *de luxe* bicycle, about the 1909 pattern, that witness repaired for him.

By the CHIEF CONSTABLE: Witness put 4 feet 7 inches of new five-ply wire into the cable of the three-speed gear, and adjusted the controls. The back tyre had a John Bull patch place on the inside by witness. He did not notice that the cycle had green mudguards, but it might have had. Witness understood that the B.S.A. motorcycle that the man referred to he had before the war.

Before Mr Cox retired, the Chief Constable said he would like, on behalf of the county, to express to him sincere gratitude for coming forward and giving evidence. Having seen the police description of the bicycle in the newspapers on Tuesday, he voluntarily attended at the County Police Office and gave valuable information, and in that way rendered a public service. He deserved their heartiest thanks.

The WITNESS: Thank you, sir.

JAMES EVANS, affirmed.

James Evans, who declined to kiss the Bible and took the oath of affirmation, supported the evidence given by his wife and father-in-law as to the happenings at Gaulby on the night of the tragedy.

Amplifying their statements, Evans said he was staying with his father in law, Mr Measures, at Gaulby, when the deceased girl called there on 5 July. About ten minutes after she arrived, witness looked out of the window and saw a strange man standing in the lane about thirty or forty yards from the house. Witness said to Bella, 'Who is the stranger in the lane?' and she replied that it was somebody she did not know, but who had caught her up on the road. Later witness went out into the lane, and could not see the man. He went back to the house again, and said to Bella, 'I think he's gone'. She said that she should wait a little longer.

Appendix I.

A little later witness was tightening up the plate on Bella's free wheel when the man (he thought) cycled down to the cottage. When the man arrived, he said, 'I thought you had gone the other way, Bella'. She made no reply to him.

The CORONER: Did he say that at once? — To the best of my recollection, the man might have heard one of us calling out 'Bella' before he got to the spot.

Witness, continuing, said he had a look at the man's bicycle, especially the back pedal brake, and that the police description of the machine was correct.[117] When deceased and the man left they were on friendly terms, and walking their bicycles. Witness went into the house and told his wife that the deceased and the man must have known each other previously.

Evans further said that he was so struck with the man that he would know him again even by his voice alone. It was squeakish, and half like a female's.[118]

When witness said to Bella, 'Who is the stranger in the lane?' she replied, 'He is a stranger to me. I picked him up on the road.'

By the CHIEF CONSTABLE: From what the cycle repairer had said, he had no doubt that the machine in the possession of the man at Gaulby was the same as the one repaired by Mr Cox. He had never seen a cycle with such a complicated back brake.

HENRY CLARKE, sworn.

Mr Henry Clarke, gunsmith, of Leicester, examined a bullet handed to him by the Coroner, and stated that in his opinion it was of an old pattern, .45 calibre. It might have been used by rifle or revolver, and was fired with black powder.

Assuming it had been fired from a revolver, the weapon would have been a large one, and the size of a service one. He would not expect any scorching of the face if fired from a distance of fifteen yards. If fired from a distance of fifty or sixty yards, it would have passed through a skull.

Indentations on the bullet showed that it must have struck the road or something hard when it was practically spent. It was possible that after a first ricochet the bullet might still have gone through the head of a person. There would be scorching of the face if the revolver were fired within a distance of five feet.

By the CHIEF CONSTABLE: The fact that the bullet was found only seventeen and a half feet from the body might be accounted for by the fact that it struck some hard body. It was possible that the bullet was fired from a rifle of an old pattern.

---

117   The *Leicester Mercury* and the *Leicester Daily Post*, 9 August 1919, give: 'Witness had a look at the man's bicycle, especially the back pedal brake, and gave the description of it circulated by the police'.
118   The *Leicester Daily Post*, 9 August 1919, and the *Leicester Journal*, 15 August 1919, give: 'The voice was "squeaky, and very much of a female mixture"'.

Light.

Mrs MARY ANN WRIGHT, mother of the deceased, confirmed the evidence she previously gave.

P.C. ALFRED HALL, sworn.

P.C. Hall, of Great Glen, gave evidence as to the steps he took when Mr Cowell reported to him the discovery of the girl's body. On searching the body, he found in a skirt pocket an empty purse and a torn handkerchief. The next morning he went to the spot at six o'clock, but discovered nothing of consequence. He made several further searches during the day, and after an hour's search at six o'clock in the evening, found the bullet produced in the middle of the road, seventeen and a half feet from where the body lay. It was lying in a hoof-mark of a horse, which appeared recently made. It was after this discovery that the bullet wound was found in the girl's head.

The CORONER, in his address to the jury, said they had come to the end of the inquiry. They had sat to enquire into the cause of this girl's death, and to find whether anybody was criminally responsible for it. There could not be much doubt in their minds that this unfortunate girl met with her death from a gunshot wound. On that point the medical evidence was absolutely conclusive. They would probably come to the conclusion that the wound was caused by the bullet produced there that day. Unfortunately – and everybody regretted the fact – it had not been possible to find the person who fired the bullet. Everything had been done by the local police, by Scotland Yard, and by the press to find the man, the man who fired that shot, but nothing, as the jury were aware, had been, up to now, brought to light.[119]

One thing, he expected, would strike them as extraordinary. They had found that a man called at a cycle dealer's in Leicester on four successive days: the second, third, fourth and fifth of July. They had heard the cycle dealer's evidence, and the Chief Constable had thanked the man for voluntarily coming forward with his statement. He (the Coroner) thought too that the man gave his evidence extremely well. He should think there could be no doubt in the jury's minds, if they accepted the evidence of Evans, that the man who went into the cycle dealer's shop on those four consecutive dates was the man who was at Gaulby on 5 July and was the man who rode off from Gaulby on that Saturday evening in company with the deceased girl. That very night, the deceased was found lying dead in the Gartree Road. Whether he was known to the deceased or not was immaterial on this point. The man who was with her at Gaulby had not come forward to offer any explanation.

Everything concerning the case had been put in the press that could be put in

---

119   An accidental but delicious moment of fateful wordplay.

Appendix I.

by it with advantage. The witness Evans had given them his opinion that the publicity which the press had given had enabled the man to get away. He (the Coroner) took an entirely different view. The publicity of the press was, in his opinion, most valuable and helpful. No doubt it was to a certain extent a double-edged weapon, but surely they could leave it to the discretion of the local police authorities, to Scotland Yard, and to the press as to how much it was proper should be published.

Having regard to the publicity which had been given, and this man having called on four successive days about the repair of his bicycle, it was most remarkable that nobody had come forward to say that the man answering the description was staying or lodging in their house on these particular nights. It was almost inconceivable that he had slept out of doors – under a haystack, or elsewhere in the open. There was nothing about his clothing to suggest it. The assumption was that he had been stopping in Leicester or close to Leicester. It seemed an astonishing thing that anybody, knowing this, should not have come forward and given some information about it. It might be that a closely related person would not give him away, but to keep a matter like that back was to render oneself liable to a charge as an accessory. That course was not taken much nowadays, but it had been taken.

There had been some comment on the query: How came it that Dr Williams did not find that this girl had been shot when he first examined the body? They must remember, however, that the telephone message to the doctor was: 'Girl found lying on the road, by her bicycle, dead'. What the doctor then did was to satisfy himself that the girl was dead, and he left it at that. It was a regrettable thing that he did not make a closer examination, but, taking all the circumstances into consideration – seeing that it was late, and that it was a dark night, and so on – there was something to be said in explanation on behalf of the doctor.

The Coroner referred in complimentary terms to the action taken by Mr Cowell. As regarded Mr Cowell's part, he (the Coroner) did not see how that witness could have done more than he did.

It seemed to him (the Coroner) that P.C. Hall went out of his way to do considerably more than one would expect from the average constable. He said that in the presence of the Chief Constable, with all respect to the members of the force. Hall had shown the smartness, keenness and alertness to be expected, if he might say so, from a detective rather than from an ordinary constable. He repeated that he said that without any disparagement to the average constable. He hoped in due time that what Hall had done would be put on the right side of the constable's account.

The Coroner then referred to the request he made to the press representatives earlier in the day to retire while some questions were being put to the witness Measures. That, he admitted, was a public court, and in the ordinary way one

Light.

did not make such a request as he made unless one had some reason for doing so. He had a good and sufficient reason, in his judgement, in asking the press to retire in that instance. At an earlier stage of the inquiry, and relating to the medical evidence, he asked the press to kindly use their discretion as to how much of that medical evidence they published in the papers; yet it struck him that something *was* put in the papers which would have been better left out, and he was going to say that he did not think what they put in would help to further the ends of justice. Anyway, he decided to exercise his discretion and felt that when he wanted to ask a witness particular questions, which it might be undesirable to be published, he might proceed to ask them *in camera*. He certainly would not have thought of asking the press to retire if he had not thought that by doing so he was considering the feelings of the people concerned in the case.[120]

In conclusion, the Coroner told the jury that he thought they would be justified in returning a verdict of wilful murder against some person or persons unknown.

After several minutes' consultation in private, the jury brought in a verdict of 'Wilful murder against some person unknown'. They added a rider that Police Constable Hall was deserving of commendation for the very smart manner in which he had dealt with the case. The Coroner said he thoroughly agreed with the rider, and the Chief Constable thanked the jury on behalf of Hall, remarking that he heartily concurred with the opinion they had expressed concerning him. Mr Holmes also reiterated his appeal to any person who could give assistance to the police to come forwards and relate what they knew.

The inquiry was then closed.

----

120   The Coroner was doubtless referring to the evidence relating to Bella's sexual history. The editor of the *Leicester Mail*, 9 August 1919, defended his decision to include the evidence in his newspaper's account of Dr Williams's testimony to the inquest: 'The medical evidence to which the Coroner refers appeared to have a material bearing on the case and was published in the public interest. The suggestion that its publication would not help to further the ends of justice is purely hypothetical.' But the editors of the *Leice ster Mercury* and the *Leicester Daily Post*, in their editions of the same date, got their jab in anyway: 'Note. The piece of evidence which Mr Bouskell referred to was not reported in the *Leicester Post* or *Mercury*.'

APPENDIX II

The Inquest Depositions.[121]

County of Leicester, Southern District, to wit.

Information of Witnesses severally taken and acknowledged upon Oath on behalf of our Sovereign Lord the King, touching the death of Annie Bella Wright at the House ~~known by the sign of~~ of Joseph Cowell in the Parish of Stretton Parva in the said Southern District of the said County, on the 8th day of July 1919, before George Edmund Bouskell, Gentleman, His Majesty's Coroner for the said Southern District of the said County of Leicester, on view of the body of the said Annie Bella Wright then lying dead in the Parish of Stretton Parva, in the said Southern District of the said County of Leicester.

MARY ANN WRIGHT, sworn, saith: I am the wife of Kenus Wright Farm Laborer of Stoughton I identify the body the Jury have viewed as being that of my daughter Annie Bella Wright. She lived at home She was single and 21 years of age. She was employed as a Rubber hand at Messrs. Bates & Cos St Marys Mills Leicester. She used to bicycle to and from her work. Between 6 & 7 o'clock last Saturday afternoon the deceased left home She said she was going to catch the Post at Evington I did not see her again alive. She was not engaged to be married but was walking out with a young man. He is a sailor and stationed at Portsmouth

[By the Chief Constable] I saw my daughter writing some letters on Saturday afternoon. I saw the envelopes in her coat pocket. Evington would be our nearest Post Office.

Signed: Mary Ann Wright

JOSEPH COWELL, sworn, saith: I am a Farmer and live at the Elms Farm Stretton Parva. Last Saturday evening about 9.20 I was driving a herd of cows along the Burton Overy Road towards Stretton Parva

When I got about 200 yards from the turning to Stretton Parva I found a girl lying

---

121 TNA: PRO ASSI 13/50. This transcription retains the irregular punctuation and erratic spelling of the copy of the inquest evidence produced for the trial. Although George Bouskell, the coroner, checked the copy against the handwritten depositions and swore to the accuracy of the copy, a few minor errors escaped his notice. These have been silently corrected here.

Light.

on the road on her left side with her head towards the centre of the road and her feet towards the hedge. I went to her and found she was bleeding from the nose. There was a large pool of blood close to the body. There was a bicycle close to her I picked her up. Her head fell back and I felt certain she was dead I placed her on the grass by the side of the road I came home and asked my wife to send some men to watch by the body whilst I went for the Police. I telephoned for Dr. Williams and then went to Great Glen for Police Constable Alfred Hall I then helped to remove the body to the cottage where it is now lying. The body which the Jury have viewed is the body which I helped to remove.

Signed: Joseph Cowell

Inquest adjourned to 25 July 1919 to the Village Hall, Glen Magna.

*

County of Leicester, Southern District, to wit.

Information of Witnesses severally taken and acknowledged upon Oath on behalf of our Sovereign Lord the King, touching the death of Annie Bella Wright at the House known by the sign of *of Joseph Cowell in the Parish of Stretton Parva in the said Southern District of the said County, on the 25th day of July 1919, before George Edmund Bouskell, Gentleman, His Majesty's Coroner for the said Southern District of the said County of Leicester, on view of the body of the said Annie Bella Wright then lying dead*

EDWARD KYNASTON WILLIAMS, sworn, saith: I am a surgeon and reside at Billesdon

About 10.30 pm on Saturday the 5th July instant I received a message by telephone from the witness Joseph Cowell to the effect that he had found a woman dead on the Gartree road close to Stretton Parva I said I would come over. I went over in my car I called at Mr Cowells house this would be about 11.15 I was told at Mr. Cowells house where the body was lying. I went in my car to the Gartree road When I got about 200 yards from the Stretton turn going towards Galby I saw several people by the side of the road and a milk float I got out of my car and found the body of the deceased was in the milk float Some one told me the deceased had been found on the road with a bicycle by her side. I got in the float made a cursory examination of the body and ascertained she was dead The body was quite warm she had not been dead 2 hours. The body was then driven in the float to a house in Stretton Parva

I then looked at the road at the place where I was told the body was removed from. I saw one large patch of blood & several smaller ones I then went in my car to the cottage where the body lay. P.C. Hall was with me I again just looked

Appendix II.

at the body but made no detailed examination. I had no suspicion at that time of any foul play. I considered at that time that the injuries were the result of a bicycle accident The next evening in consequence of what P.C. Hall told me I went to Stretton Parva about 8.15 I found ~~her~~ the deceaseds hair saturated with blood and there was much blood on her face and in her nose and mouth but not in her ears I had the head and face of the deceased washed and I made a detailed examination I found a punctured wound an inch behind and ½ an inch below the left eye I probed the wound and found it passed upwards inwards and backwards passing through the brain and through a wound of exit over the middle and upper third of the right parietal bone. The entrance wound would admit an ordinary lead pencil. The ~~would~~ wound I have just described might have been caused by the bullet produced. I made no further examination that night

The next day I made a post mortem examination of the body in conjunction with Dr. E. V. Phillips of Kibworth. The body was particularly well nourished. She had a very fair and white skin. There was a vivid circumscribed bruise about the size of a two shilling piece over her left cheek bone in the centre of which was a small punctured wound as before described. There were 2 small contusions below the right angle of her mouth a contused cut through the left upper eyelid with discolouration of the eye ball a small incision of the left cornea There were scratches on the left hand and wrist and cheek probably caused by gravel Slight discolouration of external genitals but no sign of haemorrhage. There were no signs of any bruising of the genitals The hymen was absent. There were no signs to indicate that she was suffering from syphilis. There was a discharge in the vagina of what nature I could not say There were no other bruises of marks of violence except as above described

On removing the skull cap I found the brain substance shattered a small round hole in the base of the skull through which a lead pencil would pass. There was an oval shaped hole 1½ inches by ½ an inch over the middle and upper third of the right parietal bone The viscera and all the other organs of the body were normal The uterus was not enlarged. I cut off the skin including the bruised portion from the deceaseds left cheek. I found minute portions of gravel right in the skin also some minute particles of metal There was no evidence that the discolouration was caused by gunpowder. I think the shot was fired from a distance of not more than 4 or 5 feet I cannot form an opinion as to what position the deceased was in at the time she was shot. The cause of death was shock following the injuries caused by gunshot wound Death would be instantaneous.

[By the Chief Constable] The deceaseds clothing was in perfect order and there was no evidence of any struggle having taken place or any attempt at violation.

The scratches were compatible with the theory that she had been shot whilst on her bicycle or whilst in a standing position

Signed: E. K. Williams

Light.

EDGAR VAUGHAN PHILLIPS, sworn, saith: I am a surgeon and reside at Kibworth.

In conjunction with Dr. Williams I made a post mortem examination of the body of the deceased on the 7th July instant.

I have heard Dr. Williams give his evidence as to the result of the post mortem examination. I agree with that evidence in every detail and I have nothing to add to it. I am satisfied that from the condition of the body there had been no struggle of any kind.

Signed: Edgar V. Phillips

Inquest adjourned to 8 August 1919.

*

Depositions of Witnesses taken on 8th August 1919 at Glen Magna on the body of Annie Bella Wright.

GEORGE WILLIAM MEASURES, sworn, saith: I am a Roadman & live at Gaulby.

The deceased Bella Annie Wright is my niece. On Saturday July 5th she came to my house on a bicycle She arrived about 7.15 p.m. She left her bicycle close to my cottage gate She stopped talking with me until about 8.30 The carrier Charles Palmer called about 7.15 I went to my cottage door & I noticed a strange man about 40 or 50 yards up the road I did not see a bicycle I did not like the look of him. I turned into the Cottage I said 'Bella there is a strange man up the road and the carrier does not know him' She said 'He overtook me and said he came from Great Glen and wanted to know the name of this Village' About 8 o'clock I went to my cottage door & I saw the same man walking up & down the village street I said to Bella That man is walking up & down the Street now. He is a strange man I don't like the looks of him She said I will try & give him the slip She said it in a joking way She said the man is a stranger to me Bella was then standing against the fire place ready to go. She said I will sit down a few minutes and perhaps he will be gone She sat there until about 8.15 She again got up to go and went outside to her bicycle The strange man came down the village Street pushing his bicycle He came just outside the gate He said I think 'Bella I thought you had gone the other way' I did not hear her make any reply. I only heard him call her 'Bella' once I don't think she would object to being called by her christian name I thought he was a stranger to her and I think so now.

[By the Foreman] I never spoke to the strange man.

[By the Chief Constable] I think the strange man called the deceased 'Bella' after

Appendix II.

she heard Mr. Evans call her 'Bella'.

I think I should know the man again.

[By the Coroner] I saw the deceased and the strange man leave about 8.45

Signed: George William Measures X his mark

MARGARET LOUISA EVANS, sworn, saith: I am the wife of James Evans a Collier of 6 Grove Terrace Maltby near Rotherham The last witness is my father and on Saturday July 5th I was staying with my father at Galby.

I recollect the deceased riding over on her bicycle about 7.15 p.m. that night I remember my father going to the cottage door He said that man is still up there He must be waiting for you Bella

She replied 'I don't know the man He overtaken me on the way He told me he had come from Great Glenn and wanted to know the way to some place'

My father said he is waiting up there and looks as if he is waiting for you.

She said I will wait a few minutes and see if he goes She got up and then sat down again

My husband also said there is a man up there and he looks as if he is waiting for you. My father said he looks old enough to be your father. Bella just laughed. All the time Bella was sitting down and could not see the man in the road

About 8.30 Bella got up to go and went outside the cottage gate I went with her I saw a strange man walking towards the cottage and pushing a bicycle. He walked straight up to Bella. He said you have been a long time I thought you had gone another way. She made no reply. She blushed and looked a little confused She gave me the impression that she did not want to have anything to do with the man.

Bella came in the house for a spanner My father said I don't like the look of that man I should make haste home Bella said I shall soon get in front of him. I said to Bella Now Bella do you really know that man She said I do not know the man he is a perfect stranger to me.

Bella left about 8.45 with the man pushing their bicycles. I watched them from the door They appeared quite friendly I said to my husband Bella must have known the man before My husband said Yes of course she does I should know the man again if I saw him. I should say he would be quite 40 years old 5 ft 7 in or 8 in height hair Dark turning grey his complexion was pale I should say he worked indoors or down a pit he certainly did not work in the open. cleanshaven and dark skin where he had shaved he had dark eyes he was a broad built man He was big full faced man he had a big nose. He spoke quickly with a Cockney twang. He was dressed in a gray suit and a gray cap. I could not say if the suit was shabby. He had a mackintosh rolled up & tied with string across one shoulder & under his arm The lining was a green check one.

Light.

[By the Chief Constable] The man had a very brazen look

Signed: Margaret Louisa Evans

JOSEPH COWELL (recalled), sworn, saith: When I telephoned Dr. Williams I said 'I have found a girl fallen from her bicycle at Little Stretton She is dead'

I fix the time at 9.20 when I found the body as I looked at my watch at that time

[By the Foreman] It was the head of the deceased which was lying in the large pool of blood where I first found the body

Signed: Joseph Cowell

HARRY COX, sworn, saith: I carry on business at 214 Mere Rd Highfields Leicester as a cycle dealer. On Tuesday the 8th July I went to the County Police Station & gave information after reading a description of the Bicycle in the Local Newspapers in connection with the murder of a girl at Stretton Parva I recollect that between 10 & 11 a.m. on Wednesday the 2 July a man called at my shop with a bicycle. He said 'I want my 3 speed adjusting' I looked at the bicycle and said 'I will get it done for you on Thursday' In adjusting I broke the cable I had half an hours talk with him and he said he was staying with friends in Leicester. From the way he spoke I should say he was a Londoner He spoke with a Cockney accent fairly quickly He had a squeaky voice I should say he was 35 to 40 years old about 5 ft 7 in to 5 ft 8 in height I should say he worked indoors his complexion was sallow hair dark turning grey. He was clean shaven and very dark skin where he had shaved I did not notice the colour of his eyes, his nose was ordinary. His was a big full face. He had on gray flannel trousers and a tweed 'sports' coat It was not shabby. He had on a soft felt hat an 'alpine' hat The next day he called between 10 & 11 a.m. I told him I had broken the cable He said 'put me a new one'. I told him it would be ready on Friday. He was only in my shop about 5 minutes. He was dressed the same as the previous day. On Friday he called about 11 a.m. He was dressed the same as Wednesday. He took the bicycle away & brought it back about 4 o'clock that afternoon & asked to have another inch taken out of the cable so that he could adjust it himself. On Saturday he called between 1.30 & 2 o'clock He had on a raincoat karki drill colour. Just before he left my shop he said he was fed up with messing about the town and he was going to have a run out in the Country. He rode off in the direction of Old Evington. On Wednesday the man told me he was a demobilised officer & working for a Firm in London. The Firm he said had told him he could have another 2 or 3 weeks holiday on full pay as they were not very busy. I agree with the description of the bicycle which has been circulated by the Leicestershire Police with the exception of the mud guards which I did not notice. He told me he had a B.S.A. motor bicycle.

The bicycle was a 1909 pattern

Appendix II.

[By the Chief Constable] I put in 4 ft 7 ins of new cable wire in on the Thursday. It was a bright silver coloured wire The back tyre had a John Bull sticking patch placed on the inside & a piece of outer cover patched on a weak place.

On the Friday afternoon when the man returned with the bicycle I could not say from its appearance what distance he had ridden it. The man told me he had his motor bicycle before the War.

Signed: Harry Cox

JAMES EVANS, affirmed, saith: I live at No. 6. Grove Terrace Leslie Avenue Maltby nr Rotherham and am a miner On Saturday 5th July I was staying with Mr. Measures at Galby and at about 7.30 p.m. the deceased came over on her bicycle I had never seen her before. She left her bicycle by the front gate. In about 10 minutes I looked out of the window and I saw the head and shoulders of a man He was standing 30 or 40 yards from the house I had never seen him before. I said to Bella Who is the stranger in the Lane She replied 'He is a stranger to me I picked him up on the road'

Some little time afterwards I went into the Lane I could not see the strange man I then went back into the house and said to Bella 'I think he has gone' She said 'I shall wait a bit longer'. A little while afterwards I was tightening the free wheel of her bicycle the man rose rode up on his bicycle. He got off and he said I thought you had gone the other way Bella. She made no reply I was not looking at her face. The description of the bicycle circulated by the Police is an accurate description of the Bicycle which I examined at Galby belonging to the strange man. Shortly afterwards Bella and the strange man went off together They were walking and pushing their bicycles as they went away I went into the house and said to my wife They must have known each other before. If I heard the man speak and he had his back to me I could recognise his voice. His voice was a squeaky one and a high pitched one. I should say he was nearly 40 years of age 5 ft 7 ins to 5 ft 9 ins in height dark complexion and sallow Big face round & full broad built. He was a clean shaven man but had 2 or 3 days growth on his face of black hair. He was dressed in a dirty grey suit which looked shabby but fitted well He had a fawn coloured mackintosh over his shoulder

[By the Chief Constable] I have no doubt the bicycle which Mr. Cox repaired from the description he gave me was the same machine as I saw the strange man with at Galby on the 5th July

I have never seen a bicycle with such a complicated back brake

I discussed this brake with Mr. Cox on Wednesday the 9th July

Signed: James Evans

Light.

HENRY CLARKE, sworn, saith: I am a Gunsmith and reside at Leicester

I have examined the bullet produced In my opinion it is an old pattern 45 calibre. It may be used either for a revolver or rifle

It was fired with black powder If fired from a revolver that revolver was a large one and the size of a service one. I would expect no scorching on the face if the bullet had been fired from a distance of 15 yards.

If the bullet had been fired from a revolver of average length at a distance of 50 or 60 yards it would go right through a persons head, if from a short barrel revolver 25 to 30 yards. There are 5 marks of rifling on the bullet The other marks and indentations on it in my opinion were caused by the bullet striking the road or some other hard substance. It is quite possible that the bullet might have struck the road or some other hard substance and riochetted and then passed through the head of some person.

[By the Chief Constable] There would be scorching whatever the condition of a revolver might be if fired from a distance of 5 feet If fired beyond 5 feet it would be impossible to say without seeing the weapon. From the marks on the bullet it is quite consistent with it having been fired from a rifle

Signed: Henry Clarke

ALFRED HALL, sworn, saith: I am a Police Constable in the Leicestershire Constabulary stationed at Great Glen. I was on duty on the London Road in the Parish of Glen Magna when the witness Joseph Cowell drove up to me. He said I have found a young woman lying dead by the side of her bicycle on the Burton Overy Road in the Parish of Little Stretton He said a ladys bicycle was lying in the road by her side and he said I think she has fallen off her bicycle. He also said I have picked her up and I found she was dead. I asked Mr. Cowell to go at once and telephone to Dr Williams. I went and fetched my bicycle and rode to Little Stretton. Mr. Cowell had described to me where the body was lying I found the body of a girl lying about 200 yards beyond the Little Stretton turn towards Galby on the Gartree Road and near a gate leading into a field of mowing grass Her feet were in the ditch and the rest of her body from her knees upwards was lying on the grass about 6 feet from the body and in a direct line with it and on the metal part of the road was a large pool of blood. I examined the road and also a ladys bicycle which I found leaning against a field gate with an electric torch but I could not make out anything distinctly. With assistance I removed the body to an empty cottage at Stretton Parva. In the left hand pocket of deceaseds skirt I found an empty small leather purse and a lady's handkerchief torn in the left hand pocket of her raincoat I found a box of Flag Matches. I bicycled to Oadby & reported the case to Sergt. Barrett. The next day Sunday I visited the place where the body was found at 6 a.m. This was on my own initiative I noticed a thin stream of blood running parallel with the grass on the left side of the road

Appendix II.

for a distance of 5 yards I think it was caused when Mr. Cowell moved the body I continued my examination until 8 a.m. but found nothing further. I went to the cottage and examined the bicycle & found a few spots of blood on the left side pedal about 10.30 a.m. I telephoned Supt Bowley & informed him of the finding of the body.

At 11 a.m. I again went to Little Stretton about 2 p.m. I again visited Little Stretton and searched the sides of the road also the hedges & ditches & found smears of blood on a gate. at 6 p.m. I again visited the place and after a search of upwards of one hour I found the bullet which I have produced here today. I found it in the centre of the metal part of the road 17½ feet from the pool of blood in which the body was found lying. It was lying in a hoof mark to all appearances that of a horse It rained on Saturday night I at once went on my bicycle for Dr. Williams of Billesdon I met him on the road and I told him what I had found. He asked me to go back to the cottage & wash the blood from the deceaseds face. He said he would follow me on in his car. I returned to Stretton and washed the deceaseds face and found the bullet hole in the deceaseds left cheek

Signed: Alfred Hall

Copy Verdict.

That the said Annie Bella Wright was found dead on the 5th day of July in the year aforesaid in the Gartree Road in the Parish of Stretton Parva aforesaid and that the cause of her death was a gunshot wound in the head inflicted by a man whose name is unknown and so the Jurors aforesaid do further say That the said unknown man on the 5th day of July A.D. 1919 did feloniously murder against the Peace of our said Lord the King, his Crown and Dignity, the said Annie Bella Wright and the Jurors aforesaid, upon their Oaths do further say that the said Annie Bella Wright at the time of her Death was a female person of the age of 21 years, and a Rubber Hand of Stoughton in the said County of Leicester.

G. E. Bouskell, Coroner		Walter Allen
William Harris	John Buswell	H. W. King
Nicholas Forster	John Goodman	George Coleman
James Allen R. Heath		

I certify the above to be a true copy of the Depositions severally taken and sworn before me touching the death of Annie Bella Wright.

G. E. Bouskell, Coroner.

APPENDIX III

The Rhyl Letter.[122]

——————

Morville Private Hotel[123]
East Parade
Rhyl

11th July 1919

My dearest Ronald,

I am writing after dinner to thank you for your letters & letters forwarded. We went to St Asaphs [sic] this morning – a very interesting cathedral – & pretty tiny place. The food is very good, well served breakfast – porridge, bacon & eggs – bacon & tomatoes. Marmalade, etc. Lunch cold ham lamb & beef salad. 2 sweets, cheese etc; a very good tea. Dinner fish, fine sauce, chicken, 2 vegetables, 2 sweets, cheese, everything hot. A fine pier but condemned, a pavilion but no band, but one comes Sunday. A fine promenade, good town but so few attractions. I am so glad Mr Herbert is having the Range etc seen to.[124] I have written asking Aunt Cissie to come over next week. There are endless coaching excursions but they are expeditions – however Mrs Phillips is very nice, & we are most comfortable. I hope you are well & wish you were here old man. Jojo would like the sands – kiss him for us. What is the news at home? We are interested in the Cycle mystery. The weather has been warmer & lovely today but very dull this evening, we have been out all day.

With kind love dear,
Write soon,
Your loving mother,
K. Light.

Miss Shouler's remembrances.

122 TNA: PRO ASSI 13/50.
123 *Daily Post* (North Wales), 22 November 2016: 'A Rhyl hotel dubbed "the worst in Britain" was shut down on the spot over fears people could end up being electrocuted by dangerous electrics. Fire chiefs and council inspectors also feared a fire could break out in the Fiorenzo Cazari on East Parade. The hotel – formerly known as the Morville – will not be allowed to re-open until safety work has been carried out.'
124 Probably Albert Herbert, resident at 57 Highfield Street at the time of the 1911 census.

APPENDIX IV

Report of Chief Inspector Hawkins, Scotland Yard.[125]

Metropolitan Police.
Criminal Investigation Department,
New Scotland Yard,
29th day of July, 1919.

I beg to report that at 6 p.m. on the 11th July, 1919, Detective Superintendent Taylor of the Leicestershire Constabulary called at this Office with a letter from E. Holmes Esq., Chief Constable of the County, asking for the assistance of Police re the murder of Annie Bella Wright at Stretton Parva, Leicestershire, on the night of the 5th July.

As directed by the D.C.I. with Sergeant Stephens I left with Supt. Taylor on the 12th and reported myself to the Chief Constable in the afternoon who gave me a graphic account of events up to date of the murder.

The facts are these:-

Annie Bella Wright, a girl of 22 years, daughter of Kenus Wright, a cowman, of Stoughton, near Leicester, left her home about 5.30 or 6 p.m. on the 5th July, and visited her uncle, a Mr. Measures, of Gaulby, arriving there about 7.30 p.m. leaving again about 8.30 or 8.45 p.m. and about 9.20 p.m. her body was found in the Burton Overy Road at Stretton Parva, a distance of about two miles from Gaulby, by Joseph Cowell, a Farmer of Stretton Parva. Mr Cowell informed Police Constable Alfred Hall, No. 97, of the Leicestershire Constabulary, also Dr. Williams of Billesdon. The latter arrived at 10.40 p.m. and said that the deceased had died from sudden haemorrhage and collapse, which he then attributed to an accident by her falling from her cycle. The body was taken to an empty cottage close by. The constable on the 6th had a further conversation with Mr. Cowell and ascertained the exact position in which he had found the body and the cycle. The Police Constable, after he had again viewed the body was not satisfied with the theory of the Doctor that death was caused by an accident, and later that day summoned Doctor Williams to make a further examination.

In the meantime further search was made by the Police Constable of the road and hedges to try and find some evidence to support the theory of shooting, and at about 3 p.m. 6th, he found a spent bullet about 17½ feet from where the body was found. It is suggested that the bullet fell much further away from the deceased

125   TNA: PRO DPP 1/61. Minor spelling errors have been silently corrected.

Light.

but was kicked or moved back to the spot where she fell by traffic and cattle. On the top of [a] gate close to where the body was found were blood-stains. An examination by Supt. Taylor was made on 7th and he was satisfied they had been caused by a bird which had been standing in the pool of blood from the deceased, of which it had gorged itself, then hopped about on the gate or fence, and then flew across a field of mowing grass and fell dead in an adjacent field of corn. The bird's feet (a crow) were covered with congealed blood. It was opened by Supt. Taylor with the idea of seeing if it had been shot but the conclusion was arrived at that the bird, whose crop was full of new blood, had died by choking. Certainly there was no trace of a bullet, or of a bullet or shot wound.

At about 8.40 p.m. on the 6th, Dr. Williams made a further examination of the body. He then certified that the girl had been shot through the head, that the bullet entered behind and below the left eye, and came out on the right side of the skull about three inches above the right ear.

I understand that the body on neither of these two occasions was examined to obtain evidence of rape, although there was subsequently found a discharge from the vagina. Dr. Williams also expressed the opinion that the wound could not have been self-inflicted.

A post mortem was made on the 7th July at Little Stretton by Drs. Williams and Phillips, and the result of their examination is as follows:-

Body – well nourished.

Head – hair saturated with blood and much blood on face – in nose and mouth. A vivid circumscribed bruise, the size of 2/- piece an inch behind and ½ inch below level of left eye – in centre of bruise a small punctured wound – admitting an ordinary lead pencil – passing upwards inwards and backwards to another oval wound 1½" x ½" over middle and upper 1/3 of right parietal bone. The brain between the two wounds much lacerated. There were scratches in left cheek probably caused by gravel. A contused cut through left upper eyelid, with discolouration of ball of left eye. Small incision in left cornea. Two small contusions between right angle of mouth.

Wrist – scratches on left hand and wrist.

Genitals – slight discolouration of external genitals, but no sign of haemorrhage. Hymen absent. Viscera – all normal. Uterus not enlarged. No other bruising or marks to be found on the body, or signs whatever that any struggle occurred. The discolouration on left cheek was probably not caused by powder.

The inquest was opened on the 8th July at Little Stretton by George E. Bouskell Esq., Coroner for the Southern Division of Leicestershire, but only evidence of identification was given and the inquisition was adjourned until the 25th instant. The body of Bella Annie Wright was interred at Stoughton on the 11th.

The enquiry was diligently pursued by Supts. Bowley and Taylor, and the Police

Appendix IV.

of [*sic*] both of the County and of the City, until the 11th instant, when they came to a standstill, having exhausted all the material in their possession, and it was with the object of endeavouring to assist them further that I was deputed, with Segt. Stephens, to proceed to Leicester on the 12th and to render what assistance I could in this very difficult and complicated case of murder.

It appears from the mother, Mary Ann Wright, wife of Kenus Wright, that her daughter Annie Bella, who would have been 22 years of age on the 13th of July, was employed as a factory-hand at Bates Rubber Works, St. Mary's Mills, Leicester. The family of Wrights have lived in various parts of Leicestershire for many years but had only been living at Stoughton since about April last.

The deceased was on what is termed 'the night-shift' at the Mills, commencing at 2 p.m. and finishing at 10 p.m. on the 4th. These late shifts do not work on Saturdays, therefore the girl is said to have stayed in bed until about 4 o'clock when she got up, dressed herself, had tea, wrote some letters, and about 5.30 or 6 p.m. she went down to post the letters. Before leaving the house she said to her mother, 'Mum, I am going to Evington to post these letters and have a run round on my bike'. She then left and that was the last time her mother saw her alive.

About 5.30 p.m. she said to her brother, Philip, 'Are you going out for a ride tonight?' He replied, 'No, I don't think so. I am going down into Leicester.' She said, 'I do not think I will go down tonight. I have been down there all the week,' which Philip says he took her to mean that she had been working there late all the week.

Philip Wright says that he had been for a cycle ride with his sister once during the past three months and he further says that he is of opinion that she simply asked him to go that evening to pass the evening away, and that he is sure she had no idea she was likely to meet anyone who would be offensive or who would be likely to annoy her.

Anyhow, the deceased did leave about 5.30 or 6 p.m., went to the Post Office, which is about a mile away, returned home, changed her coat and went off immediately on her bicycle, proceeding in the direction of Gaulby.

We now have it that about 7 o'clock that evening one Harry Atkins, a Cowman in the employ of Mr. Parker at Little Stretton, was out walking on the Stoughton Road and saw a girl riding a bicycle and a man, also riding a bicycle, about 50 yards at her rear. Atkins has seen the photograph of the deceased in the papers and identifies it as that of the young woman he saw riding the bicycle. He describes the man as about 30, certainly much older looking than the girl, that he seemed a bit excited and shouted, 'Hi – hi,' and that he caught the girl up when nearly opposite to him. They each got off their bicycles and walked up rather a steep hill which was in front of them. This would be about two miles from Gaulby. When they got to the top of the hill they remounted and rode away, and he did not see either of them again.

Light.

At about 7.30 p.m. a Thomas Edward Nourish of Glebe Farm, Little Stretton, a Farmer, was driving three beasts along the road top-side of Norton, about half a mile from Gaulby, when a man and a girl riding bicycles passed him. He went on to Gaulby with his beasts and turned them into a gateway before reaching his actual field. He then saw the man standing by the guide or finger-post. He was dismounted and appeared to Nourish to be waiting for the girl. After turning his beasts out Nourish went to the tobacconists shop at Gaulby and bought some tobacco. The man was still there when he entered and left the shop, but he had moved a little towards the Rectory. Nourish then went into his field and took other beasts out to take to another meadow and when he came away with these two beasts he again saw the man who was then sitting on the stile near the gate where he took the three beasts through. Nourish states he had never seen either the man or the woman before. He describes the man as 35, 5 feet 7, dark hair, turning a little grey, round featured, he had some growth and was somewhat swarthy, dressed in rather a light suit and thinks he was wearing a cap.

Nourish has seen the photograph of the deceased girl in the newspaper and thinks the girl he saw with the man is identical. He could not describe either of the bicycles but agrees with other witnesses in this case that the man looked like a townsman and certainly not like a countryman.

At about 7 or 7.30 p.m. Elizabeth Palmer, wife of Charles Palmer, Carriers of Ollston on the Hill,[126] Carriers of this District of the County of Leicester, was proceeding with her husband from Leicester to Gaulby when she saw a man and woman each riding a bicycle, who were going in the same direction as the carriers' van, and as they were driving into the village, Mrs Palmer saw this man. He was then dismounted and standing by an elderberry bush. Mrs. Palmer is sure he is the same man she saw a few minutes previously with the girl on a bicycle. She describes him as about 40 years of age, 5 feet 6 or 7, complexion sallow, dark hair turning grey, clean shaven, although he then had two or three days growth on his face, dressed in a dark mixture suit with a mackintosh slung across his shoulders, dark cap; rather stout build, rather broad face, respectable looking and looked like a townsman. She cannot describe his bicycle.

Mrs. Palmer saw the deceased go into Mr. Measures' house at Gaulby. She herself had groceries to deliver there which she handed to Mr. Measures who said to Mrs. Palmer, 'This is my niece from Stoughton'. Mrs. Palmer said, 'I thought so. I recognise her mother's features.' The girl said, 'Yes, I am like my mother, aren't I?' Whilst speaking to the girl it struck Mrs. Palmer as being strange that she was in the company of a man so much her senior, so much so that she felt like passing some remark about it but she did not do so. Bella Wright was nursing the baby of her cousin, a Mrs. Evans, and seemed quite cheerful. Mrs. Palmer then left but did not see the man again. When she passed him on approaching Gaulby she was

126   *Sic* in report. Read: Illston on the Hill.

Appendix IV.

sitting on the near side of the van and the man was standing by the tree, which is on the right hand side of the road, which is rather a narrow thoroughfare.

It seems that the deceased, after returning home to change her mackintosh or overcoat, proceeded to Gaulby to visit her Uncle and Aunt, Mr. and Mrs. Measures. (Annie Bella Wright's father and Mrs. Measures are brother and sister.) Her married cousin and her husband (Margaret Louisa and James Evans) were visiting Mr. and Mrs. Measures on a holiday, with their two children.

There was no pre-arrangement of Bella Wright's visit and though it is only about four miles from Gaulby to Stoughton she had not visited these relations since Easter last. She is said to have arrived here about 7.30. She rode up on her bicycle which she left just outside the gate, and went into the living room, sat down and stayed chatting for half an hour or more, when her uncle George William Measures, a one-legged road man in the employ of the Billesdon Rural District Council, had occasion to get up from his chair and go to the door, to use his own words, 'to stretch his legs' and also to take in the groceries from Mr. and Mrs. Palmer. As Mrs. Palmer was leaving, Mr. Measures was still at the door and he saw standing about 40 yards away in the road a strange man. He said to Mr. Palmer, 'Did you bring that man in from Leicester?' Mr. Palmer replied, 'No'. Bella Wright was in the kitchen close to the door when this conversation was going on but she did not say anything. Mr. Measures returned to the living room and said to Bella, 'There is a strange man out there but the carrier does not know him'. Bella said, 'He overtook or caught me up on the road and told me he came from Great Glenn (about 4 miles away) and said he wanted to know the name of this or some other village'. Mr Measures took it that she meant when he picked her up. About half an hour later Mr. Measures went to the door again, and again saw the same man there. He said to Bella, 'That man is still walking about out there. You must know something about him, I know.' Bella replied, 'I do not know him. He is a perfect stranger to me.' When Mr. Measures said he was still there Bella said, 'I will sit down a bit longer and see if he goes'. She did not say she wanted him to go or that she was at all afraid of him. She went on to say that her sailor boy was coming home on leave.

At about 8.30 or 8.45 she began to get ready to go and went to the gate. Mr. Measures went to the door but had occasion to return to the living room for a minute, and when he returned to the door the man was at the gate with his bicycle. Mr. Measures' son-in-law, James Evans, was doing something to Bella's bicycle. Bella came into the house for a spanner to enable Evans to tighten the free wheel of her bicycle.

Measures says that Bella appeared timid but nothing very noticeable, and that she knew that his son-in-law, James Evans, had a bicycle and could and would have accompanied her if requested. The man, Bella, and his son-in-law were outside the gate about seven yards from the front door of Measures' house for a quarter of an hour. When Bella and the man left, Measures was looking through the living

Light.

room window and saw them go away looking quite pleasant. He also agrees that the man did not look like a countryman. Mr. Measures says that about 10 minutes before Bella left he told her if he was she he would make haste home and that he did not like the look of the man, and she replied, 'I will try and give him the slip' or something to that effect, but she did not say she was afraid of him or anything of that sort.

When she arrived at Gaulby she had a bunch of gorse which it is thought she picked from the top road, which is the direct road from Stoughton to Gaulby.

Mr. Measures gives a similar description of the man and feels quite sure he would know him again, but cannot describe his bicycle. He did say to Bella, 'The man looks old enough to be your father,' and she replied, 'He is the man who caught me up on the road'.

Agnes Olive Measures aged 12, Schoolgirl, daughter of Mr. Measures, arrived home at about 8.45 p.m. on the 5th when Bella was getting ready to go home. She saw a man outside the gate holding a bicycle talking to her brother-in-law, James Evans. She heard the man say, 'This is rather a heavy machine'. That was when he was lifting his own bicycle. While James Evans was tightening up Bella's bike she saw the man whisper something to Bella and says that they both laughed, and that he said to Bella, 'I think I will put my coat on,' which he did (which probably means the mackintosh he was carrying across his shoulder).

Agnes saw the man and Bella leave together and go in the direction of Leicester Road. Bella said, 'Goodnight,' but the man did not speak. She describes the man as having rather a pointed looking nose, that his bicycle was green coloured with black mudguards and that she heard him say to someone that he had had his bicycle mended.

James Evans, son-in-law to Mr. Measures, aged 26, of 6, Grove Terrace, Leslie Avenue, Maltby, near Rotherham, employed as a miner by the Maltby Main colliery Company, supports in the main the statements made by Mr. Measures and his daughter, Agnes. He says on Saturday, 5th July, about 7.30 p.m. Bella Wright came to Gaulby. He had never seen her before that evening. They had a general conversation, particularly about cycle tyres and tubes. She said she was working at Bates Rubber Mills and could buy bicycle tubes, tyres, etc., much cheaper than they could be purchased at a shop. She nursed his baby and he agrees that she seemed quite cheerful and spoke of her boy, who was a sailor.

Soon after she arrived Evans looked out of the window and saw a strange man standing near the house. He said to Bella, 'Who is he?' She said, 'I picked him up on the road and she said something about he had come from Glenn way'.

Sometime after Evans went out into the Lane but did not see the man. He returned to the house and said to Bella, 'I think the man has gone'. She said, 'I will be getting off'.

Bella had been telling Evans about some repairs she had had done to her bicycle

Appendix IV.

and Evans went out to look at her machine, and while he was tightening the free wheel the man rode up on his bicycle and turned it round with the front wheel facing the church. He said to Bella, who was in the act of handing Evans a spanner, 'I thought you had gone the other way, Bella'. Evans says she did not make any answer and he also thinks that the man may have heard some of those around address the girl as 'Bella'.

Evans got into conversation with the man about bicycles. The man said, 'Mine is a very heavy one, it is a B.S.A.' Evans said, 'Yes, I can see that'. He waited at the gate with Bella whilst Evans went to the house and got his machine to show him. He said, 'I see yours is a three speed'. Evans said, 'Yes, and a B.S.A. also,' that he had broken the draw piece for shifting the clutches and it was still in dock. The man said he had his three speed cable recently repaired. Evans looked at the cable and saw that it had been recently repaired by new stuff or material. He looked at his back brake which seemed to work as a combine with the crank and rim with a box affair on the side of the bottom bracket. A lever worked on the box to throw the brake in or out of action. Evans said to him, 'I have never seen such a brake before, not such a complication'. The man said he had the bicycle several years. Soon afterwards Bella and the man left, each walking and pushing their own machines up the road towards the Church, which is rather a steep incline.

As Bella was leaving, Evans said, 'I will call at your place at Stoughton in the morning and repair the free wheel'. Bella said, 'I will stay in, but I am going to see Louie (her sister) sometime during the day.

When the man and Bella left Evans said they appeared to be quite friendly and pleasant with each other.

Evans goes on to say that when Bella was told that there was a man waiting about she did not seem to mind. She did not even get up from her chair to look at him. Evans further says that if Bella had said that she was at all nervous or objected to the man waiting about he would certainly have seen her home on his bike. His description of the man and particularly of the bicycle agrees with other witnesses in the case and in the event of this man being arrested we must look to Evans as one of our principal witnesses.

At 9.40 p.m. deceased was found by Joseph Cowell, a farmer, of Elms Farm, Stretton Parva. He states that about 8 p.m. he left his house to visit various fields and was bringing his cows down the Old Gartree Road (which is the road where the deceased was found) and when about 400 yards from where the tragedy happened he saw something of a yellowish looking matter in the distance which he describes as looking like a horse rug, lying by the side of the road. When he arrived at the spot he saw the body of a woman lying partly on the grass and partly in the rut of the wheel track on the road. Her feet were on the grass and the remainder of the body was askew in the road. The head was lying in a pool of blood. A lady's bicycle was also lying in the road, the front wheel towards

Light.

Leicester. The head of the body and the head of the bicycle were lying in opposite directions. The body was warm, and still bleeding from the nose. Mr. Cowell thought she had met with an accident, picked her up and laid her further back on the bank away from any passing traffic. He did not know the deceased. He returned to his house and got his wife to send someone to stop with the deceased and she in turn sent Naylor, one of their employees, and another man named Deacon, to stay by the body while Cowell got his horse and float and drove into Great Glenn to summon P.C. Hall, who asked Mr. Cowell to summon Dr. Williams whilst he went home to fetch his bicycle.

At about 10.30 Doctor Williams arrived an examined the body, but on account of insufficient light, it was removed to an unoccupied cottage where a more minute examination was made and Dr. Williams said that deceased had died from sudden haemorrhage and collapse.

Mr. Cowell further states that just before entering the high road as he was walking across one of his fields he saw a man and a woman each riding a cycle pass along the road in which the deceased was found. He could not identify either and could not say whether the dead girl was the girl he saw riding with the man on the bicycle. One thing of importance he does say, that when he arrived on the spot all the clothing on the body appeared to be in perfect order. Enquiry was made amongst the neighbouring farmers and farm hands but no one can say that they heard a shot fired. It is more than probable that Mr. Cowell was in a position to hear the shot, but the fact of his being a little deaf may account for his not hearing the report of firearms.

The bullet has been examined by a local Gunsmith, a Mr. Henry Clarke, of Henry Clarke & Sons, 30, Gallowtree Gate, Leicester, Gunsmiths. He describes the bullet as a 'rim-fire No. 44 bullet' fired either from an old-fashioned rifle or a revolver, he rather favours a revolver. The bullet he describes as a foreign bullet, fired with black powder, certainly not a service bullet. He would expect such a bullet if fired from 15 or more yards to cause no scorch on the flesh, if fired from a long barrelled revolver it would kill effectively about 50 or 60 yards, short barrel 25 to 30 yards. It must have been a large revolver, almost Service size, but the bullet is certainly not a Service bullet.

Apart from the finding of the spent bullet, the hedges on the roads have been cut for miles, but so far no trace of any firearm or anything else in connection with the murder has been found.

With the able assistance of the local Police we have scoured the whole of Leicestershire. We have interrogated every known relative and personal friend of the deceased, and her family, but not one of them can give any idea of any one they would consider capable from any cause whatever of taking the life of this girl.

We have kept James Evans in Leicester, whose home it will be remembered

Appendix IV.

is at Maltby, near Rotherham, and he has kept observation at various places in Leicester, particularly at her last place of employment, viz St. Mary's Mills, where some hundreds are employed, but he has failed to see anyone whom he could identify as the man he saw at Gaulby with the deceased on the evening of the 5th July.

It appears that on the 28th June what is termed a 'Shops Outing' of this Factory was given to the employees and they were taken in brakes to Foxton Locks. They left about 10 in the morning and came through a village named Oadby about 10 at night on their return to Leicester. It appears that Bella Wright joined the party at Oadby, a point nearest to her home at Stoughton, and left there when the brakes arrived at about 10.15 p.m. She was evidently under the influence of drink. A soldier and a young man in Mufti were standing close by at the junction of Stoughton and London Roads when some of the girls shouted to these two young men asking them to see this girl home. Bella walked on but was seen to be overtaken by the young man in mufti. Considerable difficulty was experienced in locating this young man but on the 16th of July we found William Bertie Wood aged 24, of 26, Cross Street, Oadby, who made a statement shortly to this effect. He is a blacksmith by trade but at present employed as a jobbing gardener at Stoughton Grange by Mr. Burn, of Carisbrooke Road, Leicester. About 10.15 p.m. on the 28th June, he was standing at the junction of Stoughton and London Roads, with his brother named Norman, aged 29, when a brake containing some of the employees of Bates Rubber Works drew up alongside. He describes them as all being merry. One of the girls got off the brake and one or two of the other girls said, 'Would you mind seeing her safely home?' The girl was walking on towards Stoughton. He said he could see she had had too much to drink and thought the girls wanted him to see her safely home so hurried up and overtook her. He says the journey took him about half an hour across the fields, and that he did not go up to her house. He says that he was met by inhabitants of Oadby named Jim Masser, and a girl (name unknown), and a Mr. Lewis Ludlam and his wife, that he said, 'Goodnight,' to these parties in passing, that he saw the girl home and that he has never seen her before or since, but she did say that her name was Bella Wright.

With regard to the man seen with the girl on 5th July. It appears that a man answering his description went between 10 and 11 a.m. on Wednesday, 2nd July, to Mr. Harry Cox, of 214, Mere Road, Highfields, Leicester, Cycle Dealer, and asked him to repair his bicycle by adjusting his three speed gear. In a conversation that morning with Mr. Cox he said he was a demobilised officer, and Mr. Cox says he looked as though he might be. The man said he had had a month's leave, that he was working for a Firm in London before the war and after he had had a month's leave he went back, and the Firm told him to go for another two or three weeks on pay if he liked, so he came to Leicester to visit some friends.

In addition to the three speed adjustment he asked to have a 'John Bull' sticky

Light.

plaster put in the inside of the outer cover of the back wheel, which was done.

On the 3rd July he called in about the same time. Mr. Cox told him he had broken his cable and the man asked that a new one be put in. On the 4th he went in about the same time and paid 4/9 for the job and rode the machine away, but took it back in the afternoon and asked Mr. Cox to take an inch off so that he could adjust it himself if it stretched which Mr. Cox promised to do and told the man it would be ready on the Saturday morning, 5th. He came in between 1.30 and 2 p.m. on the 5th and took the machine away. He said he was going to have a run out in the country, he was fed up with messing about the town. He rode off towards Old Evington in the direction of Stoughton and Stretton Districts, and that is the last Mr. Cox saw of him.

Mr. Cox has given a description of the bicycle and the man, which tallies with the other witnesses, with the exception that he is not at all sure whether the mudguards on the bicycle were black or any other colour. In the course of conversation the man told Mr. Cox that he had a B.S.A. motor cycle at home.

It will be seen from the foregoing particulars that our only witnesses to date as regards the description of the green bicycle are Mr. Cox and Mr. Evans. The former, of course, can speak with all the facts with regard to the repairs and the general character of the bicycle, but it does seem that Evans, who has a peculiar amateur ability for cycle repairing and riding, made even a more minute examination of the details of the machine.

With regard to the man there is ample evidence and hope that he can be identified by Cox, Evans, Measures, the girl Measures and Mrs. Palmer, but at present we have no evidence of anyone seeing the girl after she left with the man at Gaulby, and although there is a very strong inference that that man who had his bicycle repaired at Cox's and the man seen at Gaulby are identical it is certainly not conclusive that he committed the murder.

It is not difficult to define a sound theory for the motive, but it does seem to me to be one of three.

* That deceased, who according to medical evidence was not a virgin, resented overtures and suggestions made to her by this stranger and in consequence he took her life.

* She unfortunately made the acquaintance of a madman who shot her for no real reason whatever.

* She may have had immoral relations with a man sometime previously and that man may have contracted venereal disease and he may have thought rightly or wrongly that he had contracted that disease through his connection with Bella Wright.

The first theory is based upon these facts. Deceased was engaged to one Archibald Ward, an assistant stoker on H. M. Ship 'Diadem' at Portsmouth. His statement

Appendix IV.

has been taken and he says that he expected to be demobilised in August next and that there was an arrangement between himself and Bella before he joined up in April last that the moment he was free of the Navy they should marry, although incidentally the correspondence received by her from him, and by him from her, has been carefully examined but there is no mention of the impending marriage in the letters, neither was it known to the parents or relatives that such a ceremony was in contemplation, and it may be, knowing that her sweetheart was likely to be demobilised in August, that she was anxious to keep clear of trouble and thus declined and resented immoral suggestions.

Going back to the 2nd July, it is quite clear that the wanted man was staying in or around Leicester from that date until the 5th, the day of the murder, yet although enquiries have been made at Hotels, Inns, Lodging Houses, etc. and various strong appeals have been made in the London and local press, and circulars giving description of men and bicycles, offering a reward for information have been distributed to all Police Forces in the United Kingdom, but so far we have had no useful suggestions from the public as to where the man may have resided on any or all of these dates.

At this moment everything goes to show that what the girl stated to her relatives at Gaulby, that the man was a stranger whom she picked up on the road, is true.

Little Stretton, where the murder was committed, is about seven miles outside of Leicester.

In Leicester there is a population of about 280,000. There are about eight fairly large villages around Little Stretton with an aggregate population of something like twenty or thirty thousand people. The description of the suspected murderer is one which tallies with a very fair percentage of men particularly those recently demobilised. In normal times the local Police have a very fair knowledge of who is in their respective areas, but latterly such an influx of men have returned to towns and country villages that it is more difficult to know who are strangers and who are not. Men being away for four or five years naturally have so altered that their identity in many cases is not always so easy to establish.

The County Police have concentrated the whole of their efforts to try and locate the suspected man but so far without success.

The description of the suspected man is given as age 35 to 40, 5ft 7-9 inches, usually clean shaven, but on the 5th July had about 3 or 4 days growth, which is described as making him look swarthy, hair dark turning grey, broad round full face, stiff built, described as having a squeaky voice and to speak in a low tone, dress: grey mixture suit, grey cap, collar and tie, and black boots, wearing cycle clips, and in possession of a rain proof coat or mackintosh, with green plaid lining. The description of the bicycle which he was riding is as follows:- A gent's B.S.A. green enamelled frame, black mud guards, usual plated parts, up turned handle bars, 3 speed gear, control lever on right handle bar, lever front brake,

Light.

back pedalling brake work from crank and of unusual pattern, open centre gear case, Brooks saddle with spiral springs of wire cable. The 3-speed control had recently been repaired with length of new cable.

The adjourned inquest was resumed on the 25th and after Dr. Williams and Dr. Phillips had given evidence at the post mortem examination, the enquiry was further adjourned until the 8th August.

Dr. Williams said that he found that the deceased had a punctured wound about 1 inch behind and ½ inch below the level of the left ear. He probed the wound and found it passing upwards, inwards and backwards. It passed through the brain to a wound of exit at the right side at the back of the head.

The wound would just about admit an ordinary lead pencil. He was of the opinion that the bullet (produced) might have caused the wound. He went on to say that the body was well nourished. The skin was peculiarly fair and white. The hair was saturated with blood. There was also blood in the nose and mouth, but not in the ears. He noticed externally that there was a bruise over the left cheek bone, about the size of a 2/- piece.

In the centre there was a small punctured wound as previously described. There were two small contusions below the right angle of the mouth and contused cut through the left upper eyelid with discolouration of the eyeball. There were scratches on the left hand and wrist also on the cheek. There were probably caused by gravel. There were no other bruises or marks of violence, which he held might have been caused by a fall when she was shot. He was of opinion that she had not been subjected to any rough handling, that he was sure, having regard to the peculiar delicate nature of the skin, he would have found discoloured marks or bruises.

The doctor went so far as to say that he found no signs of resistance, her clothes were not disarranged. She was wearing a bow which was only fastened by a flimsy pin and this was found intact.

Internally the brain was shattered. There was an oval shaped hole 1½ inches in the skull. He had dissected portions of the skin including the bruise taken from the left cheek, in it he found gravel and small particles of metal. In his opinion the shot could not have been fired from more than 4 or 5 feet away. He could not find any evidence of gunpowder, and could not say whether the deceased was actually riding her bicycle when shot, but he inclines to the theory that she must have been either riding or in an erect position.

There was a slight discolouration of the genitals, no sign of any bruising of the genitals and the hymen was absent. There was a discharge from the vagina, but not sufficient to indicate that she was suffering from syphilis, neither could he say whether she was suffering from gonorrhoea or not, further that he could not say the nature of the discharge.

Dr. Williams, in conclusion, said that the actual cause of death was shock

Appendix IV.

following gunshot wound and death must have been instantaneous.

Dr. E. V. Phillips of Kidworth[127] agreed with what Dr. Williams had said, but desired to emphasise the point that there had not been any struggle. If there had, there would have been much bruising, bearing in mind the nature of the deceased's skin.

Before the adjournment the Chief Constable (E. Holmes Esq.) made a strong appeal to the Press to again appeal to the Public to come forward with any information that would help to trace the man that called at the cycle shop in Leicester on 2nd, 3rd, 4th and 5th July, adding that it was clear that the man was living near at the time, although it might have been only temporary.

I am strongly of opinion that if it had not been for the persistent manner in which P.C. 97 Alfred Hall followed up his suspicion that Bella Wright had been foully murdered, the case would have been treated by Dr. Williams as one of accidental death.

The case was not certified to be one of murder until about 8.40 p.m. 6th instant, or nearly 24 hours after the body had been found. The aid of New Scotland Yard was not sought until the afternoon of the 11th, when the County Police had come to a dead end with their enquiries. In spite of these delays I venture with every respect to give as an opinion that the enquiry was not very materially affected in so far as bringing about an arrest. I am more than convinced that as far as the local Police are concerned they acted with a promptness and thoroughness that must have brought about, in the ordinary conduct of a case, a satisfactory result had they a sound clue to work upon.

The moment the cruel deed was perpetrated and the murderer got clear of the scene no connection or material of any sort was left to work upon, and unfortunately the case from that aspect has not altered. There is at the time of reporting not a vestige of enquiry that has been left undone.

We have made very many enquiries and interviewed numerous people in London and throughout Leicestershire, but all without result or progress towards tracking the wanted man and so far every available point has been exhausted.

I beg that a copy of this report and a copy of the statements be sent to the Director of Public Prosecutions, also that a copy of the report be sent to E. Holmes Esq., Chief Constable of Leicestershire, the latter is already in possession of a copy of the statements.

[Signed] A. Hawkins
Chf Inspr
[Countersigned] Fred Thomas
Supt.

---

127   *Sic* in report. Read: Kibworth.

APPENDIX V

The Death of George Light.

EDITOR'S NOTE.

The prosecution brief reported that Ronald Light's father had 'committed suicide after his son's conviction by court marshal', but the dates did not add up.[128] *Light's father, George, died in the circumstances described below on 21 September 1916 – a little less than a year before Light's court marshalling. George had been to London 'to try and see' the prodigal Ronald on Monday 18 September, which was, depending on which date one accepts (both are given in the brief) either ten days after Ronald had enrolled with the Honourable Artillery Company, or the very day on which he enrolled. Ronald's father was plainly worried about him; but any connection between those feelings and his death (which was never found to be suicide) seems to have been the product of mere speculation by the police.*

*

Colliery Manager's Death.
Mysterious Fall from a Window.

Yesterday Mr E. G. B. Fowler (Borough Coroner) held an inquest, at the Town Hall, touching the death of Mr George Henry Light (60), colliery manager, residing at Park View, Granville Road, Leicester.

At the outset the Coroner said deceased during the past few weeks had been worried about his only son, who had been a second lieutenant in the Royal Engineers, but for some reason or other had resigned his commission, and then joined the Army as a private. On Monday, Mr Light went to London to try and see his son, and returned home. On Thursday morning he got out of bed and went into a spare room, was subsequently found lying in the vestibule outside, and died in a couple of hours from injuries received.

The evidence of Mrs Light, the widow, was taken at the house.

Dr Chapel said he had been attending Mr Light for gastritis. He occasionally suffered from insomnia. Witness did not think Mr Light had any suicidal tendencies. He saw him on Wednesday night, when he appeared to be very cheerful, though he was somewhat worried owing to his not having seen his

---

128 TNA: PRO DPP 1/61.

Light.

son. Witness was called to the house on Thursday morning, and found Mr Light suffering from injuries, external and internal, caused by falling out of a window. Death was due to shock following injuries. So far as he could judge he was not a man who would take his own life.

Mary Webb, servant at Park View, deposed to unlocking the front door at 7.15 on Thursday morning, and finding Mr Light. She said, 'What has happened?' or 'Where have you been?' and he said, 'I don't know, Mary'. The window of the spare room was open. She had noticed nothing unusual about him recently. Replying to the Foreman, witness said deceased was wearing pyjamas and a dressing gown. She came to the conclusion that he felt faint, and went to the window for fresh air, and then fell out.

By the Coroner: She had known him faint before.

The jury returned a verdict of 'Death from shock and internal injuries, caused by falling from a window, but there was not sufficient evidence to show how he came to fall'.

The Coroner said Mr Light was a most respected gentleman. He was well known to him, and it was particularly painful to him to have to hold the inquest upon a respected friend.[129]

---

129   *Leicester Daily Post*, 23 September 1916.

APPENDIX VI

Report of the War Office Committee of Enquiry into 'Shell-Shock'.

———

EDITOR'S NOTE.

In August 1920, a little over two months after Ronald Light's acquittal, an enquiry was convened under the following terms of reference:

> *To consider the different types of hysteria and traumatic neurosis, commonly called 'shell-shock'; to collate the expert knowledge derived by the service medical authorities and the medical profession from the experience of the war, with a view to recording for future use the ascertained facts as to its origin, nature, and remedial treatment, and to advise whether by military training or education, some scientific method of guarding against its occurrence can be devised.[130]*

Criminal offences perpetrated by sufferers of the condition were therefore beyond the remit of the committee, but some of the evidence and commentary, here and there through the report, may cause the reader to think of Ronald Light.

*

From the evidence of F. Burton Fanning, Esq., M.D., F.R.C.P., M.R.C.S.

'If the neurotic element had been kept out instead of forced in there would have been very much less "shell-shock". A tremendous number of neurotics resented having been passed, and they had never the slightest intention of trying to make soldiers of themselves. An enormous proportion amongst the men who broke down had been neurotics previously.'

… 'A large number of fellows broke down long before they had finished their training. The patient's attitude of mind was wrong prior to service. They had never taken exercise, they had not been prepared for muscular exercise, they had always lived a sedentary life. They knew they could not stand the long marches, and they never intended to.'

He used to have a hundred to two hundred of these neurotic men at Cambridge.

---

130 *Report of the War Office Committee of Enquiry into 'Shell-Shock', 3.*

Light.

'They were marched out with non-commissioned officers, and before they had gone one hundred yards some of them would begin to turn giddy and faint, and I am sure it was only from auto-suggestion. A large proportion of his [*sic* – my?] people gave as a cause of nervous break down, horses. They had never had anything to do with horses in civil life. They did not know one end of a horse from another, and they were put to attend them and ride them.'[131]

*

EDITOR'S NOTE.

Among the complaints made about Light during his commission in the army was that he 'openly expresses a dislike for riding'.[132]

*

From the evidence of Squadron Leader W. Tyrrell, D.S.O., M.C., Royal Air Force Medical Service.

'"Shell shock" I define as exhaustion of the nervous energy which determines will-power and self-control, with the resultant loss of control. It resembles a paralysis of the inhibitory nervous system. I approach the problem by comparing a man's store of nervous energy to a capital and current account at the bank.

'A man instinctively masks his emotions almost as a matter of routine. In trifling everyday affairs this is involuntary and automatic with a negligible expense of nervous energy. In minor crises the expenditure of nervous energy increases relatively with the man's estimate of the importance and necessity for concealing the emotion. This expenditure is usually out of his current account, consequently it is not missed and has no untoward effect. In great crises – fear, birth, death, marriage, murder, personal disgrace or dishonour – the emotion called forth is abnormal. The necessity for camouflage or repression is increased in ratio with a corresponding rise in expenditure of nervous energy, which quickly uses up the current account and draws upon the capital account for reinforcement.

'A continuous series of great crises without intervals for replacing spent energy ultimately exhausts the capital account, and you get a run on the bank, followed by loss of control, hysteria, irresponsible chattering, mutism, amnesia, inhibition of the senses, acute mania, insensibility, *etc.*, with the diagnosis of nervous breakdown or 'shell shock'. The credit balance of

---

131   *Report of the War Office Committee of Enquiry into 'Shell-Shock'*, 22.
132   TNA: PRO WO 339/52768.

Appendix VI.

nervous energy varies in individuals just as banking balances do. Some become bankrupt and succumb before they draw on their current account, or even scent the battle. Most real men take a lot of depressing, and even when really and justifiably exhausted their hearts are in the right place. They have spirit and soul, and so they draw on an overdraft, if necessary, and manage to carry on. A very few appear to have an inexhaustible store. They usually get killed, and always earn the description that they did not know what fear was, which is a misnomer. All men know fear. Some conceal it better than others. A few bury it out of sight, but it is there all the same.' ...

During the war he had no experience of 'shell-shock' in depots or barracks.

'In rest billets it was usually associated with the history of insomnia, nightmares, hysteria, mutism, amnesia, melancholia, petty crime, and, in some cases, by self-inflicted wounds. In the field by melancholia, depression, hysterical fits, uncontrollable shivering and wringing of the hands, staring eyes, blindness, amnesia, irresponsible chattering, acute mania, sudden insensibility, self-inflicted wounds, generally to the left hand or the feet; fear, and the very characteristic look of furtive fear – the hunted animal.

'An observant and knowledgeable medical officer who has put himself into the right and proper relationship with the troops (officers and other ranks) under his charge, can often detect very early the signs of approaching breakdown. Summed up in change of character:

'The wild fighting type becomes quiet and moody.

'The sullen type becomes excitable and talkative.

'The careful man becomes suddenly reckless.

'The previously well-behaved man perpetrates petty crimes, *etc.*'[133]

*

'Behaviour Characteristics, used in the training of recruits in the U.S. Navy during the war.

1)   Resentfulness to discipline or inability to be disciplined.

2)   Unusual stupidity or awkwardness in drills or exercises.

3)   Inability to transmit orders correctly.

4)   Personal uncleanliness.

5)   Criminal tendencies.

6)   Abnormal sex practices and tendencies, including masturbation.

133   *Report of the War Office Committee of Enquiry into 'Shell-Shock',* 30-32.

Light.

7) Filthy language and defacement of property.

8) Distinct feminine types.

9) Bed-wetters.

10) Subjects of continual ridicule or teasing.

11) Queer or peculiar behaviour.

12) All recruits who show persistently, the following characteristics: Tearfulness, irritability, seclusiveness, sulkiness, depression, shyness, timidity, anti-social attitude, over-boisterousness, suspicion, dulness [sic], sleeplessness, sleepwalking.

13) Chronic homesickness.'[134]

---

134   *Report of the War Office Committee of Enquiry into 'Shell-Shock'*, 183.

APPENDIX VII

The Bowley Statement.

___

EDITOR'S NOTE.

The Bowley Statement, an account of the death of Bella Wright given by Ronald Light after the conclusion of his trial for her murder, is a recent addition to the enigma of the Green Bicycle Case. For some discussion of its authenticity, see Brown's 'The Green Bicycle Mystery', pages 229-233. I can supplement this discussion with the observation that the paper on which the statement was typed was manufactured by Joseph Town and Sons of Leeds – a finding disclosed by its distinctive watermark, and one which is not inconsistent with the purported date of the document. None of the documents of Leicestershire Police origin in TNA: PRO DPP 1/61 discloses the same watermark, but it should be noted that they all emerged from the office of Edward Holmes, the Chief Constable of the Leicestershire Constabulary, and his official letter paper was pre-printed with his name, address and telephone number. The watermarks featured on the examples of Holmes's letter paper preserved within the DPP file are: 'Climax Superfine Parchment'; 'Spicer Brothers'; 'Royal Vellum'; 'Verona Linen'; and 'British Bond'.

I am grateful to Leicestershire Police and the Leicestershire & Rutland Record Office for their permission to reproduce the statement here.

*

County Police Station,
Leicester,
14th June, 1920.

At about 11 a.m. this day, RONALD VIVIAN LIGHT (who was on 11th instant acquitted of the Murder of ANNIE BELLA WRIGHT, at Stretton Parva, on 5th July, 1919,) came to this Office to arrange for his property to be handed back to him. I talked with him for about an hour-and-a-quarter about his Trial and about the Murder generally. He and I were together in my Office with the door closed. I pointed out amongst other things that I could not swallow his story of his leaving the girl where and how he said he had done, knowing as I did, of his fondness for women and his past history in this respect. I returned to this subject time after time and told him that I did not believe he had wilfully shot her and that I never had believed that of him.

Light.

When Light was in my custody I had endeavoured to make him as comfortable as was possible, and had allowed him certain privileges which he missed when on remand at Prison. In consequence of this he was on good terms with me and said, "Well you are a good Sport, if I tell you something can I depend upon your keeping it to yourself"? I said, Yes, strictly. He said, - "Well I'll tell you, but mind it must be strictly confidential, no other person knows it and if you divulge it I shall, of course, say I never told you anything of the kind. He went on to say - I did shoot the girl but it was completely accidental, we were riding quietly along, I was telling her about the War and my experiences in France, I had my Revolver in my Raincoat pocket and we dismounted for her to look at it. I had fired off some shots in the afternoon for practice and I had no idea there was a loaded cartridge in it, we were both standing up by the sides of our bicycles, I think she had dismounted on the right of her machine and that the two bicycles were between us. I took the Revolver from my Coat pocket and was in the act of handing it to her, I am not sure whether she actually took hold of it or not, but her hand was out to take it when it went off. She fell and never stirred, I was horror struck, I did not know what to do, I knew she was dead, I did not touch her, I was frightened and altogether unnerved and I got on my bicycle and rode away, I went by Great Glen, I saw some courting couples between Stretton and Glen and I slowed down somewhat so that I should not be unduly noticed, I thought that as no one knew me I should get clear away, and as time went on I thought it would never be found out. I cannot account for the shot unless it was that the Revolver was fully cocked, the least touch would fire it then. Mary Webb's evidence was quite true, and whenever the subject of the Murder was brought up I always said as little as possible and commenced to talk of something else. I did not know the girl, I had never met her before that evening. What I said about her asking me for a Spanner was quite true I first saw her at the top of the hill, I screwed her bicycle up and we went down the hill then started to go up the next hill where Atkins saw us. I did not make any improper suggestion to her either on the way to Gaulby or after leaving there. I did not mention that at all, that might – and probably would, have happened later. If I had intended shooting her I should never have done it close up to the village, it was much more lonely along the road we had passed. I do not remember the two little girls, they must have mistaken me for someone else. I asked Light about the bullet – He said – I do not believe that the bullet found in the road is the one which was shot by the Revolver as it would have travelled much further, and from the position in which we were standing it could not have struck the ground, and if it had struck a tree it would have buried itself in the tree, and besides it would not have been found at that angle. It was, I think, in October that I threw the bicycle in the Canal. I unscrewed everything as far as I could before leaving home, I then walked with the machine to the Canal and got on the towing-path at Walnut Street Bridge, it would be about 10 o'clock when I got there. I first threw in the mudguards, then the gearcase, then the chain,

Appendix VII.

then the Cranks & pedals and so on until I had thrown it all in, the holster was full of cartridges to sink it. I said – If you had left the Revolver in the holster that would have kept it down – Is that in there too? He said – No, I had it with me and it was loaded. I was in such a nervous state that if anyone had interfered with me I should have been guilty of murder, I should have shot him. I remember a man passing me as soon as I had got on the towing path, I pretended to be doing something at my bicycle and he did not speak to me. I said – Where is the Revolver? He replied – It is in the Canal but not there, I threw that and another in near to Belgrave Gate. I said Did your Counsel know All this? He said No, I told Mr. Powers I was not at Gaulby at all, and it was not until later that I was persuaded to tell them part of the truth. I told them the story I told in Court. I was asked about it being an accident but I adhered to the story that I left the girl at the two roads. I dared not admit the shot, I was afraid of a verdict of Manslaughter. I said You ran a great risk. He said – I suppose I did but I would rather have my neck stretched than do ten years in prison. I asked Light to give permission to tell the Chief Constable what he had told me. He declined to do so but eventually, after much pressing, he said – You can do so after a while but not at present. I said – Does your Mother know? He said My God no, I would not let my mother know it for the world. No one on this earth knows it but us two, and if you tell I shall say I never said anything of the kind.

L. Bowley
<u>Superintendent</u>.

INDEX.

Index.

Index.

evidence, 52, 79; permits Light to be seated during opening speech, 22, 55; commends PC Hall, 64; reproves Birkett for leading witness, 23, 64; rectifies formal omissions in Crown case, 26–7, 73–4, 79, 87; criticises D.P.P., 80; questions witnesses (PC Hall, 26, 73–4; Joseph Orton, 74; Mary Webb, 78; Dr Williams, 27, 79; Henry Clarke, 26, 82, 83, 87; Ronald Light, 91, 94, 95, 97, 98, 101, 102, 104–5, 106–7, 108, 110–11); advises jury on prisoner's entitlement to reserve defence, 108–9; requests measurements of crime locality, 99; receives telegram, 111n; reprimands press photographer, 123; summing up, 36, 123–6; praises Marshall Hall's defence, 17n
Houghton on the Hill, Leicestershire, 100–1
Howe, Sergeant (of Leicestershire Constabulary), 59

identification parades, 13–15, 14n, 26, 84–5, 86
Illes, Detective Sergeant Harold: evidence at trial, 86
inquest on body of Bella Wright: coroner's jurisdiction, 8; process, 8–9; viewing of body, 8; first day, 131–4, 164; second day, 134–40, 174; third day, 140–50; evidence given *in camera*, 142, 149–50; coroner's closing address to jury, 148–50; jury verdict, 9, 150, 159; depositions, 151–9

John Bull (journal), 41 & n
Jones, Brian, 12

Keay, William: evidence at trial, 61–2, 111

leading questions, 23
legal aid, 19
Leicester: Bates's Rubber Works, 2, 132, 165, 171; Harper & Sons (bicycle firm), 31n; Highfield Street (No 54), 3–4, 30–1, 37–8, 75; Mecklenburg Street (*later* Severn Street), 31n; police station, 13–14, 38–9; St Mary's Wharf, 11, 63, 80
Leicester Castle: identification parade at, 14; as venue for trial, 18; *see also* trial
Leicester Daily Post: on death of George Light, 177–8; coverage of murder case, 68, 104 & n; as inquest source, 133n, 147n, 150n; as trial source, 65n, 74n
Leicester Journal, 133n, 147n

Leicester Mail: Sarah Ward's account, 2n; coverage of murder case, 85–6; as inquest source, 132n, 133n, 135n, 136n, 138n, 139n, 150n; as trial source, 58n, 65n, 84n, 97n, 100n, 101n, 121n
Leicester Mercury: coverage of murder case, 94, 104 & n; as inquest source, 135n, 137n, 138n, 141n, 142n, 144n, 147n, 150n; as trial source, 63n, 91n
Light, Catherine (mother), 3–4, 37–8, 41, 105, 109; writes to Ronald from Rhyl, 107 & n, 161
Light, George (father), 96, 109; death, 177–8
LIGHT, RONALD: family background, 2; schooling, 2, 30; graduates as civil engineer, 2–3; draughtsman in Derby, 3, 31; purchases green bicycle, 11–12, 57, 74–5; lodges with Morris family, 71; enlists with Royal Engineers and discharged, 3, 31–2; service revolver, 16, 33, 60, 70, 87–9, 95–7; and Miss Tunnicliffe incident, 16n, 60, 70, 87, 96; accused of fire starting, 32; gunner with Honourable Artillery Company, 3, 32, 88; court martialled and imprisoned, 32, 177; death of father, 177–8; deployed to France, 32; invalided home with health problems, 3, 32, 88–9, 109; shellshock, 3, 109; lives with mother in Leicester, 3–4, 57, 89; interest in cycling, 3; possible prior relationship with Bella Wright, 22, 35, 36, 44, 117–18, 120–1; visits bicycle repair shop, 57, 89, 97, 145–6, 171–2; physical appearance and voice, 145, 147; allegedly pesters young girls, 10, 13, 23, 55, 64–6; spotted riding with Bella, 13, 55–6, 68, 75, 144, 165–7; waits outside Gaulby cottage, 7, 13, 56, 68–70, 140–4, 146–7, 167–9; his version of events, 33–4, 90–4, 99–103, 110–11; returns home, 4, 34, 58, 76, 77, 94, 103; reaction to mentions of murder, 70, 77, 105; policy of concealment and failure to come forward, 43, 58, 94, 104–6, 107, 108, 122, 124–5; throws bicycle and holster in canal, 33, 95, 97–8, 108, 184–5; disposes of clothes, 77, 106–7, 111; schoolmaster at Cheltenham, 12, 31n; bicycle traced to, 12; questioned by police, 12, 59, 86, 108; identity parades, 13–14, 84–5, 86; charged and held in custody, 59, 86; police enquiries into Light's background and sexual history, 28,

Index.

Index.

Index.

NOTABLE BRITISH TRIALS SERIES.

Notable British Trials Series.

Notable British Trials Series.

* New series.

In preparation:

Henry Hunt (ed. Caitlin Kitchener)

Eliza Fenning (ed. Kate Clarke)

The Mannings (ed. Linda Stratmann)

Frederick Baker (ed. David Green)

CPSIA information can be obtained
at www.ICGtesting.com
Printed in the USA
JSHW041047050421
13291JS00001B/15